PRINCIPLES

OF

PENAL LAW.

Est enim unum jus, quo devincta est hominum societas, et quod lex constituit una: quæ lex est recta ratio imperandi atque prohibendi: quam si quis legum Lator ignoret, is est injustus. Cic. de Legibus.

THE SECOND EDITION.

BY

[WILLIAM EDEN, Baron Auckland]

THE LAWBOOK EXCHANGE, LTD.
Clark, New Jersey
2009

ISBN-13: 978-1-58477-951-3
ISBN-10: 1-58477-951-9

The quality of this reprint is equivalent to the quality of the original work.

THE LAWBOOK EXCHANGE, LTD.
33 Terminal Avenue
Clark, New Jersey 07066-1321

Please see our website for a selection of our other publications and fine facsimile reprints of classic works of legal history:
www.lawbookexchange.com

Library of Congress Cataloging-in-Publication Data

Auckland, William Eden, Baron, 1744-1814.
Principles of penal law / [William Eden]. -- 2nd edition.
p. cm.
Originally published: London : Printed for B. White, in Fleet-Street; and T. Cadell, 1771.
Includes bibliographical references.
ISBN-13: 978-1-58477-951-3 (cloth : alk. paper)
ISBN-10: 1-58477-951-9 (cloth : alk. paper)
1. Criminal law--Great Britain. 2. Punishment--Great Britain. 3. Criminal procedure--Great Britain. I. Title.
KD7869.A95 2009
345.42--dc22

2008044663

Printed in the United States of America on acid-free paper

PRINCIPLES

OF

PENAL LAW.

Est enim unum jus, quo devincta est hominum societas, et quod lex constituit una: quæ lex est recta ratio imperandi atque prohibendi: quam si quis legum Lator ignoret, is est injustus. Cic. de Legibus.

THE SECOND EDITION.

LONDON:

PRINTED FOR B. WHITE, IN FLEET-STREET; AND T. CADELL, IN THE STRAND.

MDCCLXXI.

A

SUMMARY

OF THE

CONTENTS.

CHAP. I.

Of the Origin of Legiſlation.

CHAP. II.

Of Penal Laws.

CHAP. III.

Of the Infliction of Death.

CHAP. IV.

Of Banishment.

CHAP. V.

Of Forfeiture, and Corruption of Blood.

CHAP. VI.

Of Impriſonment.

CHAP. VII.

Of Corporal Punishments, and of Infamy.

CHAP. VIII.

Of Fines.

CHAP. IX.

Of the Diſpoſal of the dead Body of the Criminal.

* * *

CHAP. X.

That it would not compleat the deſign of this work, to have ſtated only the right of puniſhments: That it is alſo neceſſary to conſider the ſeveral ſpecies and degrees of criminality.

* * *

CHAP. XI.

Of Crimes.

§ 5. But

CHAP. XII.

Of Crimes relative to Religion.

CHAP.

CHAP. XIII.

Of Crimes relative to the Law of Nations.

CHAP. XIV.

Of Treaſons.

§ 8. Of

* * *

CHAP. XV.

A Digreffion relative to the Englifh Trials in Cafes of high Treafon.

CHAP. XVI.

A further Digreſſion relative to the gradual Improvements of criminal Proceſs.

§ 12. Re-

* * *

CHAP. XVII.

Of other Crimes immediately relative to the State.

CHAP. XVIII.

Of Murder.

By

CHAP. XIX.

Of Duelling.

CHAP. XX.

Of Suicide.

CHAP. XXI.

Of other Crimes relative to the Perſons of Individuals.

CHAP. XXII.

Of Crimes relative to Property.

CHAP. XXIII.

Of Crimes of poſitive Inſtitution.

CHAP. XXIV.

Of the Compoſition and Promulgation of Laws.

CHAP.

CHAP. XXV.

Of the Execution of Penal Laws.

CHAP. XXVI.

Of the Importance of this Subject.

PRINCIPLES

OF

PENAL LAW.

CHAP. I.

Of the Origin of Legiſlation.

§ 1. THE mutual dependence of mankind upon each other is neceſſary to their mutual preſervation; and the conſciouſneſs of this neceſſity is, in the firſt formation of ſocieties, the inſtinctive principle of union. But reaſon co-operating with inſtinct carries the aſſociation ſtill further, and points out the inſufficiency of a ſtate merely gregarious. The unlimited enjoyments of Individuals are found incompatible with the exiſtence of a collective Body; rules of conduct and covenants are introduced; and the moral duties of benevolence, juſtice, and adherence to compacts, become as evident to human underſtanding, as they are eſſential to human happineſs.

Here then commences the obligation of civil laws: the impulſes of appetite ceaſe to be the ſole motives of action; power is no longer the meaſure of property; and the natural herd is refined into a political government. Legiſlation is inſtituted; and the baneful exceſſes of the paſſions are ſubjected to various modifications of reſtraint. Magiſtracies are eſtabliſhed; and the promulgation of puniſhments is extended to All, by the common conſent of All, for the benefit of All.

And thus it is, that the ſyſtem of civil liberty is eſtabliſhed on the aggregate of thoſe portions of natural liberty, which are given up by the conſtituent members of ſociety. But it is not to be ſuppoſed, that this effect is inſtantaneous: I ſhall hereafter have occaſion to ſhew, that the infancy of civilization is tedious, and its progreſs towards maturity ſubjected to many difficulties. The gratification of private reſentment, and the purſuit of private ſatisfaction, are at firſt the ſole objects of criminal proceſs; and the offended party is his own avenger. It is long, before the ſelfiſh paſſions are ſoftened into an habitual acquieſcence in the general diſpenſations of Law; before injuries to individuals are conſidered, and made puniſhable, as injuries to the ſociety at large. This change, in which the public intereſt is recognized to be the great end of penal juriſdiction, though founded in reaſon, is contradictory to the moſt active propenſities of human nature, and therefore is ſubmitted to with reluctance.

It is from this aſſumed period of improved civilization that I am now to proceed.

§ 2. To what extent the authority of legiſlative regulations may be carried, and how far the obedience of the ſubject is demandable, are queſtions of ſpeculation, which the temperate diſpoſition of modern governments hath rendered rather curious than uſeful. It is ſufficient to obſerve, that every cauſeleſs or unneceſſary reſtraint of the Will is an infringement of that political freedom, to which every member of ſociety is entitled; and poſſible caſes may certainly be propoſed, which no authority on earth can juſtify.—

[a] *Phalaris licet imperet, ut ſis*
Falſus, et admoto dictet perjuria tauro,
Summum crede neſas animam præferre pudori,
Et propter vitam vivendi perdere cauſas.

The accompliſhed Athenians enacted, that in ſieges the aged and infirm ſhould be put to death: an Engliſhman would not think himſelf compellable by any Law to plunge the poniard into the boſom of his helpleſs Father. The ſame Athenians in the height of the moſt refined effeminacy conſidered the Expoſition of their children as a practice juſtifiable, and blameleſs; and Solon, the moſt celebrated of the Sages of Greece, gave to it the ſacred permiſſion of law. Among the Spartans this unnatural ſpecies of murder was conducted by a ſtate-committee, appointed to determine, whether the child were proper to be reared, as likely to become uſeful to the community; or to be deſerted, as of an infirm, and unpromiſing conſtitution. Vain were the ſmiles of innocence, and the cries of helpleſſneſs. [b] Cuſtom had murdered natural

[a] Juv. viii. 81.

[b] *The force of habitual prejudices is wonderful*; a truth, which will frequently recur to the Reader in the courſe of the following enquiry. Plutarch, the humane, good-natured Plutarch, recommends it as a virtue in Attalus, that he expoſed all his own children, in order to leave the crown

tural affection; and the Babe was abandoned by its Parents to the Mercy of Wolves and Bears. The hearts of modern mothers bleed at the idea.

§ 3. As to the more confined question, to what degree punishments may be carried; or how far a Man may subject himself and his fellow-citizens to the infliction of pains, the loss of honors and property, the horrors of imprisonment, and the deprivation of life; the answer may in some measure be collected from those writings of Divine authority, to which I shall hereafter refer: At present it may be sufficient to appeal to the unwritten law of God imprinted on the heart of Man; to that natural sympathy better felt than expressed, which forbids us to give unnecessary

crown to the son of his brother Eumenes; signalizing in this manner his gratitude and affection to Eumenes, who had left him his heir in preference to that son.

Perhaps (says Mr. Hume) by an odd connection of causes, this barbarous custom might contribute to render those times more populous. By removing the terrors of too numerous a family it would engage many people in marriage; and such is the force of natural affection, that very few in comparison would have resolution enough, when it came to the point, to carry into execution their former intentions. China, where this practice still prevails, is the most populous country that we know.

Essays, 4to, p. 218.

Pain to each other; or, in fuller words, to extend the ſeverity of puniſhments beyond what is eſſentially neceſſary to the preſervation and morality of ſociety; general terms, of which a definition will reſult from the ſubſequent detail.

State-puniſhments are to be conſidered then as founded on, and limited by, firſt, natural Juſtice; ſecondly, public Utility: and it will be ſhewn, that, in the purſuit of thoſe great ends, Wiſdom and Mercy ſhould go hand in hand.

CHAP. II.

Of penal Laws.

§ 1. THE prevention of crimes ſhould be the great object of the Lawgiver; whoſe duty it is, to have a ſevere eye upon the offence, but a merciful inclination towards the offender. It is from an abuſe of language, that we apply the word "Puniſhment" to human inſtitutions: Vengeance belongeth not to man. Criminals, ſaid Plato[e],

[e] De Legibus, p. 977.

are

are punifhed, not becaufe they have offended; for what is done can never be undone: but that for the future the criminals themfelves, and fuch as fee their punifhment, may take warning, and learn to fhun the allurements of vice. "[d] Meti Suffeti, inquit Tullus, fi ipfe "difcere poffes foedera ac fidem fervare, vivo "tibi ea difciplina a me adhibita effet: nunc, "*quoniam tuum infanabile ingenium eft, Tu tuo* "*fupplicio doce humanum genus ea fancta cre-* "*dere, quæ a te violata funt.*" It is the end then of penal laws to deter, not to punifh.

§ 2. But let not for this purpofe the feverity of the penalty be augmented in proportion to the increafe of the temptation; which is a cruel and miftaken policy.

"*Qui vi rapuit, fur improbior videtur* [e]." Such was the maxim of the Roman law, which punifhed the open, daring thief with whipping, and the pilferer by fine only. The Englifh law, adopting a lefs equitable idea, hath made it death [f] to take privately from the pocket a hankerchief, or other thing of the value of twelvepence; but any Larceny

[d] Liv. Hift. l. i. c. 28.
[e] ff. 4. 2. 14. 12.
[f] 8 Eliz. c. 4.

(below the degree of robbery by putting in fear) committed openly, and avowedly on the person, to any extent, and even in a dwelling-house or out-house, under the value of forty shillings, is [g] within the benefit of clergy.

Under the same perversion of distributive justice it is made [h] only a transportable offence, "to assault another with an offensive weapon, or by menaces, demanding money, goods or chattels, with a felonious intent to rob:" whereas by another [i] statute it is death without benefit of clergy, merely "to write an anonymous Letter, signed with a fictitious name, demanding money, venison, or other valuable thing."

§ 3. The punishment should be proportioned to the flagitiousness of the crime; but the flagitiousness of the crime diminishes in proportion to the facility, with which it may be committed [k]: for that facility in general constitutes the degree of the temptation.

Were

[g] 1 Hawk. P. C. p. 97.

[h] 7 Geo. II. c. 21. [i] 9 Geo. I. c. 22.

[k] By the flagitiousness of a crime, I mean its abstract nature and turpitude, in proportion to which the criminal should be considered as more or less dangerous to society. And surely, in the eye of the Lawgiver, who as a

Man

Were I to leave the ſupport of this poſition to the internal evidence of its own truth, or to the mere unaſſiſted dictates of moral ſentiment, it might appear perhaps preſumptuous; becauſe contradictory to the moſt ingenious and elegant writer on the law of England.

" The ſeverity of our law in certain in-" ſtances (ſays that [l] writer) ſeems to be ow-" ing to the eaſe with which ſuch offences are " committed." Again [m]—" It is but reaſon-" able, that, among crimes of equal maligni-" ty, thoſe ſhould be moſt ſeverely puniſhed, " which a man has the moſt frequent, and " eaſy opportunities of committing; which " cannot be ſo eaſily guarded againſt as others; " and which therefore the offender has the " ſtrongeſt inducement to commit: accord-

Man muſt make allowances for the imbecillities of mankind, the abſtract turpitude of the offence decreaſes in proportion to the inducements which naturally influence the mind of the offender.

C'eſt le triomphe de la Liberté, lorſque les loïx criminelles tirent chaque peine de la nature du crime: tout l'arbitraire ceſſe; la peine ne deſcend point du caprice du legiſlateur, mais de la nature de la choſe; et ce n'eſt pas l'homme qui fait violence à l'homme.

L'Eſprit des Loix, xii. 4.

[l] See the Commentaries on the Laws of England, b. iv. p. 241.

[m] Ib. b. iv. p. 16.

"ing to what Cicero obſerves, [n] *ea ſunt* "*animadvertenda peccata maximè, quæ diffi-* "*cillimè prœcaventur.*" He then proceeds to ſeveral Examples, on which it may be ſufficient to obſerve, that when "it is made capital for a ſervant to rob his maſter" in certain caſes, which extend not to a ſtranger committing the ſame offence againſt indifferent perſons; and, when "it is a ſpecies of treaſon for a ſervant to kill his maſter, or for a wife to kill her huſband, which act in others is only murder;" we are not in thoſe caſes to ſuppoſe the frequent opportunities of perpetrating the offence to have excited the peculiar ſeverity of the law [o]. The malignity of the fact is the true meaſure of the penalty; and that malignity is in theſe caſes aggravated by the groſs breach and flagrant abuſe of domeſtic confidence [p]. Cicero has certainly ſaid, *quod*

[n] Orat. pro. Sexto Roſcio, c. 40.

[o] *Commune eſt hoc malum, communis metus, commune periculum. Nullæ ſunt occultiores inſidiæ, quam eæ quæ latent in ſimulatione officii, aut in aliquo neceſſitudinis nomine. Nam eum, qui palam eſt adverſarius, facile cavendo vitare poſſis. Hoc vero occultum, inteſtinum, ac domeſticum malum, non modò non exiſtit, verùm etiam opprimit, antequam proſpicere atque explorare potueris.*

Cic. in Verrem, II. l. i. c. 15.

[p] Upon this principle, by a declaration of Lewis the XVth, A. D. 1724, Le vol domeſtique ſera puni de mort.

This

quod ea sunt animadvertenda peccata maximè, quæ difficillimè præcaventur: but the learned Commentator should have cited also the context, which supports the very principle for which I contend; "*ad cujus enim fidem ali-*" "*quis confugiet, cum per ejus fidem læditur cui*" "*se commiserit? tecti esse ad alienos possumus;*" "*socium cavere qui possumus? quem etiam si*" "*metuimus, jus officii lædimus*:—"*Nam neque*" "*mandat quisquam ferè nisi amico: neque*" "*credit nisi ei quem fidelem putat. Perditissimi*" "*est igitur hominis, simul et amicitiam dissolvere,*" "*et fallere eum, qui læsus non esset, nisi credi-*" "*disset.*"

§ 4. From these positions, "that the penalty ought to be increased in proportion to the outrage of the crime," and "not in proportion to the temptation which misleads the mind of the criminal;" I would by no means infer, "that the penal sanction relative to every particular offence should be mitigated in proportion to the facility with which that offence may be committed."

This was only the renewal of a very ancient Law made by Lewis the IXth, A. D. 1270, which considers this offence as a species of treason. "Hons, quand il emble a son Saignour, et il est a son pain et à son vin, il est pendable; *car c'est maniere de trahison.*" Code penal. 103.

Political

Political wiſdom is the reſult of experience, rather than of theory. And the hiſtory of every ſtate will ſhew to us, that in ſome caſes the emergencies of ſociety make it expedient to place great ſeverities in oppoſition to the ſtrongeſt temptations; that in others it is neceſſary to puniſh the offence without any reſearch into its motives; and that in every caſe it is impracticable for Lawgivers to aſſume the divine attribute of animadverting on the fact, only according to the internal malice of the intention.

The ſafety of the Public is the ſupreme law of policy: and when Legiſlature is thus neceſſitated in any degree to deviate from the principles of juſtice and humanity, we muſt ſubmit to the deviation merely as to an occaſional reſult from the imperfections of our nature. But the principles of juſtice and humanity are unchangeable: and to thoſe principles I appeal, when I controvert the poſition, "that among crimes of equal malignity, thoſe ſhould be moſt ſeverely puniſhed which the offender has the ſtrongeſt inducement to commit." A poſition! which, if generally eſtabliſhed, would lead to ſanguinary and cruel conſequences.

§ 5. "That

§ 5. "That Legiſlature may juſtify the infliction of whatever degree of ſeverity is neceſſary for the prevention of any particular crime;" is alſo a poſition, which, when offered without limitation, I conceive to be both morally and politically falſe. It is a pretence, which, if once ſuffered to hurry us beyond the bounds of humanity, is ſubject to no other reſtraint.

§ 6. When the rights of human nature are not reſpected, thoſe of the citizen are gradually diſregarded. Thoſe æras are in hiſtory found fatal to Liberty, in which cruel puniſhments predominate. Lenity ſhould be the guardian of moderate governments: ſevere penalties, the inſtruments of deſpotiſm, may give a ſudden check to temporary evils; but they have a tendency to extend themſelves to every claſs of crimes, and their frequency hardens the ſentiment of the people. *Une loi rigoureuſe produit des crimes.* The exceſs of the penalty flatters the imagination with the hope of impunity, and thus becomes an advocate with the offender for the perpetrating of the offence.

The convicts, who have ſtolen [q] cloth from the tenters, fuſtian [r] from the bleaching ground, or a lamb from their landlord's paſture, knew the law to have aſſigned death, without the benefit of clergy, to each of their offences: but, in the depth of ignorance and profligacy, mere inſtinct informed them, that common humanity would recoil at the idea, and they relied for their ſecurity on the ingenuity of mercy to evade the law.

§ 7. Legiſlators ſhould then remember, that the acerbity of juſtice deadens its execution; and that the increaſe of human corruptions proceeds, not from the moderation of puniſhments, but from the impunity of criminals.

§ 8. In the promulgation of every new offence, let the lawgiver expoſe himſelf to feel what wretches feel; and let him not ſeem to bear hardeſt on thoſe crimes, which, in his elevated ſtation, he is leaſt likely to commit. " [s] Si les ſupplices en uſage dans " preſque tout l'orient font horreur à l'huma-

[q] 22 Car. II. c. 25. § 3.
[r] 4 Geo. II. c. 16. and 18 Geo. II. c. 19.
[s] De l'Eſprit, t. ii. p. 68.

" nité,

" nité, c'eſt que le Déſpote, qui les ordonne, " ſe ſent au deſſus des loix. Il n'en eſt pas " ainſi dans les republiques ; les loix ſont tou- " jours douces, parce que celui qui les établit, " ſ'y ſoumet." If this reaſoning be founded in truth, it furniſhes a mortifying inference, that men are naturally cruel, when they can be ſo with ſafety.

§ 9. Penal laws are to check the arm of wickedneſs; but not to wage war with the natural ſentiments of the heart.

Contrary to this principle is the [t] ſtatute, which, making the concealment of infamy evidence

[t] 21 James I. c. 27. which recites, " That women, delivered of baſtard children, *to avoid their ſhame, and to eſcape puniſhment*, do ſecretly bury, and conceal the death of, their children, alledging, if the child or children be afterwards found, that they were born dead; whereas it falleth out *ſometimes* (although hardly it is to be proved) that the ſaid children were murthered by the ſaid women." For the prevention of this miſchief, it is hereby enacted, " That *in every caſe* the ſaid mother ſo offending ſhall ſuffer death as in caſe of murder, except ſuch mother can make proof by one witneſs at the leaſt, that the child, whoſe death was by her ſo intended to be concealed, was born dead."

The modern expoſition of this ſtatute is a good inſtance, that *cruel laws have a natural tendency to their own diſſolution in the abhorrence of mankind.* It is now the conſtant practice of the courts to require, that the body of the evidence of murder, compels unhappy women to break through the becoming pride and modesty of their sex, and to be the first officious publishers of their own shame. Harsh is the construction of treasons [u], which subjects

the child shall be found, before any conviction can take place; and, if it should happen, that the mother had any child-bed linen, or other preparatives in her possession, prior to her delivery, it is generally admitted as a proof, that no concealment was intended. Moreover, it is not unusual to require some degree of evidence that the child was actually born alive, before the ungenerous presumption, that the mother was the wilful author of the death of her new-born infant, is permitted to affect her. These humane deviations from the harsh injunction of the statute have nearly amounted to a tacit abrogation of it.

The expressions of the Swedish Law on this subject are very severe—"Mulier impudica, quæ ex illegitimo concubitu uterum gestat, nec hoc ante partum aperit, latebras quærens quo furtim enitatur partum, et deinde abscondit, percutiatur securi, et in pegmate comburatur, *non attento prætextu mortuum vel ante justum terminum editum fuisse.*"

There is a law to the same purport in France; which may also be found in the "Observations on the ancient statutes," p. 425; and I find that it is strictly enjoined by an ordinance of Henry III. and by a declaration of Lewis XIV. to be published once in every three months in all the parish churches.

Code penal. Paris, 1755, 8vo. titre 29.

[u] A. D. 1689, Lady Lisle and Mrs. Gaunt were convicted of high treason, and executed: the former for harbouring a dissenting priest, who had been concerned in the Duke of Monmouth's rebellion; the latter for giving refuge to another rebel, on whose evidence, voluntarily offered, the conviction was grounded. The man was pardoned

jects to that sentence full of horrors the son, husband, and father, for the protection given to the wife, parent, and child.

The laws of Japan oblige the person accused to give an answer to the accusation; if his answer be false, he is punished with death. This is a violation of the first principle of self-preservation.

§ 10. It is one of the unavoidable imperfections of legislatures, that they are necessitated to assign the same name and penalty to whole classes of crimes, each of which differs from the other by an infinite variety of unsearchable circumstances. Yet some offences are so intimately, and so undistinguishably classed in their nature, that it is difficult to conceive any possible reason for a diversity in their punishment.

doned for his treachery; she was burned alive for her charity.

I make no observations on their respective trials; because the proceedings of our criminal courts, at this æra, are so disgraceful, not only to the nation, but to human nature, that, as they cannot be disbelieved, I wish them to be buried in oblivion.

See Hume's Hist. vi. 385.—Burnet i, 649.

It seems a ſtrange incongruity, that the offence of counterfeiting foreign coin legitimated by proclamation, ſhould work [w] a corruption of blood; which is ſaved [x] by ſpecial proviſo in the offence of counterfeiting the current coin of the kingdom. Again, it is a clergyable felony by our law to deſtroy or damage the bridges of Brentford or Black-friars: but it is death to commit the ſame offence on the bridges of London, Weſtminſter, or Putney. There is a ſimilar unaccountable diſtinction between priſon-breakers convicted of [y] perjury, or committed for [z] entering black-lead mines with intent to ſteal; and ſuch as are convicted of, or committed for any other offence within clergy. God forbid, that I ſhould inſinuate a neceſſity to drag all this variety of diſcordant inſtances to the ſame bloody line of uniformity! Their cruelty appears to me equal to their inconſiſtency; and it would not perhaps be difficult to prove their folly equal to their cruelty.

§ 11. Laws made on the ſpur of the occaſion, ſhould have a ſhort and limited dura-

[w] Foſter, p. 226.
[x] 5 Eliz. c. 11. and 8 & 9 W. III. c. 29, &c.
[y] 2 Geo. II. c. 25. § 2.
[z] 25 Geo. II. c. 10.

 tion;

tion; otherwiſe in the courſe of years it will be ſaid, "*magis ſæculum ſuum ſapiunt, quam rectam rationem.*"

It is ſtill a Felony to ſteal a hawk, and death to aſſociate one month with Egyptians [a], or to wander, being a ſoldier or mariner [b], without a teſtimonial under the hand of a Juſtice.

§ 12. Obſolete and uſeleſs ſtatutes ſhould be repealed; for they debilitate the authority of ſuch as ſtill exiſt and are neceſſary. Neglect on this point is well compared by Lord Bacon to the cruelty of Mezentius, who left the living to periſh in the arms of the dead.

Perſons carrying ſubjects out of the northern counties [c], or giving black mail for protection, Jailers forcing priſoners to become approvers [d], Maſons confederating to prevent the ſtatutes of labourers [e], Purveyors in certain caſes [f]

[a] 5 Eliz. c. 20. p. 23. See the declaration of Lewis XIV. contre les Bohemiens, et ceux qui leur donnent retraite. Code penal. p. 114.

[b] 39 Eliz. c. 17.

[c] 43 Eliz. c. 13.

[d] 14 Ed. III. c. 10.

[e] 3 Hen. VI. c. 1.

[f] 28 Ed. I. Stat. iii. c. 1.

though purveyance is aboliſhed, are all capital offenders: and none ſhall bring pollardz and crockardz (which were foreign coins of baſe metal) into the realm, on pain of forfeiture of life and goods [g]. The alterations in our government have rendered theſe particular proviſions totally ineffective; but there are other obſolete ſtatutes, which exiſt, the poſſible inſtruments of miſchief in the hand of tyranny.

§ 13. Civil and criminal laws muſt accumulate, and become complicated, in proportion to the increaſed riches of the ſtate, and to the ſecurity given to the liberties, lives, honours, and properties of the people. Deſpotic ſtates admit a ſimplicity of legiſlation, the forms and principles of which depend on the caprices of a weak and ignorant Monarch, whoſe breaſt is the repoſitory of precedents: but it ſhould be the primary object of free governments, to have the outlines of their privileges fixed and determinate. When the laws for this purpoſe are explicit, it is the duty of the Judge ſtrictly to conform to them; when they are otherwiſe, it is the immediate duty of the Legiſlator to aſcertain them.

[g] 27 Ed. I. ex Rot. in Turr.

It

It is not therefore ſufficient, that the deciſion of the fact be guarded from the influence of fear and affection: the adjudication of the law ſhould be a certain conſequence of that deciſion. But, when the penalty preſcribed bears an evident and exceſſive diſproportion to the offence, the humanity of the Judges will be intereſted in the evaſion of it, "*et magis valebunt acumina ingeniorum, quam auctoritas legis*[h]." And this is a conſideration, which, excluſive of every motive of humanity, ſhould induce the lawgiver carefully to diſcuſs the different modes of puniſhment, as applicable to the different degrees of moral and political guilt.

CHAP. III.

Of the Infliction of Death.

§ 1. IT is impoſſible to read the hiſtories of executive juſtice in different governments without ſhuddering at the very idea of thoſe miſeries, which men, with unrelenting ingenuity, have deviſed for each

[h] Bac. de Augm. Scient.

other. In ſome countries it hath been uſual to ſow up criminals in the warm ſkins of beaſts, and in this condition to expoſe them to wild dogs; in others the limbs are torn aſunder by horſes; in others recourſe is had to crucifixions, burnings, boilings, flayings, famiſhings, impalements, and other modes of deſtruction, equally ſhocking to decency and humanity.

> " Merciful heaven!
> " Thou rather with thy ſharp and ſulphurous bolt
> " Split'ſt the unwedgeable and gnarled oak,
> " Than the ſoft myrtle: O but man, proud man,
> " Dreſt in a little brief authority,
> " (Moſt ignorant of what he's moſt aſſur'd,
> " His glaſſy eſſence) like an angry ape,
> " Plays ſuch fantaſtic tricks before high heaven
> " As make the angels weep [i]."

§ 12. This imputation of tyranny and cruelty hath at different periods been applicable to every government, of which we have any authentic hiſtory. Livy, in reſpect to his countrymen, hath endeavoured to eſtabliſh a different inference in his account of the puniſhment of Metius Suffetius [k]; " *Exinde,* " *duabus admotis quadrigis, in currus earum*

[i] Shakeſpeare, Meaſ. for Meaſ.   [k] L. i. c. 28.

" *diſtentus*

"*distentus illigatur Metius; deinde in diversum* "*iter equi concitati, lacerum in utroque curru* "*corpus, quâ inhæserant vinculis membra, por-* "*tantes. Avertêre omnes a tantâ fœditate* "*spectaculi oculos. Primum, ultimumque illud* "*supplicium apud Romanos exempli parum me-* "*moris legum humanarum fuit; in aliis gloriari* "*licet, nulli gentium mitiores placuisse pœnas.*" We know that national benevolence ought to be the concomitant of national liberty, and are therefore inclinable to give credit to this assertion; but it will not be found in any degree reconcileable to the united testimony of many other Historians. The modes of capital punishment, used by the Romans, were at least as numerous, and as exceptionable, as those of other nations. The head of the malefactor was in some cases fastened within the furca, and in this attitude he was whipped to death [l]; and this was distinguished by the name of [m] *supplicium more majorum.* In other

[l] *C. C. Caligula curatorem munerum ac venationum per continuos dies in conspectu suo catomis verberatum, non prius occidit, quam offensus putrefacti cerebri odore.*

Sueton. in vitâ Calig. c. 27.

[m] *Codicillos præripuit Nero, legitque se hostem a senatu judicatum, et quæri ut puniatur more majorum: interrogavitque quale esset id genus poenæ. Et cum comperisset, nudi hominis cervicem inseri furcæ, corpus virgis ad necem cædi; conterritus ferrum jugulo adegit.*

Sueton. in vitâ Neron. c. 49.

caſes, as in the execution of Antigonus, the whipping terminated in beheading [n]. Crucifixion, or the *ſervile ſupplicium*, was in uſe during many centuries, and firſt abrogated by Conſtantine; the ſentence alſo inflicted whipping, "*verbera intra aut extra pomœrium, arbore infelici ſuſpendito* [o]." The criminal was naked in the execution of theſe different puniſhments. Parricides [p] were ſewed up in a leathern ſack, with an ape, a cock, a ſerpent and a dog, and ſo caſt into the ſea. It was alſo uſual to cover ſome offenders with a mantle dawbed over with pitch, and then to ſet fire to it; *Cogita*, inquit Seneca [q], *illam tunicam alimentis igneis illatam et intextam*. The Emperors introduced a puniſhment called "*Serræ-diſſectio* [r]". *Damnatio in gladium*, or ſentence to the public combats, and *damnatio ad beſtias* [s], were alſo frequent; and the latter appears to have been very fatal to offenders; "*præclara ædilitas!* ſaid Cicero, *unus Leo, ducenti Beſtiarii.*"

[n] Dion. l. xlix.

[o] Liv. l. i. & Val. Max. l. i. c. 7.

[p] *Cujus ſupplicio non debuit una parari*
Simia, nec ſerpens unus nec culeus unus. Juv. l. viii.
See alſo, Dig. 48. ad Leg. Pomp. & Cic. Orat. pro Sext. Roſcio.

[q] Ep. 14. [r] Sueton. in vitâ Calig. c. 27.

[s] Dig. 48. 19. 11. 3.

Theſe

Theſe cruelties were founded on the twelve tables of the Decemvirs, and were contrary to the republican ſpirit. Accordingly by the Porcian law, made in the 454th year of Rome, by Porcius Lecca the Tribune, it was ordained, that no Citizen ſhould be put to death. This exemption was in the extreme of lenity, and erroneous in its foundation. Capital executions are in all ſtates neceſſary.

§ 3. Nothing, however, but the evident reſult of abſolute neceſſity, can authorize the deſtruction of mankind by the hand of man.

The infliction of Death is not therefore to be conſidered, in any inſtance, as a mode of puniſhment, but *merely* as our laſt melancholy reſource in the extermination of thoſe from ſociety, whoſe continuance among their fellow-citizens is become inconſiſtent with the public ſafety.

§ 4. We may pronounce it then contrary both to ſentiment and morality, to aggravate capital executions by any circumſtances of terror or pain beyond the ſufferings inſeparable from a violent death.

The

The punishment of the murderer after tryal and conviction was by the Athenians left to the relations of the deceased, who might put him to death if they thought proper; but they were not permitted to use any degree of torture, or to extort money [t]; Excellent restrictions! which taught the prosecutor to seek justice, not revenge; in wrath to remember mercy; and to feel less, what he in his own interests had suffered, than what the Offender was about to suffer.

It was a custom among the Jews to give wine mingled with myrrh to the malefactor at the time of his execution; in order, as it is said, to cause a stupor, and deaden the sensibility of the pain.

I transcribe the following passage from the English State-tryals. "Hugh Peters, being carried on a sledge to the scaffold, was made

[t] Demosthenes hath given a full explanation of this law, which ordered the murderer, if put to death, to be executed in the district, or parish of the deceased; εν τη του πεπονθοτος πατριδι: "*sequitur in lege* λυμαινεσθαι δε μη. "*quibus verbis significatur, non licere flagris cædere homi-* "*cidam, vincire, laniare, lacerare ora, manus, populari tem-* "*pora raptis auribus, &c.*" Pet. Leg. Att. p. 611. Demosth. Orat. adv. Aristoc. p. 410.

to ſit thereon within the rails, to behold the execution of Mr. Cook. When Mr. Cook was cut down, and brought to be quartered, Col. Turner ordered the Sheriff's men to bring Mr. Peters near, *that he might ſee it*; and bye and bye the hangman came to him all beſmeared in blood, and, rubbing his bloody hands together, he tauntingly aſked, "Come how do you like this work, Mr. Peters? how do you like it?" He replied, "Friend, you do not well to trample on a dying Man [u]."

Shall we plant thorns in the path of Miſery? God forbid! Such refinements of inhumanity are admiſſible only in governments ſo abominable in their Conſtitution, as to make the mere loſs of life deſirable.

[u] This is not the only inſtance of ungenerous inſults towards the Republican ſufferers at the Reſtoration. "The Regicides (ſays Biſhop Burnet) had at that time been odious beyond expreſſion, yet *the odiouſneſs of the crime began to be much flattened by the frequent executions.*"

And therefore when Sir Henry Vane was brought to the ſcaffold; leſt his words ſhould leave impreſſions on the hearers to the diſadvantage of the government, drummers were placed under the ſcaffold, who, as ſoon as he began to addreſs the people, upon a ſign given, ſtruck up with their drums. After being thus repeatedly interrupted, and even when he was taking leave of his friends, "he gave over and died with ſo much compoſedneſs, that it was generally thought, that the Government had loſt more than it had gained by his death." Vol. i. p. 164.

§ 5. So-

§ 5. Solemnity indeed is requisite, for the sake of example; but let not death be drawn into "lingering sufferance;" detain not the excruciated soul upon the verge of eternity. It was consistent only with the brutal insanity of Caligula to order the executioner to protract the death of the mangled criminal, *perpetuo, notoque jam præcepto,* "*Ita feri, ut se mori sentiat.*"

§ 6. Lawgivers should remember, that they are, mediately, and in effect, the executioners of every fellow-citizen, who suffers death in consequence of any penal statute; and there are certain contrasted points of view, in which it may be of use to them to consider criminals at the approach of death.

"[w] Master Barnardine, what hoa! your
"friend the hangman! you must be so good,
"Sir, to rise, and be put to death: Pray,
"Master Barnardine, awake, till you are ex-
"ecuted, and sleep afterwards."

The wretch, to whom this last summons is so ludicrously addressed, is represented to us, "as a man, that apprehends death no

[w] Shakespeare, Meas. for Meas. Act. iv. Sc. 3.

more

more dreadfully, but as a drunken dream; carelefs, recklefs, and fearlefs of what's paft, prefent, or to come."

The crimes of fuch a man may perhaps have made him unfit to live; but he is certainly unfit to die. The fafety of the community, and the prefervation of individuals, may call for his execution; but the bofom of humanity will heave in agony at the idea, the eye of religion will turn with horror from the fpectacle.

Suppofe the fufferer on the contrary to have been a valuable member of fociety, and to have erred only from fome momentary impulfe of our imperfect nature; one, who in the recollection of reafon hath found repentance; who refigns with chearfulnefs that life, which is become a forfeiture to the law, and looks up in confidence to heaven for that forgivenefs which is not to be found on earth. The laft footfteps of fuch a man, are watered with the tears of his fellow-citizens; and we hear from the mouth of every fpectator,

"Yes, I do think, that you might pardon him,
"And neither heaven, nor man grieve at the mercy."

CHAP.

CHAP. IV.

Of Baniſhment.

§ 1. THE Romans permitted an accuſed *Citizen*, in every caſe *before* judgement to withdraw himſelf from the conſequences of conviction into voluntary exile.

" *Exilium* (inquit Cicero) [x] *non ſupplicium*
" *eſt, ſed perfugium, portuſque ſupplicii. Ita-*
" *que nulla in lege noſtra reperietur, ut apud*
" *cæteras civitates, maleficium ullum exilio eſſe*
" *multatum. Sed cum homines vincula, neces,*
" *ignominiaſque vitant, quæ ſunt legibus conſti-*
" *tutæ; confugiunt, quaſi ad aram, in exilium;*
" *qui, ſi in civitate legis vim ſubire vellent, non*
" *prius civitatem, quam vitam amitterent. Quia*
" *nolunt, non adimitur his civitas; ſed ab his*
" *relinquitur atque deponitur.*"

§ 2. Tranſportation [y] was totally unknown to the common law of England; but the antient

[x] Orat. pro A. Cæcin. c. 34.

[y] We may eaſily form a probable gueſs as to its firſt introduction into our laws; for by ſtat. 39 Eliz. c. 4. it was enacted, " that dangerous rogues, and ſuch as will not be reformed of their roguiſh courſe of life, may lawfully

tient practice of abjuration of the realm bore a ſtrong reſemblance to the Roman inſtitution. "This was permitted, ſays Sir E. Coke, "when the felon choſe rather, *perdere pa-"triam, quam vitam.*" The oath of perpe-

fully by the Juſtices in their Quarter-ſeſſions be baniſhed out of the realm and all other the dominions thereof, into ſuch parts beyond the ſeas as ſhall be for that purpoſe aſſigned by the Privy Council: *or otherwiſe be adjudged perpetually to the Gallies of this Realm.*" And further, every rogue ſo baniſhed, and returning without licence, was made guilty of felony, but within the benefit of Clergy. And for the better indemnifying of ſuch rogues ſo returning, it was alſo enacted that prior to their baniſhment they ſhould be "thoroughly burned upon the left ſhoulder with a hot burning iron of the breadth of an Engliſh ſhilling, with a great Roman R upon the iron, for a perpetual mark upon ſuch rogue during his or her life." See Raſtall's Statutes, p. 429.

But Tranſportation more nearly as now practiſed ſeems to have taken place about the time of the Reſtoration. For, ſaith L. C. J. Kelyng, p. 45, "Copeland (the priſoner) alledged, that he had done nothing but what he ought to do to ſerve his friend; and this favourable circumſtance was allowed to be put into the King's pardon, amongſt thoſe priſoners of that nature who were to be ſent beyond the ſea; *it having been lately uſed*, that for felonies within clergy, if the priſoner deſire it, not to give his book, but procure a conditional pardon from the King, and ſend him beyond ſea to ſerve five years in ſome of the King's plantations, and then to have land there aſſigned to him, according to the uſe in thoſe plantations for ſervants after their time expired; with a condition in the pardon to be void if they do not go, or if they return into England during ſeven years, or after without the King's Licence."

tual

tual banishment was then administered to him by the Coroner in the church, or church-yard, to which he had fled; and a cross was delivered into his hand for his protection on his journey. This custom no longer subsists; for the privileges of sanctuary [z] being taken away by the act of Ja. I. the abjuration, as at the common law, being founded thereon, was virtually abolished.

§ 3. At present, banishment is in England, as in Russia [a], more frequently inflicted as a mode of punishment, than permitted as an act of mercy. But in Russia it is made subservient to political utility; and those, who have by their misconduct lost all claim to the indulgence of their countrymen, are compelled to undergo a separation from all domestic connections, the rigours of a horrid climate, and the unhealthiness of mines, in

[z] A very particular description of sanctuary and abjuration may be found in "Le Grand Coustumier," f. 13. § 81. See also the Mirror, c. 1. § 13.

[a] L' exil en Siberie porte avec soi une sorte de reprobation; il rend un homme si malheureux, que quoiqu'il vive au milieu de ses semblables, tout le monde le fuit; personne n'ose avoir avec lui aucune espece de liaison; mais c'est moins à cause du crime qu'on lui suppose, que par la crainte qu'on a du despôte.

Voyages en Sib. t. i. p. 236.

the

the place of better citizens, who muſt otherwiſe be neceſſitated to accept ſo ſevere a lot.

On the contrary, every effect of baniſhment, as practiſed in England, is often beneficial to the criminal, and always injurious to the community. The kingdom is deprived of a ſubject, and renounces all the emoluments of his future exiſtence. He is merely transferred to a new country; diſtant indeed, but as fertile, as happy, as civilized, and in general as healthy, as that which he hath offended.

It would not be incredible then, if this puniſhment ſhould be aſſerted in ſome inſtances to have operated even as a temptation to the offence; in many inſtances hath its inſufficiency been a fatal argument for the multiplication of capital penalties.

§ 4. It deſerves ſerious and immediate conſideration, how far, and by what means, this defect in our law may be redreſſed. It might perhaps be practicable to direct the ſtrict employment of a limited number of convicted felons in each of the dock-yards, in the ſtannaries, ſaltworks, mines, and public buildings of the kingdom. The more enormous offenders might be ſent to Tunis, Algiers, and other Mahometan ports, for the redemption of Chriſtian ſlaves: others might be compelled to dangerous expeditions; or be ſent to eſtabliſh new colonies, factories, and ſettlements on the coaſts of Africa, and on ſmall iſlands for the benefit of navigation. It muſt however be confeſſed, that it is not eaſy to determine upon theory the ſucceſs of political innovations; it is indeed impoſſible for a ſpeculative writer in his cloſet to collect the proper materials for this purpoſe. Practicable ſchemes on ſuch ſubjects can only be obtained from merchants and others, who are qualified by experience to point them out, and have the inducement of intereſt to promote their ſucceſs.

§ 5. I cannot diſmiſs this ſubject without expreſſing a doubt, relative to the propriety of puniſhing with death a return from tranſportation; eſpecially where the original offence was not capital. It certainly is not juſtified by neceſſity; for it is eaſy, if requiſite, to ſend the delinquent abroad again, without any conſiderable degree either of expence or trouble. Will it be ſaid, that he deservedly suffers for the breach of a compact, which he is supposed to have made? In many instances the transportation is not in the nature of a conditional pardon, but directed by positive law [b]; in no instance is

[b] In support of this assertion I shall cite some authorities; *previously observing*, that "exclusion from society is the proper punishment of those only, who are become objects of terror to their fellow-citizens in consequence of very heinous crimes, either not equivalent to the *ultimum supplicium*, or of which they have been convicted by disputable and unsatisfactory evidence."

By 6 Geo. I. c. 23. and 4 Geo. I. c. 11. any persons convicted of larceny either grand or petit, and entitled to clergy, may in the discretion of the court be directed to be transported to America for seven years; and if they return within that time, it shall be felony without benefit of clergy.

By stat. 10 Geo. II. c. 32. the penalty of transportation for seven years is inflicted on the second offence of stealing deer in any uninclosed forest; and for the first offence upon such as come to hunt there, armed with offensive weapons.

By 26 Geo. II. c. 19. § 11. persons convicted of assaulting any magistrate or officer, &c. in the salvage of any vessel or goods, are to be transported for seven years.

Ibid. c. 33. § 8. persons convicted of solemnizing matrimony without banns or licence, &c. shall be transported for fourteen years.

Also, by 5 Geo. III. c. 14. persons stealing or taking fish in any water within a park, paddock, orchard or yard, and the receivers, aiders, and abettors shall be transported for seven years.

I have not selected these as the *most* exceptionable instances; there are many others, in which transportation is inflicted upon offences by no means so heinous in their nature, as to require the extirpation of the criminal from the society of his fellow-citizens.

ſuch a compact reconcileable to the law of nature.

On the whole, is not ſuch ſeverity inconſiſtent with that leading principle, which forbids penal laws to attack the natural ſentiments of the heart? "*Duri eſt non deſiderare* "*patriam. Cari ſunt parentes, cari liberi,* "*propinqui, familiares; ſed omnes omnium* "*caritates patria una complexa eſt: pro quâ* "*quis bonus dubitet mortem oppetere?*

§ 6. By ſtat. 20 Geo. II. c. 46. it is made a felony, without benefit of clergy, for rebels under ſentence of tranſportation to go into France or Spain; and the ſame ſeverity is extended to all the friends of ſuch perſons, keeping or entertaining any correſpondence with them by letters, meſſages, or otherwiſe.

In the wording of this clauſe, there is not any ſaving of even the moſt innocent interchanges of friendſhip. Shall then the lawgiver infringe all the ties and privileges of humanity? Shall he point the ſword of juſtice againſt the boſom of fidelity? To ſuch a lawgiver I would ſay, "Conſult your own

" heart, and inflict not chastisement on ac-
" tions, which a good mind cannot disap-
" prove!"

CHAP. V.

Of Forfeiture and Corruption of Blood.

§ 1. *NEC vero me fugit, quam sit acerbum parentum scelera filiorum pœnis lui: sed hoc præclarè legibus comparatum est, ut caritas liberorum amicitiores parentes reipublicæ redderet* [c].

On a superficial glance, it seems harsh in a moral view, to extend the disgrace and infamy of the guilty ancestor to the innocent descendant; and to involve a whole family in the punishment of one criminal. In a political light, it seems contrary to the principles of freedom, to institute irregular fluctuations of property, and to leave so baneful a tool to the misapplication of possible tyranny, or the rage of civil troubles. A very ingenious answer hath been given to

[c] Cic. ad Brutum, Ep. xii.

theſe objections by a late learned perſon; from whoſe excellent argument (without adopting all the concluſions for which he ſo ably contended) we muſt at leaſt collect, that the law of forfeitures, when properly directed and reſtrained, is a ſalutary terror in defence of the ſtate, neither cruel nor impolitic.

Was it ever alledged againſt the puniſhment of death, that "its conſequences cannot in any caſe be confined to the criminal; but muſt of neceſſity go beyond him, to ſome connected with him by friendſhip, intereſt, or nature?"[d]—Society is ſupported by this neceſſity, whilſt individuals ſuffer by it. *Omne magnum exemplum habet aliquid ex iniquo, quod contra ſingulos utilitate publicâ rependitur*[e]

But it will be ſaid, that the collateral conſequences of forfeiture are not the creatures of neceſſity, but of poſitive inſtitution. Be they ſo; it is neither unjuſt nor unwiſe to convert human partialities to the promotion of human happineſs. Deſcendible honours,

[d] Conſid. on the Law of Forfeiture, p. 10.

[e] Tacit, Annal, l. xiv.

and

and the expectations of inheritance, are the gifts of society, conditional gifts, and therefore revocable, and may be modified by the public discretion for the public benefit.

§ 2. These arguments are offered in defence only of forfeitures immediately affecting the criminal; and it may seem a sufficient severity, that the children are thereby reduced to present poverty.—It is not so easy to reconcile either to reason or benevolence, that corruption of blood, a further consequence of English attainders, by which the inheritable quality is for ever extinguished.

The grandfather possesses an estate in fee; his son commits treason, and is executed; this attainder is a never-ceasing bar to the claim of the grandchild, and his posterity. A father seised of an estate in fee dies, leaving two sons the elder of whom is attainted; the younger cannot succeed, though the immediate descendant of innocent ancestors; nor can the children of the elder. Why, it will be said, should the impediment of blood stop the course of descent as to estates, over which, the criminal, as he never had any possession, could have no influence? It is an obvious anſwer, that the law requires the claimant by deſcent to prove himſelf heir to the perſon laſt ſeiſed; and in theſe caſes a link of the deſcending chain is irrecoverably loſt.

We muſt not however argue from ſpecial caſes againſt general ſyſtems. Perfection unexceptionable cannot be the reſult of human diſpenſations; and it would turn this beautiful fabric of our liberties to a fantaſtical, confuſed ſcene of prepoſterous diſtinctions, if it were allowable to ſet up perſonal compaſſion, and private hardſhips, in oppoſition to the conſiſtency of legal principles.

§ 3. Yet there are caſes, in which it is difficult for the artificial inferences of reaſon to give ſatisfaction to the natural dictates of ſentiment.—A criminal is attainted, in the year 1770, for an offence, then only diſcovered, but committed in the year 1760.—Suppoſe him, in this interval, to have alienated one half of his eſtate to a fair purchaſer, and to have contracted *bonâ fide* debts, equivalent to the other half. The *Alienée* muſt be diſpoſſeſſed, and the honeſt creditors are left without remedy; for "the forfeiture of lands "(ſays the law) has a relation to the time "of "of committing the offence, so as to avoid "the intermediate charges and convey-"ances."

Again, if the Husband and Wife be possessed jointly of a term of years in land, and the husband drown himself, the land shall be forfeited to the King; and the wife must lose the benefit of the survivorship. For, by the act of casting himself into the water, which is the cause of the felony committed, he forfeits the term; and this gives a title to the King, in preference to the wife's title by survivorship, which could not accrue till the instant of her husband's death [f].

Many of the inferior felonies subject the offender to the forfeiture of goods and chattels only; whence results a very unequal distribution of justice: A rich trader, and an affluent country-gentleman, being involved precisely in the same species and degree of guilt, the children of the former are reduced to beggary, while the family of the latter retain all their opulence.

[f] Blackst. Comment. iv. 190. Plowden 260. This was determined in the case of Lady Margaret Hales, wife of Sir James Hales (one of the Judges of the Common Pleas) who drowned himself in the third year of Q. Eliz.

The death of the anceſtor, before conviction and judgment, diſcharges, as to the real eſtate, all proceedings and forfeitures. So that the law furniſhes a temptation to the Criminal to ruſh uncalled for into the preſence of the Almighty, with all his imperfections on his head, and the addition of Suicide to the catalogue of his offences.

Valerius Maximus gives us an example of the effect of a temptation of the ſame kind. He tells us, that Licinius Macer, at the concluſion of his trial, perceiving Cicero ready to give judgement againſt him, ſtopped his breath with a handkerchief, and expired; and that the eſtate was thereby ſaved to his ſon Licinius Calvus, afterwards an Orator of great eminence[g]. In the latter ages of the Roman law, a diſtinction was made, inflicting forfeiture on thoſe who killed themſelves under the accuſation of a capital crime.

§. 4. Bills of attainder may with propriety be mentioned under the title of this chapter: they are exertions of thoſe extraordinary legiſlative powers, which ought to be uſed

[g] Val. Max. ix. 12.

only

only on the preſſures of real and urgent neceſſity; but never to be deſecrated to the gratification of political reſentments.

One of Henry the Eighth's parliaments attainted the Counteſs of Saliſbury, the Marchioneſs of Exeter, and two Gentlemen, without any trial or even citation to appear, and without better proofs, than the unſupported ſuggeſtions of the wretched ſycophant Cromwell. This inſtrument of regal tyranny fell a ſacrifice to the ſame iniquitous meaſures himſelf. He was in the year following declared Vicar-general of the kingdom; and, a few weeks afterwards, under an attainder of the ſame parliament, without trial, examination or evidence, condemned to death, and executed[h].

It is impoſſible to apologize for the many bloody ſtains, which we find indelibly affixed upon Engliſh hiſtory, by this paſſionate and irregular mode of puniſhing. Even Strafford, whom, as an Engliſh ſtateſman, we may, as Engliſhmen, abhor, muſt in candour be confeſſed to have fallen a victim to the indiſcreet rage of an Engliſh parliament. "We have

[h] Burnet, vol. i. p. 278.

"lived,

" lived, my lords, (ſaid he at the concluſion
" of his eloquent defence) happily to our-
" ſelves at home: we have lived glorioully
" abroad to the world: let us be content
" with what our fathers have left us: let
" not our ambition carry us to be more
" learned, than they were, in killing, and
" deſtructive arts. Were it not for the
" intereſt of theſe pledges, which a Saint
" in heaven left me, I ſhould be loth"—
(here he pointed to his children, his voice faultered, and his weeping ſtopped him)
" what I forfeit for myſelf, it is nothing:
" but, I confeſs, that my indiſcretion ſhould
" forfeit for them, it wounds me very deeply.
" You will pardon my infirmity: ſomething
" more I ſhould have ſaid; but I ſee I ſhall
" not be able, and therefore I ſhall leave
" it."

" Such (ſays the philoſophical Hiſtorian) were the capacity, genius, and preſence of mind, diſplayed by this magnanimous ſtateſman, that, whilſt argument, and reaſon, and law had any place, he obtained an undiſputed victory: and he periſhed at laſt overwhelmed, and ſtill unſubdued, by the undiſguiſed violence

lence of his fierce and unrelenting antagonists." *Weak is the effect of eloquence on the predeterminations of party!* The parliament proceeded in the attainder; but in a few weeks remitted to the children the more severe consequences of the sentence[i].

[i] The following note, which was copied from the Lord Primate Usher's Almanack, furnishes matter for much reflection.

" *May* 11, 1641.

The King wishes me to deliver unto my Lord Strafforde to-morrow,

1. That if the King's own life were only hazarded thereby, he would never have given passage unto his death.

2. *That the Execution without extream danger cannot be deferred.*

3. That he was moved by the Lords for his wife and children, and intended to dispose his entire estate upon them.

4. That, if his son be capable, he will take special notice of him for his imployment and preferment, (which I must tell none but him.)

5. That for Lord Chancellor, Lowther and Derry, he stops the proceedings until they give good reason for their authority.

6. L. Dillon's ability above all the natives.

7. *Earle of Ormond shall be Knight of the Garter in his place.*

8. Carpenter to be at liberty to look to his estate, or any one whom he shall appoint to have care of his children.

May 12. The Lord Strafforde beheaded at Tower-hill."

See the Strafforde Letters, vol. ii. p. 418.

That,

That, "*whoever deserves to die, and dies by an act of the whole Legislature, dies justly,*" is a position, which in the construction of unprejudiced reason is certainly true: but it should be remembered, that many requisites must concur to shew, that the party prosecuted *deserves to die*; requisites, which, in most cases of attainders, have been too precipitately assumed. But I return to my subject.

§ 5. Upon the whole, though it be not unequitable, "that those contingent advantages, which the civil qualifications of the blood have brought into view by the desert of one Ancestor, should be intercepted by the crimes of another [k]:" yet it is with pleasure, I see the approach of that day, when the posthumous rigours of forfeitures will cease, and the impediments of descent no longer affect a blameless posterity.

The Stat. 7 Ann. c. 21, provides, that, after the death of the then Pretender, no attainder for treason shall extend to the disinheriting of any heir, nor to the prejudice of the right, or title of any person, or per-

[k] Considerations on the Law of Forfeiture.

sons,

ſons, other than the right or title of the offender, or offenders, during his, her, or their natural lives only; giving alſo a power of entry after their deaths, as if ſuch attainder had never happened.

It was thought expedient, in the year 1744, to ſuſpend the operation and effect of this ſtatute, till after the deceaſe of the preſent Pretender and his brother.

This ſuſpending clauſe was debated with great warmth, and profuſion of learning, between Sir Dudley Ryder, and Mr. Fazakerly; by the latter of whom it was contended, to be virtually ſubverſive of the conditions of the Union, inconſiſtent with the ſpirit of our conſtitution, with the dictates of humanity, and the principles of policy. It was firſt moved in the upper houſe by Lord Bathurſt, ſeconded by Lord Hardwicke, and was there alſo the ſubject of much eloquence.

In fact, when the act of Union paſſed in the fifth year of the Queen, this point had been left undetermined; but, upon a tacit undertaking, well underſtood on the part of the Scots, (who had no intention to make them-

themſelves liable to Engliſh attainders) that it ſhould be afterwards adjuſted. The ſubſequent Act was accordingly framed "for improving the union of the two kingdoms[1]." But, as a total immunity from the forfeiture of real eſtates was not founded on any requiſition of Scotland, either expreſſed or implied, it is difficult to conceive the reaſon which induced the parliament to carry the remedy ſo far beyond the grievance then in contemplation.

The mere execution of the criminal is a fleeting example; but the forfeiture of lands leaves a permanent impreſſion: It is indeed one of our beſt conſtitutional ſafe-guards, when applied with diſcretion to the preſervation of moral conduct, and uſed without violence to the correction of guilt. *This branch of the penal ſyſtem will not therefore be ſuffered to fall from the body of our law without*

[1] Stat. 7 Ann. c. 21. the preamble is in the following words. "Whereas nothing can more conduce to the improving the union of the two kingdoms, than that the laws of both parts of Great Britain, ſhould agree as near as may be, eſpecially thoſe Laws which relate to High Treaſon and the proceedings thereon, as to the nature of the crime, the method of proſecution and trial, and alſo the *forfeitures and puniſhment* of that offence; which are of the greateſt concern both to the King and the Subject."

ſerious

serious consideration: but we may safely conclude, that the corruption of blood, with all its endless consequences, will have a speedy and total abolition; as any further intervention of Parliament therein would be contrary to that sacred regard, which is due to national compacts.

§ 6. But it should be observed, that this Provision extends to Attainders, only in cases of high Treason: they will still operate in full force upon the crimes of petty treason, and on many of, if not all, the higher felonies.

If such an inconsistence be suffered, it will make the English law the very reverse of the system of Arcadius; who, leaving treasons liable to the utmost severities, speaks of other offences in the following words: "*Sancimus* "*ibi esse pœnam, ubi & noxia est; propinquos,* "*notos, familiares, procul a calumniâ submovemus, quos reos sceleris societas non facit.* "*Nec enim affinitas, vel amicitia, nefarium* "*crimen admittunt: peccata igitur suos teneant* "*auctores; nec ulterius progrediatur metus,* "*quam reperiatur delictum.*"

CHAP. VI.

Of Imprisonment.

§ 1. IMprisonment, inflicted by law as a punishment, is not according to the principles of wise legislation. It sinks useful subjects into burthens on the community, and has always a bad effect on their morals: nor can it communicate the benefit of example, being in its nature secluded from the eye of the people.

These objections are obviously true; but their influence on the Laws of England hath not been uniform. It is not unusual, by the positive institutions of this land of liberty, to punish offenders by confinement: in many cases, temporary; in others, as in the instance of striking at any person in the King's courts of justice, of rescuing a prisoner, and in every case of Præmunire, perpetual. And in this light, as a mode of punishment, it was considered in the earlier ages of our Law; of which I find the following instance in the statute

ſtatute of Weſtm. the 2d, [m] A. D. 1285. "*Qui monialem a domo ſuâ abducat, licet monialis conſentiat, puniatur per priſonam trium annorum, et ſatisfaciat domui, a quâ abducta fuerit, competenter.*"

§ 2. It is the proper end of cuſtody, to keep thoſe, who are accuſed of injuries to ſociety, amenable to the deciſions of juſtice. But, as accuſations are not proofs, and as innocence is to be preſumed in every ſtage of the charge [n], previous to the conviction of guilt; the utmoſt tenderneſs and lenity are due to the perſon of the priſoner. And here it ſhould alſo be obſerved, that it is contrary both to public juſtice and public utility, to throw the accuſed and convicted, the inno-

[m] 13 Ed. I. c. 34.

[n] The power of taking bail, which in effect is only a milder ſpecies of cuſtody, is a conſequence of this preſumption; and appears to have exiſted in every poliſhed ſyſtem of laws, with regard to all offences except thoſe of the higheſt enormity, in which nothing leſs than the perſon of the accuſed is thought to be a ſufficient pledge for his future appearance. Such particularly is the idea of our law, and ſuch was the language of the Roman Digeſt. "*In vincula non conjiciendus eſt reus, qui fidejuſſores dare poterit, niſi tam grave ſcelus eum admiſiſſe conſtet, ut neque fidejuſſoribus, neque militibus committi debeat.*"

Dig. l. xlviii. t. 3. 3.

cent and the guilty, indifcriminately, into the fame Dungeon.

From a numberlefs variety of accidental circumftances, which happen in the courfe of human tranfactions, it muft fall to the lot of many, to become Infolvent. Debtors therefore, though certainly a fpecies of Criminals, fhould in general be confidered rather as unfortunate, than culpable [o]. Humane treatment they have a claim to; nor can we confiftently with any good principle, either of morals or government, refufe the fame to perfons accufed, or even to the moft atrocious convicts. It will follow, that a fpecial care fhould be taken, that the neceffary miferies of a jail may not be aggravated by the unreftrained cruelty of the jailer.

§ 2. I might refer to the very excellent provifion of the civil law on this fubject [p];

[o] It feems to be a defect in our government, but incapable perhaps of any practicable remedy, that the conduct of infolvent perfons, prior to their infolvency, is not, except in the inftance of Bankrupts, fubjected to fome legal mode of inquiry. The cafe of a confined debtor, whofe confinement is the mere confequence of inevitable misfortunes, without any mixture either of criminality or neglect on his own part, is extremely pitiable, and contradictory to every juft principle of legiflation.

[p] Domat's Civil law, v. ii. p. 287.

but

but ſuch peculiar attention hath been ſhewn to it both by the common, and ſtatute law of England, that nothing more can be deſired; except that improvement in the airineſs and extent of the buildings, which the induſtrious refinement of a ſenſible age is ſoon likely to produce.

The appointment of jailers reſts with the ſheriff, who is in ſome degree reſponſible for their good behaviour [q], and intereſted therefore in the choice of proper perſons; from whom he is alſo required to exact very ample ſecurity. The body of a man dying in priſon is not to be interred, until the Coroner's inqueſt hath examined it [r]: and, in point of law, if a priſoner dies in dureſs of the jailer by hard confinement, and ſeverities unneceſſary to the ſafe cuſtody, it is murder [s]. Theſe preventives of ſecret tyranny

[q] Dalt. c. 118. 4 Rep. 34. [r] 3 Inſt. 52. 91.

[s] Strange, 856, and 884. The caſes of Caſtel *v.* Bambridge and Corbet; and of the King *v.* Huggins. Mr. Juſtice Foſter, p. 322, hath inadvertently ſtated the opinions collaterally given by the court in theſe caſes, as the poſitive deciſions of the court againſt the defendants: whereas, in the firſt caſe, there being no pretence to charge either of the appellates, the jury brought them in "Not guilty:" and in the other caſe, "it is the judgment of the "court on the ſpecial verdict, that the priſoner Huggins "is Not guilty and therefore he muſt be diſcharged."

 have

have been well preferved to the fubject by frequent profecutions, the effects of ufeful and compaffionate enquiries, occafionally inftituted by the two houfes of Parliament. And laftly, the abufes, extortions, and infults of jailers towards the unfortunate perfons in their cuftody, are more particularly guarded againft by a late very comprehenfive ftatute [t]; the provifions of which are very beneficial both to debtors and criminals, though more efpecially intended for the former.

§ 3. This extraordinary anxiety of our law in favour of prifoners is by no means fuperfluous; for it muft be confeffed that jailers are in general a mercilefs race of men.

The Count de Lauzun paffed the long interval from the year 1672 to 1681 in the prifon of Pignerol. It has been well obferved [u], "that, with pen, and ink, and paper, albeit "a man cannot get out of prifon, he may do "very well within, and at laft come out a "wifer man than he entered;" but thefe confolations did not fall to the lot of the Count

[t] 32 Geo. II. c. 28. [u] Sterne.

de

de Lauzun.—At a diſtance from the voice of friend or relation; without any ſounds except his own ſighs; without any light except the glimmering through the ruins of the roof; without books, means of occupation, or poſſibility of exerciſe; a prey to hope deferred, corroding languor, and uninterrupted horror; he at laſt, as the only means of avoiding inſanity, had recourſe to the expedient of taming a ſpider.—“ Miſery, ſays Trinculo, makes a “ man acquainted with ſtrange companions.” The ſpider received his flies every morning with gratitude, carried on his webs through the day with alacrity, and engaged the whole attention of his benefactor; until the jailer, converſant in ſcenes of wretchedneſs, and conſequently ſteeled againſt every tender ſenſation, accidentally diſcovered this amuſement of his priſoner, and in the wantonneſs of tyranny officiouſly deſtroyed the ſubject of it. M. de Lauzun afterwards declared, that he conceived his agony on this occaſion to have been more painful than that of a fond mother on the loſs of a darling child.

CHAP. VII.

Of Corporal Punishments, and of Infamy.

§ 1. WE are told, that in Sparta it was thought a very disgraceful sentence to the criminal, to lose the privilege of sending his wife to another man, or to be confined to the society of virgins.

The authenticity of the fact is immaterial, if the inference be admitted; which is, that, *in a moderate and virtuous government, the idea of shame will follow the finger of the law*; and that, whatever species of punishment is pointed out as infamous, will have the effect of infamy. *Existimatio est dignitatis illæsæ status, legibus ac moribus comprobatus, qui ex delicto nostro, auctoritate legum aut minuitur, aut consumitur* [w]. The punishment of strangling is deemed honourable by the Ottoman family, who think it infamous, that their blood should be spilt upon the ground; in England, it is

[w] Dig. l. i. t. 13. 5. § 1.

thought

thought a more reſpectable death to be beheaded.

§ 2. Let legiſlators then remember, that the ſtamp of ignominy is intruſted to their diſpoſal; and let them uſe with œconomy, and diſcretion, this beſt inſtrument for the promotion of morality, and the extirpation of vice.

Shame loſes its effect, when it is inflicted without juſt and cautious diſtinction; or when, by the wantonneſs of oppreſſion, it is made familiar to the eye. The ſenſibility of the people, under ſo extravagant an exertion of power, degenerates into deſpondency, baſeneſs, and ſtupidity: their virtue is of forced extraction, the child of fear, with all the meanneſs of the parent entailed upon it. The tranquillity of ſuch a ſtate, ſays Monteſquieu, is the mournful ſilence of a city, which the enemy is about to ſtorm.

The preſent Empreſs of Ruſſia is aware, that immoderate efforts are the ſymptoms of inſufficiency, and have always more fury than force; that the ſecurity of the prince decreaſes in proportion to the exorbitance of his deſpotiſm;

tiſm; and that the national ſenſibility is the beſt ſpring of national power. But a few years ago, prior to the reign of the late Empreſs Elizabeth, it was no more diſgrace to a Ruſſian nobleman to receive a public flogging from the arm of the hangman, than it is at this moment to a miſerable Japoneſe to pay with his ſkin the coſts of a civil action, thought nugatory by the judge. The Muſcovites no longer wed their wives with a whip inſtead of a wedding ring; and Ruſſia riſes into the reſpect of Europe. The Japoneſe ſtill ſubmit to the daily diſcipline of the laſh; and Japan continues the contempt of the world.—The cudgel (ſays du Halde) is the Governor of China; the Chineſe (ſays the writer of Lord Anſon's voyage) are eminent for timidity, hypocriſy, and diſhoneſty.

§ 3. Corporal puniſhments immediately affecting the body, and publickly inflicted, ought to be infamous in the eſtimation of the people; ſo ſhould degradations from titles of honour, civil incapacities, brandings, and public exhibitions of the offender: all which penalties ſhould be applied with

with great caution, and only to offences infamous in their nature.

§ 4. In any caſe, to fix a laſting, viſible ſtigma upon the offender, is contrary both to humanity and ſound policy. The wretch, finding himſelf ſubjected to continual inſult, becomes habituated to his diſgrace, and loſes all ſenſe of ſhame. It is impoſſible for him to form any irreproachable connection; for virtue, though of a ſocial nature, will not aſſociate with infamy [x]. Yet this practice of branding hath prevailed in every known ſyſtem of laws; as with us at preſent, in the puniſhment of many offences; and in

[x] The Preamble of ſtat. 5 Ann. c. 6. is a ſtrong inſtance in ſupport of this poſition.—"Whereas by ſtat. 11 "& 12 W. III. § 6. it is enacted that all and every perſon "and perſons, who ſhould be convicted of any Theft, "and ſhould have the Benefit of Clergy allowed there-"upon, or ought to be burnt in the hand for ſuch of-"fence, inſtead of being burnt in the hand, ſhould be "burnt in the moſt viſible part of the left cheek neareſt "the noſe: *and whereas it hath been found by experience,* "*that the ſaid puniſhment hath not had the deſired effect, by* "*deterring ſuch offenders from the further committing ſuch* "*crimes and offences, but on the contrary, ſuch offenders, be-*"*ing rendered thereby unfit to be entruſted in any honeſt and* "*lawful way, become the more deſperate:* Be it there-"fore enacted, that the aforeſaid clauſe ſhall be and is "hereby repealed."

all

all cafes, when the offender, not being a clergyman, is admitted to the benefit of clergy. In like manner by the laws of France, "*Ceux & celles, qui après avoir été* "*condamnés pour vol, ou flétris de quelque au*-"*tre crime que ce foit, feront convaincus de rè*-"*cidive en crime de vol, ne pourront être con*-"*damnès a moindre peine que, fcavoir lès* "*hommes aux galeres à tems, ou à perpétuité,* "*et lès femmes à être de nouveau flétries d'un* "W. *fi c'eft pour récidive de vol, ou d'un fimple* "V. *fi la premiere flétriffure a été encourue pour* "*autre crime*[y]. *Et ceux qui feront condamnés* "*aux galeres à tems ou a perpetuité* pour "quelque crime que ce puiffe être, *ferront* "*flétris, avant d'y être conduits, dès trois let*-"*tres* G. A. L. *pour, en cas de récidive en* "*crime qui mérite peine afflictive, être punis de* "*mort*[z]." So alfo among the Romans, it was ufual, but only when the crime was infamous in its nature, to affix fome branding, or ignominious letter, on the forehead of the criminals; and perfons fo branded were afterwards called, *infcripti* or *ftigmatici*, or, by a

[y] Code penal. 8vo. A. D. 1755, p. 105. Declaration du Louis XV.

[z] Ibid. p. 138.

more

more equivocal term, *literati* [a]. One might almost say that those literary acquisitions were in some instances voluminous: for Zonaras relates that Theophilus the Emperor caused twelve verses to be inscribed on the foreheads of two monks; and we find in Petronius, "*quod implevit Eumolpus frontem Encolpi & Gytonis ingentibus literis, & notum fugitivorum epigramma per totam faciem liberali manu duxit.*"

§ 5. There are two kinds of infamy, the one founded in the opinions of the people respecting the mode of punishment, the other in the construction of law respecting the future credibility of the delinquent: the law of England was erroneous, when it declared the latter a consequence of the punishment, not of the crime [b].—There still exist some unrepealed statutes, which inflict perpetual infamy on offences of civil institution [c]. But in general the rigour of this doctrine is now

[a] Cœl. Rod. l. vii. c. 13. *Nulli Samiis literatiores.* Plaut. Cas. II. vi. 49. "*Si hic literatus me sinat.*"

I was mistaken in supposing that this expression had been adopted by stat. 4 H. VII. c. 13. which recites "that divers persons *lettered* had been more bold to commit mischievous deeds, &c." That word clearly relates only to scholars and the clergy.

[b] Coke, Litt. 6. b. [c] 2 & 3 Edw. VI.

reduced to reaſon[d]; and it is holden that, unleſs a man be put in the pillory, or ſtigmatized, for *crimen falſi*, as for perjury, forgery, or the like, it infers no blemiſh on his atteſtation. It may be highly penal to engroſs corn, or to publiſh a pamphlet offenſive to government; but mercantile avarice, and political ſedition, have no connection with the competence of teſtimony; the credit of an oath can only be overbalanced by the nature and weight of the precedent iniquity. Such was the reaſoning of the Roman law. "*Ictus fuſtium infamiam non im*-" *portat, ſed cauſa, propter quam id pati me*-" *ruit; ſi ea fuit, quæ infamiam damnato*" *irrogat*[e]."

§ 6. I ſay nothing of baſtinadoes, mutilations, and a variety of other modes of corporal puniſhment, equally inconſiſtent with decency and humanity: ſuch refinements of cruelty put the whole ſpecies, rather than the criminal, to diſgrace.

Artaxerxes moderated the ſeverity of the laws of Perſia, by enacting[f], that the nobility

[d] Gilbert's Law of Evidence, p. 143.
[e] Dig. 48. t. xix. § 26. [f] Plutarch.

who

who debaſed themſelves, inſtead of being laſhed, which had been the practice, ſhould be ſtripped, and the whipping be given to their veſtments; and that, inſtead of having the hair plucked off, they ſhould only be deprived of their high-crowned Tiaræ.

§ 7. The Engliſh conſtitution, ever anxious to preſerve the virtuous pride of the people, hath uſed this branch of the penal code with a reſerve ſo ſcrupulous, that it may almoſt be doubted, whether more attention hath not been ſhewn to the protection of this principle, than to the preſervation of life: for corporal pains might certainly with good effect be ſubſtituted, in ſome caſes, in the room of capital judgments.

Yet, without any very ſtrict ſcrutiny into our ſtatute books, one may point out many proviſions ſtill exiſting, which are diſguſtful to humanity, and offenſive to common ſenſe.

It is eaſy to conceive, why the hand which gives a blow in a court of juſtice ſhould be cut off by edict of law; the analogy between the offence and the penalty is evident: though it was at leaſt a condeſcenſion to minutenesses in that parliament, which, "to "give more solemnity to the operation, "ordered the master-cook, and serjeant of the larder to attend with dressing knives; the serjeant of the wood-yard to furnish a chopping-block; the yeoman of the scullery to attend with a pan of coals, and the serjeant-farrier to bring hot irons to sear the stump." But it is not so easy to acquiesce in the propriety of punishing a blow given in a church-yard, with the loss of an ear[h]; though we are told, that it was intended to obviate the quarrels of Protestants, and Papists, at the first establishment of the Reformation. Under a similar disregard to relative propriety, Henry the First seems to have enacted "*quod falsarii monetæ oculos et genitalia amitterent, absque aliquâ redemptione*[i]." Less absurd was the conduct of Severus, who punished a notary for the exhibition of a forged plead-

[g] Stat. 33 Hen. VIII. c. 12.

[h] 5 and 6 Edw. VI. c. 4. or, "having no Ears, the offender shall be branded with the letter F in his cheek."

[i] Wilkins, Leg. Anglo-sax. p. 304. Knyghton, p. 2377. and in the Annales de Margan, sub anno 1124. "Monetarii autem numero XCIV jussu Regis in Normanniâ consistentis die Epiphaniæ Genitalibus privati sunt." And in the Records about the time of the Conquest, it is very frequently said, in regard to other offences, that the convict "pro felonia suâ fuit occœcatus, et ementulatus, et bona sua eschaet. Regi."

ing,

ing, by ordering the nerves of his fingers to be cut, that he might never be able to write again; as was alſo a Law of Edward the Firſt, how unjuſtifiable ſoever on account of its cruelty, againſt the third offence of theft from the lead mines in Derbyſhire; "that a knife ſhould be ſtruck through the hand of the criminal fixed on the table; and that in this agony and attitude he ſhould continue, till he had freed himſelf by cutting off his hand [k]."

The eighth of Eliz. c. 3. puniſhes with impriſonment, and the loſs of the left hand, the ſending of live ſheep out of the kingdom, or the embarkation of them on board of any ſhip; and this too, without any exceptions of the neceſſary proviſions for the ſhip's crew: the ſecond offence is made only a clergable felony.—Sir Edward Coke thinks [l], that the benefit of clergy might be pleaded, as well in caſe of cutting off the hand, as in caſe of felony; if ſo, and if the offender were fortunate enough to have learnt to read, he could never have ſuffered under this act.

[k] Fuller—and Obſerv. on the ancient Statutes, p. 380.

[l] 3 Inſt. 104.—Staunford 37. b. is referred to by Sir Ed. Coke; but I have not been able to find any ſuch opinion.

The 14th of Eliz. c. 5. directed vagabonds to be ſeverely whipped, and burned through the ear with a hot iron, the compaſs of an inch; and for the ſecond offence to ſuffer death. This was a temporary act, and not continued in force.

It will not eaſily be credited by thoſe, who do not poſſeſs the Statute which I am about to mention, yet it is certainly true, that by *Stat.* 10 *Geo. III.* [m] *c.* 19. *A. D.* 1770, "every "perſon whatſoever, taking, killing, or de-

[m] It is remarkable, that this Statute was made at a time, when "the Commentaries on the Laws of England" muſt be ſuppoſed to have been very recently peruſed by every Member of the Legiſlature. The writer of that admirable work hath, with peculiar anxiety, ſhewn "the neceſſity of not deviating any further from our ancient conſtitution, by ordaining new penalties to be inflicted upon ſummary convictions."

And ſurely, the corporal puniſhment of an Engliſhman, by the ſuffrage of one perſon only, is inconſiſtent with every idea of Engliſh Liberty. Yet this unſatisfactory mode of trial was inſtituted for the promotion of ſpeedy juſtice; and as a ſpecies of mercy to Delinquents, who, in trivial miſdemeanors, might otherwiſe be ruined by the expence and delay of frequent proſecutions by indictment: but it hath been extended in a degree truly formidable. The Courts Leet and Sheriff's Tourns are fallen into diſuſe, and the juriſdiction of individuals is aggrandized beyond meaſure: a juriſdiction, which, by its burthenſome conſequences becoming diſguſtful to men of fortune and education, too often falls into the hands of the mercenary and the ignorant.

"ſtroying

" ſtroying any hare, pheaſant, partridge, " moor-game, &c. or uſing any dog, gun, " &c. for that purpoſe, between an hour after " ſun-ſetting, and one hour before ſun-riſing, " and convicted thereof *before one* or more " juſtice or juſtices, *upon the oath of one* or " more witneſs or witneſſes; ſhall for the " firſt offence be impriſoned, not leſs than " three months, for other offences not leſs " than ſix months; and either for the firſt, " or any other offence, *be once publicly whip-* " *ped* in the town, where the jail or houſe " of correction ſhall be, within three days " from the time of his commitment, between " the hours of twelve and one o'clock in the " day." And this is enacted even *without any reſervations, or diſtinctions, as to the rank, quality, or fortune of the offender.*

The tacit diſapprobation of mankind conſigns ſuch laws to diſregard and oblivion: but they ſhould be repealed, to prevent every poſſibility of oppreſſion on the one hand, and to ſtifle all hopes of impunity on the other.

CHAP. VIII.

Of Fines.

§ 1. PEcuniary penalties form the last, and best class of those salutary restraints of law, which alone render national liberty either valuable or permanent. It is a wise and merciful institution, which converts the little attachments of selfishness, into the strong holds of society. Let the inordinate sallies of profligacy be controuled in their first efforts; and the frequency of capital, and corporal punishments will soon become unnecessary: that frequency, so fatal to the present, and future happiness of the sufferers, so subversive of every sentiment of national benevolence!

§ 2. There exists however to this mildest mode of punishment a plausible objection, which makes it seemingly repugnant to the genius of a government, formed and supported on maxims of freedom: *the quantum of the fine must in most cases be left to the discretion of the Judges.*

The

The value of money and property is subjected to daily and unforeseen fluctuations: the circumstances of the offenders, like the circumstances of their offences, are infinitely various. It is impossible therefore, in this age of refinement, to imitate the simplicity of the Ancient Britons, to annex specific penalties to specific classes of crimes, and to establish a wholesale traffic between criminals and courts of justice.

Howel Dda found no difficulty in saying [n], that the fine for murdering a Chancellor should be 189 cows; for killing the Queen's cat, as much wheat as would cover her, when suspended by the tail; for a perjury, three cows; for the rape of a maid, twelve cows; of a matron, eighteen; and in cases of seduction, "*Vir, si factum denegaverit, jurabit super campanam ecclesiæ malleo destitutam; quod si fassus fuerit, compensabit denariis totidem, quot nates fœminæ operiantur.*"

I see no reason, except what arises from their internal absurdity, to doubt the authen-

[n] Leges Wallicæ, p. 116. 202, &c.

ticity of theſe laws [o]; or to ſuppoſe, that they were not the moſt ſerious efforts of Welſh Juriſprudence. For on this point, the ſame want of common delicacy, and common ſenſe, is very conſpicuous in the Inſtitutes of our good King Alfred [p]; and in the ancient Codes of the Burgundians, and of Sweden, and indeed of all the German nations. They had no ſettled rule of diſtinction between accidental damages, and intentional injury; between voluntary, and involuntary acts. "It was (ſays a learned Writer) the firſt indication of the approach of theſe nations towards politeneſs, that their compoſitions for injuries done to women were generally doubled [q]."

In ſhort, in the ages of imperfect civilization, "Juſtice ſeems to have been adminiſtered, merely to give a protection to the criminal againſt the party injured [r];" and this protection was given to the former, in con-

[o] They were made, A. D. 914. Adhibitis populi frequentibus comitiis in Casâ Candidâ ſuper fluvium Taf. Spelm. Gloſſ. p. 362.

[p] Leg. Anglo-ſax. p. 37.——Civil. Reg. Sueciæ, t. xi. c. 12.

[q] Lord Kaims's Law-tracts, p. 32, &c.

[r] L'Eſprit des loix, l. xx. c. 20.

ſideration

ſideration of the fine, which the latter was obliged to receive[s]. This was called a compoſition, and the reſentment of the offended family was cancelled. Such is the character given by Tacitus of the Germans: "*Suſcipere inimicitias ſeu patris, ſeu propinqui neceſſe eſt: nec implacabiles durant; luitur enim etiam homicidium certo armentorum ac pecorum numero, recipitque ſatisfactionem tota domus.*"

We find alſo in Homer frequent mention of the price of blood as paid to the repreſentatives of the deceaſed; and the ninth book of the Iliad is founded entirely on the efficacy of preſents in the expiation of an injury.

[s] By ſuch means individuals were firſt taught to acquieſce in the general diſpenſations of law, and by degrees to conſider injuries to themſelves as injuries to ſociety. But, prior to the eſtabliſhment of theſe compoſitions, "Every offended Baron buckled on his armour, and ſought redreſs at the head of his vaſſals. His adverſary met him in like hoſtile array. Neither of them would ſubmit points in which their paſſions were warmly intereſted, to the ſlow determination of a judicial enquiry. Both truſted to their ſwords for the deciſion of the conteſt; the kindred and dependants of the aggreſſor, as well as of the defender, were involved in the quarrel."

See Dr. Robertſon's Hiſt. of the Emperor Charles the Fifth, v. i. p. 44.

§ 3 In the courſe of ſociety, riches muſt branch into very unequal proportions; and ſtated fines to ſpecified crimes muſt become ſubjects of mockery and indifference to ſome offenders, of ruin and deſolation to others and their families.

A modern Lawgiver ſhrinks therefore at the recital of the ancient amercements: he feels, that the Law on this point cannot, conſiſtently with reaſon, be fixed, and determinate. The enormity and tendency of the crime, the malice and wilfulneſs of the intention, the inconſiderateneſs and ſuddenneſs of the act, the age, faculties, and fortune of the offender, form a chain of complex queſtions; which can be reſolved only by the evidence of each ſeparate charge, and for which no human foreſight can provide.

Here then ariſes a neceſſary appeal to the breaſt of the judge; an appeal, which, under the families of Tudor and Stuart, became occaſionally the inſtrument of extortion and tyranny: but which was, even in thoſe reigns, (for the Bill of Rights was only declaratory of the old conſtitutional privileges) ſubjected by the law of England to ſuch wiſe regulations, and

and barriers, as ought to have ſecured to the ſubject every benefit of certainty.

It is the uſage of the courts, ſuperinduced on the clauſe of Magna Charta relative to civil amercements [t], never to extend the fine of any criminal ſo far, as to take from him the implements, and means of his profeſſion, and livelihood; or to deprive his family of their neceſſary ſupport. If the produce of his property, under thoſe humane reſtrictions, be thought inadequate to the degree of the offence, ſome corporal puniſhment is inflicted, or ſtated impriſonment: the impropriety of the latter, as a penal judgement, I have already obſerved. As a further ſafeguard againſt poſſible oppreſſion, all grants and promiſes of

[t] C. 20. Liber homo non amercietur pro parvo delicto, niſi ſecundum modum delicti, et pro magno delicto amercietur ſecundum magnitudinem delicti, *ſalvo contenemento ſuo*, et mercator eodem modo *ſalvâ mercandiſâ ſuâ*, et villanus eodem modo amercietur *ſalvo wainnagio ſuo*. ſi inciderint in miſericordiam noſtram; et nulla predictarum miſericordiarum ponatur niſi per ſacramentum proborum hominum de viſneto; comites et barones non amercientur niſi per pares ſuos, et non niſi ſecundum modum delicti.

The idea of leaving to the defendant the tools in trade and huſbandry, and the beaſts of the plough, appears to have been taken from the Roman law.

See Gilbert's Forum Romanum, p. 25. and Wood's Civil Law, p. 334.

fines,

fines, and forfeitures, of particular perſons, before conviction, are illegal [u] and void.

§ 4. The wiſdom of our Law, having thus amply ſecured the property, and perſonal freedom of the ſubject, hath rarely thought it adviſable to affix certain ſums to ſpecified crimes: I ſhall however mention one inſtance to the contrary; which, on account of its ſingularity, deſerves attention.

The 37th H. VIII. c. 6. intituled, "the bill for burning of frames," and ſtill in exiſtence; for the better prevention alſo of "the cutting out of beaſts tongues, and the damms of ſtew-ponds; the cutting off the ears of his Majeſty's ſubjects, and the heads of conduit pipes; the barking of apple-trees, and divers *other like kinds* of miſerable offences, to the great diſpleaſure of Almighty God, and of the King's Majeſty;" gives treble damages, recoverable by action of Law, to

[u] Bill of Rights, ſtat. 1 W. and M. ſtat. ii. c. 2. But it was long before holden by Sir Edward Coke to be an illegal practice. "For when a ſubject obtaineth a promiſe "of the forfeiture, many times undue means, and more "violent proſecution is uſed for private lucre, tending to "deſtruction, than the quiet and juſt proceeding of law "would permit, and the party ought to live of his own, "until attainder." 2 Inſt. 48.

the

the party injured, and a fine of x l. ſterling to the King's Majeſty.

This ſtatute wants no obſervation upon it; except, that I have not ſtated it on account of the equivocal idea of treble damages for an ear: treble damages have in all caſes the ſound of abſurdity, though not uncommonly preſcribed in ſtatutes, which give penal Actions.

§ 5. *The excellence of the Penal ſyſtem conſiſts in the reaſonable ſelection of the objects of its coercion, in the moderate and judicious application of its penalties, in the perſpicuity of its expreſſion, in the notoriety of its mandates, and in the certainty of its execution.* But it may be rendered ſtill more perfect by the addition of certain ſalutary precautions, which ſavour in ſome degree of puniſhment, though intended in their general purport merely for the prevention of crimes.

And here it is with pleaſure, that I take the opportunity of mentioning an inſtitution full of Wiſdom and Humanity, of ancient uſe in England, and very imperfectly known to any other country. That wiſe inſtitution

of

of our Anceſtors I mean, which, dividing the people into certain claſſes, compelled the ſeveral neighbourhoods or diviſions of men to become mutual pledges for the good behaviour of the individuals, who compoſed them; and conſequently, when any offence was committed within their diſtrict, either to produce the offender, or become liable to ſuch penalty as might be thought proportionable to the injury offered to the peace of Society. *Securitas fiebat ſcilicet, quod de omnibus villis totius regni ſub decennali fide-juſſione debebant eſſe univerſi; ita quod ſi unus ex decem foris-fecerit, novem ad rectum eum haberent:* [w] *ſumma et maxima ſecuritas, per quam omnes ſtatu firmiſſimo ſuſtinebantur!*

The additional facility of mutual intercourſe between the different provinces of the kingdom, the improving uniformity of language which aroſe from that intercourſe, the increaſing numbers of the people, and their unſettled inhabitancy occaſioned by the purſuit of commerce, ſeverally contributed to throw this plan of police into gradual diſuſe. In its original extent it is become perhaps

[w] Wilkins, Leges Edwardi, c. 20.

im-

impracticable; but ſome of its beſt veſtiges are ſtill viſible in our Laws.

In general, every perſon, as even a wife againſt her huſband or a huſband againſt his wife, who hath cauſe to apprehend that another will do any corporal hurt to him, hath a right to compel ſuch perſon to give ſecurity to a magiſtrate, that he will not do any act, that ſhall amount to a diſturbance of the peace; and this is called *a recognizance of the peace*[x]. It is in the nature of a conditional debt, payable only to the King, but in which both the King and the ſubject are ſuppoſed to have an intereſt [y].

The complainant muſt verify upon oath, that his application to the Magiſtrate is not made from motives of malice, or to give vexation; and, if the perſon complained of ſhall refuſe, or be unable to find ſufficient ſurety, he ſhall be committed to priſon.

[x] 1 Hawk. P.C. 126. Commentaries, b. iv. c. 18.

[y] For which reaſon it ſeems an abſurd poſition in our law, that a recognizance may be diſcharged by the demiſe of the king; or that it may be releaſed by the party at whoſe complaint it was taken.

It is alſo uſual, upon the conviction of certain Miſdemeanours, to make *ſureties for the future good behaviour* of the offender, a part of the puniſhment. And it is holden under the Stat. 34 Edw. III. c. 1. that the Magiſtrate hath a diſcretionary power to take ſuch ſurety from all perſons of evil fame, or, in other words, whom he ſhall have juſt cauſe to ſuſpect to be dangerous, quarrelſome, or ſcandalous; as from thoſe, that ſleep in the day, and go abroad in the night; and ſuch as keep ſuſpicious company. All ſuch perſons are preſumed to have been in ſome degree criminal in their conduct; and conſequently to be the proper objects of that preventive juſtice, which is calculated for the amendment of offenders, the example of others, and the ſecurity of the ſtate.

CHAP. IX.

Of the Disposal of the dead Body of the Criminal.

§ 1. THE Roman Law permitted the murderer to remain on the gibbet after execution, as a comfortable sight to the friends and relations of the deceased[z].

Nec furtum feci, nec fugi, si mihi dicat
Servus: Habes pretium; loris non ureris, aio.
Non hominem occidi: Non pasces in cruce corvos[a].

The Mosaical Law directed the body of the criminal to be buried on the day of his death, "that the land might not be defiled[b]."

[z] *Ut et conspectu deterreantur alii, et Solatio sit cognatis interemptorum.* ff. 48. 19. 28. § 15.—A. D. 1741, when the English Regency made an order to hang the murderer of Mr. Penny in chains, they inserted therein "that it was on the petition of the relations of the deceased." St. Tr. vol. x. 39.

[a] Horat. Epist. l. I. ep. xvi. 46.

[b] Deuteron. xxi. 23.

It cannot with any propriety be ſaid, that there is inhumanity, but it may be doubted, whether there be wiſdom, in the adoption, which the Laws of England have made on this point, of the reſcripts of the Emperors, in preference to the command of Moſes.

We leave each other to rot, like ſcare-crows in the hedges; and our gibbets are crowded with human carcaſes. May it not be doubted, whether a forced familiarity with ſuch objects can have any other effect, than to blunt the ſentiments, and deſtroy the benevolent prejudices, of the people?

§ 2. The ignominious burial of perſons guilty of ſuicide might perhaps, if ſtrictly executed, form ſome check on the ſin of ſelf-murder; but, in this caſe, Juries are more generally guided by the momentary impulſe of compaſſion, than by a proper attention to the general benefit.

§ 3. To the diſſection of criminals it is impoſſible to offer any ſolid objection. Modern ages will confine it to the dead, and turn a deaf ear to the anatomiſt, who laments the Æra of his own exiſtence, " *Ubi, præ iniquitate*

iniquitate temporum, vivos homines diſſecare non licet[c]."

§ 4. There is a ſeeming liberality of ſentiment in the propoſal, to ſubject certain claſſes of criminals to medical experiments for the benefit of mankind. England was by theſe means enabled to extend inoculation through Europe, and conſequently to ſave the lives of millions.

I am apprehenſive, that I diſſent from a very learned writer[d], when I aſſert, that ſuch a plan can never with any propriety receive the legiſlative ſanction.

If the experiments be without hazard, they are unneceſſary; becauſe equally practicable on the innocent and on the guilty: if of a nature to maim and diſable; they are cruel and impolitic: if dangerous to the life; the uncertainty of the event deſtroys all the ſolemnity of the example in the eyes of the people. The criminal himſelf too expects the deciſion, under all the heated anxiety of a gambling adventurer; and meets the perils of

[c] Vide Corn. Celſ. in Præfat.

[d] Obſervations on the ancient Statutes, p. 353.

death in a ſtate of mind, very unſuitable to the dictates and temper of Chriſtianity.

The modern advancement of medical knowledge, and the benevolence of its profeſſors, make ſuch aids uſeleſs and ineligible.

* * *

CHAP. X.

A General Idea of the Connection between Puniſhments and Crimes.

WHEN we follow the unreſtrained courſe of our thoughts, inſtead of laying down premiſes, and deducing concluſions from them, we reaſon from concluſions only: we begin our reſearches at the mouth of the ſtream, and thence inveſtigate the ſpring.

The political liberty of a ſtate conſiſts in the ſecurity of the people; that ſecurity bears a proportion to the juſtice, and wiſdom of the penal code, which protects innocence by the

the chaſtiſement of guilt. But the juſtice, and wiſdom of every penal law depend on its analogy to the particular quality of the crime, to which it applies. The puniſhment then becomes an eſtabliſhed conſequence, unconnected with the caprice of authority, and flowing from the very nature of the offence.

It is not ſufficient therefore to have ſtated the right of puniſhment, and the different claſſes of puniſhments; it is alſo neceſſary to conſider the ſeveral ſpecies of crimes, their definitions and gradations.

The ſuperſtructure, as the moſt ſtriking object, firſt caught my attention; it remains to examine the foundation.

* * *

CHAP. XI.

Of Crimes.

§ 1. CRIME is diſtinguiſhable from ſin[e]: for every crime muſt be a poſitive breach, or wilful diſregard, of ſome exiſting public law. But many offences againſt earthly authority are no otherwiſe ſinful in the eye of Heaven, than as infractions of that implied contract of obedience to the legiſlature, to which every member of ſociety is ſubjected: and there are many ſpecies of ſin, which, in a legal ſenſe, cannot be criminal, becauſe in their nature not obvious to human accuſation.

§ 2. The mere ſpeculative wantonneſs of a licentious imagination, however dangerous, or even ſanguinary in its object, can in no caſe amount to a crime. It is a paſſion inſeparable from the eſſence of the human mind,

[e] This diſtinction, ſays a learned writer of the laſt century, was known both to the Greeks and Romans, in the words ἁμάρτημα, ἔγκλημα, *Peccatum*, *Crimen*.

to

to delight in the fiction of that, the actual existence of which would please.

Dionysius the tyrant is said to have punished with death one of his subjects, for dreaming that he had killed him. This was hardly more iniquitous, than the execution of the gentleman[f], who, having a white deer in his park, which was killed by Edward the Fourth, wished the deer, horns and all, in the belly of him that counselled the King to kill it; "whereas in truth no man counselled the "King to it:" or than the attainder, and execution of Algernon Sydney, on the evidence of private, and unpublished papers, without any proof, or even a suggestion of their intended publication; without even an averment, that they were relative to the treasonable practices charged in the indictment[g].

§ 3. Crimes have no existence prior to the resolution to do some criminal act, and are punishable only when that resolution is

[f] Markham Ch. J. rather chose to quit his office, than consent to this. Baker's Chr. 229. Hale's Hist. P. C. i. 115.

[g] In which case it is thought, that they might have been read in evidence. Foster, p. 191.

capable of proof: but criminality even in this ſtage is only inchoate, and in all caſes therefore, except treaſon, is treated with a moderated ſeverity by our law; which benevolently ſuppoſes a poſſibility of recollection, and repentance, in every moment previous to the actual completion of the deſign.

This poſſibility was excluded by ſtat. 25 Eliz. which made it felony "to wiſh or de-"ſire the death, or deprivation of the Queen, "*or any thing to that effect*."

Qui deliberant, deſciverunt, ſaid Tacitus. Sir Heneage Finch gave a bloody interpretation to this expreſſion, when he inferred[h], that "to *doubt* or *heſitate* in a point of allegiance, "is direct treaſon and apoſtacy."

When the will is ſaid to be equivalent to the deed, it ſhould always be underſtood, that there hath been an actual, determinate endeavour, ſo far co-operating with the intention, that no new exertion of the mind could have intervened to prevent the effect of the crime[i], though that effect may caſually

[h] State Trials, vol. ii. p. 230.
[i] Pufendorff, p. 782.

have

have failed; as if a man ſhould ſtab another with intent to kill, though by the ſkill of the ſurgeon the wound ſhould not prove mortal, or diſcharge a bullet at his head, though he ſhould miſs his aim.

§ 4. Thus every criminal charge muſt be founded on ſome fact, with the evidence of which every trial ſhould commence. If that fact be eſtabliſhed beyond the power of refutation, it then becomes neceſſary for the perſon accuſed to have recourſe to the ſeveral ſuggeſtions, which are allowed by reaſon, morality and religion, to be matters of mitigation or excuſe.

We find in every ſyſtem of laws a great variety of elaborate diſtinctions, on the different gradations from the completeſt guilt, which is the accumulated reſult of both fact and intention, to innocence, which conſiſts in a total deficiency of a miſchievous will.

The colour of the accuſation aſſumes a new tint, whether the perſon accuſed be reſponſible, as principal or as acceſſory; whether principal in the firſt degree, as actual perpetrator, or in the ſecond, as aiding and abetting:

whether as acceſſory before the fact, or after; whether juſtifiable on the ſeveral pleas of misfortune, ignorance, or compulſion: laſtly, if there be a want of diſcernment or underſtanding, there cannot exiſt a malignity of mind; for ſuch perſons the law itſelf ſhould anxiouſly apologize, on the appearance of their incapacity, whether it ariſes from the courſe of nature, as in the nonage of infants; or from the viſitation of God, as in the caſes of ideots and lunatics.

But when the meaſure of proof is full; when the act and intention [k] have both co-operated to eſtabliſh the guilt of the offender; when every poſſibility of extenuation or excuſe is precluded; then, and not before, let the arm of juſtice be ſtretched forth, and let that penalty be rigorouſly inflicted, which the law hath proportioned to the denomination of the crime.

[k] By the common law, *an intention to commit a felony amounted to the ſame crime in no inſtance.* And therefore in the caſe of Holmes, who ſet fire to his own houſe in the city of London, with intent to burn the houſe of his neighbour; as the fire did not extend beyond his own houſe, this was adjudged not to amount to the crime of Arſon. I ſhall hereafter have occaſion to mention ſome particular ſtatutes which depart from this rule. Holmes's caſe is in Cro. Car. 577.

§ 5. It

§ 5. It is impoſſible to delineate any ſyſtematic, or graduated ſcale of crimes, applicable to every legiſlation; for crimes are of temporal creation, and to be eſtimated in proportion to their pernicious effects on ſociety. Municipal laws muſt be adapted to the temper and influence of the climate, the ſtate of commerce, the occupations, number, and riches of the people; in ſhort, to the nature, principles, and neceſſities of each particular government. The ſame fact is therefore liable to a different conſtruction under every different legiſlation. Solon made idleneſs a crime; and this, in the infancy of a democracy ſo well regulated as that of Athens, was not unreaſonable. In Holland it is a capital crime to kill a ſtork; but ſuch a proviſion in the dry, mountainous parts of Germany would be groſsly abſurd. The ſafety of the ancient Gauls conſiſted in the mere brutal activity of their bodies: "it was criminal therefore, ſays Strabo, and puniſhable, for the young men to exceed the meaſures of their girdle, for it was conceived to be a proof of idleneſs and gluttony." In the warmer countries, which want the reſtriction of the true religion, we ſee polygamy eſtabliſhed, or the uſe of ſeraglios permitted. Lawgivers are but men; and the wiseſt of them will too often be influenced by their conſtitutional paſſions, though perhaps inſenſibly, in the laws which they frame. But in the temperate climate, which we inhabit, where the ſexes are equally qualified for the pleaſures of ſentiment; and where it is not unuſual for the wife, the miſtreſs, and the friend, to exiſt in the ſame perſon; ſuch pluralities would as ill agree with the temper and diſpoſition of the people as with the dictates of the religion which they profeſs.

§ 6. Crimes then being relative to the nature of each particular government, they are incapable of general definitions: but it is very poſſible to eſtabliſh certain leading principles, which ſhould be ever preſent to the attention of human juriſdictions.

The Preſident de Monteſquieu hath conſidered crimes, as prejudicial to religion, to morals, to the tranquillity of the public, and to the ſecurity of individuals. This diviſion ſeems liable to objections, though it may not be eaſy to make a better. I ſhall avoid therefore the arrogance of the attempt, by purſuing the detail without any methodical diviſion of the ſubject.

CHAP. XII.

Of Crimes relative to Religion.

§ 1. RELIGION hath been wisely established by law, as useful and necessary to society; and is so wrought into the very frame of our government, as to become a main part of the constitution. The magistrate therefore, though the well-being of the state be his peculiar object, is by no means exempted from a due concern for the religion of his country.

§ 2. But it is no consequence from these premises, that men should be debarred liberty of conscience, and the free use of reason and inquiry; much less can any argument be drawn from them in favour of persecution. Freedom of thought is the prerogative of human kind; a quality inherent in the very nature of a thinking being; a privilege which cannot be denied to him or taken from him. Montaigne therefore had good cause for saying, in his familiar way, "that it is setting up one's own "opinions very high, to direct another to be "roasted

" roaſted alive for them." He ſpoke feelingly; for all the ſtates of Europe were at that time blazing with religious martyrdoms: and it ſeemed to be the fundamental principle of all ſects to execrate and extirpate each other.

§ 3. Even England, the ſeat of national liberty and benevolence, became the bloody ſcene of intolerance and perſecution; the miniſters of peace and chriſtianity were the active diſpenſers of death and deſolation; and the perpetrators of the moſt malignant murders were clad in the pure mantle of religion.

The accompliſhed and ſentimental Sir Thomas More cauſed Lutherans to be whipt, tortured, and burnt alive in his preſence[1]. Cran-

[1] It ſeems almoſt neceſſary to produce ſome inſtance in ſupport of this aſſertion; and therefore I tranſcribe the following from Biſhop Burnet, on whoſe hiſtorical fidelity we may rely as to all tranſactions except thoſe of which he believed himſelf to have been an eye-witneſs.—" The clergy now reſolved to make an example of one James Bainham a gentleman of the Temple: he was carried to the Lord Chancellor's houſe, where much pains were taken to perſuade him to diſcover ſuch as he knew in the Temple who favoured the new opinions; but, fair means not prevailing, More made him be whipt in his preſence, and after that he ſent him to the Tower, where he looked on, and ſaw him put to the rack." Bainham was afterwards burnt. Hiſt. of the Reform. vol. I. p. 165.

mer led Arians and Anabaptiſts to the ſtake. Bonner, Biſhop of London, tore off the beard of a weaver, who refuſed to relinquiſh his tenets; in another inſtance of the ſame kind, he ſcourged a man until his arm ached with the exerciſe; and held the hand of a third to the candle, to give him a ſpecimen of burning, till the ſinews and veins ſhrunk and burſt. Even Wriotheſly, the Chancellor of England, directed a young and beautiful woman to be ſtretched on the rack, for having differed with him on the real preſence; with his own arm he tore her body almoſt aſunder, and cauſed her afterwards to be committed to the flames. In fine, infants, born at the ſtake, were thrown into the fire with their parents, as partaking of the ſame hereſy.

Human nature appears deteſtable under ſuch repreſentations; which (as they are well deſcribed by a philoſophical writer) ſink men below infernal ſpirits in wickedneſs, and below beaſts in folly.

Henry the Eighth, whoſe caprice was the bloody ſtandard of the national faith[m], ruled

[m] It was made high-treaſon *to believe* this Prince to have been married to Anne of Cleves.

all

all ſects by turns with a rod of iron: his ſcholaſtic ſubtlety was equal to his cruelty; and we are told, that, in one inſtance, he found ſufficient reaſons for ſending three papiſts with three proteſtants, their companions, in the ſame proceſſion to the ſtake. His daughter Mary, with leſs ingenuity, poſſeſſed the ſame rancorous and implacable zeal. And we accordingly learn, that in the ſpace of three years, under the auſpices of Biſhop Gardiner, ſhe committed two hundred and ſeventy-ſeven proteſtants to the flames. Human ſacrifices were at this period more frequent in the metropolis of England, than they had ever been in either Carthage, or Mexico: and in all theſe inſtances, the future damnation of the heretic was believed to be the inevitable conſequence of his death.

Ye rev'rend fathers,
Whoſe beards the ſilver hand of time had touch'd,
Whoſe learning, and good letters peace had tutor'd,
Whoſe white inveſtments figur'd innocence,
The dove and very bleſſed ſpirit of peace,
Wherefore did ye ſo ill tranſlate yourſelves
Out of the ſpeech of peace, that bears ſuch grace,
Into the harſh and boiſt'rous tongue of war,
And civil maſſacre? who ſhall believe
But ye miſus'd the rev'rence of your place,

Under the counterfeited zeal of God [n],
In deeds most damnable [o]?

This frenzy had subsisted here for more than a century [p]: I find the following account of the execution of Lord Cobham, A. D. 1418.

"Than was he layd upon an hurdle, *as* "*though he had been a moost heynouse traytoure* "*to the crowne* and so drawne forth into "Sainct Gyles Felde, wheere as they had set "up a new paire of Galowes. than he was "hung up in a chayne of yron and so con-"sumed alyve in the fyre, *and so he departed* "*hence moost christenly*. how the priestes that "tyme fared and cursed, requiring the peo-"ple not to pray for hym, but to judge hym "dampned in hell, for that he departed not

[n] Deorum numen prætenditur sceleribus. Liv. xxxix. c. 16.

[o] Shakespeare.

[p] But it appears, from Godfridus Coloniensis, who wrote A. D. 1234, to have prevailed much earlier on the Continent. "Eodem die, quo quis accusatus est, seu "juste, seu injuste, nullius appellationis, nullius defen-"sionis refugio proficiente, damnatur, et flammis injici-"tur." This was founded on the following constitution of the Emperor Frederic: "Damnati per ecclesiam judici sæculari relinquentur, animadversione debitâ puniendi, clericis a suis ordinibus primo degradatis." See also Matt. Paris, p. 429, and Hales Hist. P. C. i. 383.

"in

"in the obedience of the Pope, it were too "long to wryte. And thy was done in the "yeare of our Lord MCCCC and XVIII[q].

The writ *de Hæretico Comburendo* ſeems to have been founded on the 2 Hen. IV. c. 15: it was firſt uſed with effect againſt William Sawtre, A. D. 1401, who had been condemned for hereſy by the Convocation of Canterbury, and whoſe ſentence had been confirmed by the Houſe of Peers: it concluded in the following words, "*ac ipſum hæreticum in eodem igne realiter comburi facias, in hujuſmodi criminis deteſtationem, aliorumque Chriſtianorum manifeſtum exemplum.* This writ was iſſued ſo late as the year 1611, by James the Firſt, againſt Bartholomew Legat[r], an Arian, on a conviction before the Ordinary. Having ſubſiſted three centuries, it was at laſt aboliſhed, with all proceedings thereon; and all capital puniſhments in purſuance of eccleſiaſtical cenſures, by 29 Charles II. c. 9.

[q] See the tryal and examination of Sir John Oldcaſtle collected by John Bale.

[r] On which occaſion it was adjudged by Fleming, Tanfield, Williams, and Croke, that the Dioceſan may convict of hereſy, and that thereupon the writ "de hæretico comburendo may iſſue." 12 Co. Rep. 92.

It

It is perhaps to be wiſhed, that this ſtatute had gone one ſtep further, and taken from the ſpiritual arm every exerciſe of penal juriſdiction.

I have given this detail of hiſtorical facts, merely as a ſubject of curious ſpeculation. The banners of pious cruelty ſeem now to be for ever laid aſide. Philoſophy and benevolence are become the companions of religion.

§ 4. Still, however, and conſiſtently both with reaſon and civil liberty, all intentional affronts to the national rites, and all manifeſt impieties vauntingly committed, are conſidered as criminal, and in their nature ſubject to the ſecular cognizance: yet not as crimes immediately fatal to ſociety, and calling for the extirpation of the criminal; but as infractions of the public tranquillity and diſturbances of the eſtabliſhed ſyſtem.

The Engliſh legiſlature is now aware, that it is not the office of the magiſtrate to ſtir up the zeal, and blow the coals of perſecution; that ſeverity ought not in any inſtance to be extended to the peaceable exerciſe of different opinions; that the Law ought not to be made the ſcourge of conſcience, nor compulſion to be added to intolerance. Miſdirected piety is no longer within the province of our tribunals; though ſometimes, from the principle of the civil eſtabliſhment, properly ſubjected to certain civil diſabilities.

"Hear this, ye nations;" and let not in any caſe the ſacred truths of the Goſpel be forced upon mankind by the contaminated hand of the executioner! let not in any caſe an unhappy attachment to hereditary religious errors, confirmed by the prejudices of education, be made a capital crime! The attempt to over-power by terrors the miſapprehenſions of the mind is unnatural and prepoſterous. Uniformity in opinion cannot be the reſult of force; general orthodoxy cannot be the creature of mandatory Law; nor can "*the pains of death in ſupport of religion* " *ever have any effect but to deſtroy*[s]."

§ 5. It would be uncandid however not to confeſs, that the Laws of England at this day ſubject Popiſh Prieſts, in many caſes, to

[s] L'Eſprit des Loix.

perpetual imprisonment[t]; in others, to the pains of high-treason. It is also high-treason[u] to pervert, *or even to be perverted*, to the see of Rome. A second refusal to take the old oath of Supremacy is liable to similar severity[w]. Such Laws are rarely exerted; but their existence is a national reproach.

A free government may naturally hold in abhorrence a religion, the principles of which are founded in slavery; but a free government forgets its own principles, when it gives to involuntary opinion, the denomination and punishment of the most enormous guilt.

In that age of bigotted enthusiasm, when ecclesiastical tyranny was placed in competition with civil government; and when it was attempted, with impudent and unwearied diligence, to subject the internal Sovereignty of the realm to the supposed universality of the papal power; the indignation of our ancestors was at length awakened, and the unnatural position of "*imperium in imperio*" was encountered by many sharp and severe Laws. The motive hath ceased, but the effects re-

[t] Stat. 27 Eliz. c. 2. [u] 3 Ja. I. c. 4. 23 Eliz. c. 1.
[w] 5 Eliz. c. 1. § 11.

main: and our ſtatute books are at this day crowded with inflictions of forfeiture, and perpetual impriſonment, (under the name of præmunires) on Papal proviſors, importers of any *Agnus Dei*, croſſes, beads, or other commodities of the church of Rome. Can it be a queſtion, whether theſe laws ought alſo to be repealed?

§ 6. Sorcery, by the conſtruction of the common Law, was a ſpecies of hereſy [x]. Under this idea, A. D. 1441, the writ *de hæretico comburendo* was iſſued againſt Margery Goodman of Eye in Suffolk; and ſhe was accordingly burnt for conſultation with the Devil. Witchcraft alſo was treated with extreme ſeverity in very early times: in Scotland [y], A. D. 840, a Law was made to puniſh it by cutting out the tongue; and in England, by

[x] "Sorcery et Devinal ſont membres de hereſie." Mirror, c. 1. § 5.—Fleta. "Chriſtiani apoſtatæ, ſortilegi, et *hujuſmodi*, comburi debent." The word "hujuſmodi," which in this ſentence ſeems of a very alarming nature, is not more exceptionable than certain expreſſions, which frequently occur in the Engliſh ſtatutes: ſuch as "*divers other like kinds of miſerable offences.*" "*Any thing to the ſame effect.*" "*Other offences of the like ſort, &c.*" We frequently find the ſame vague appendix in the Roman Law. "*Aliudve quid ſimile ſi admiſerint.*"

[y] Concil. Brit. p. 341.

the laws of Æthelſtan, A. D. 928, it was made a capital crime[z]. We find a preſentment of ſorcery *inter placita Reg. Rich.* I; and in the Year Books there is an appeal of Necromancie in the 18th year of Edw. II. There are alſo many ancient writs in Rymer *de ſortilegis capiendis*. It ſuited the ſanguinary temper of Henry VIII, as well as the pedantry of James the Firſt, to give written deſcriptions of this offence; we accordingly find very learned edicts againſt prophets, ſorcerers, feeders of evil ſpirits, charmers, and provokers to unlawful love[a]. Sir Edward Coke thinks[b], "that it would have been a great defect in government, to have ſuffered ſuch

[z] See alſo a Law temp. Hen. I. in Lambard, c. 71. William of Neuburgh, who wrote A. D. 1181, gives a very grave account of a witch who obtained a victory at ſea in favor of Suerus King of Normandy, by commanding the waves to ſuck in the greateſt part of the adverſe fleet; "which was accordingly done." P. 236.

On the 23d of Auguſt, 1728, ſeveral perſons were burnt alive at a town in Hungary, *becauſe* a large woman, who had confederated with them in the art of witchcraft, did not, when put into the ſcale, weigh more than four ounces.

[a] See the Roman Law "de his qui amatorium poculum dant." Plutarch alſo exclaims warmly againſt women uſing "τὰ φίλτρα ὅτι διερεθίστικα εἰς τὰ κατ᾽ ἀφροδίτην."

[b] 3 Inſt. 45.

 deviliſh

devilish abominations to pass with impunity." But the lawgivers of this generation have prohibited[c] all prosecutions of a crime which doth not appear to have any existence; and have by the same statute ordered all pretenders to such preternatural abilities to be exalted on the pillory above the rest of mankind. *That knavery, which endeavours to impose on credulity, is surely a proper object of correction*; for which reason also, false and pretended prophecies are properly punishable, though they are too frivolous in their nature to require any extraordinary severity. They were punished capitally by 1 E. VI. c. 12; which was repealed by Q. Mary: and now, by 5 Eliz. c. 15, the penalty for the first offence is a fine of 100 l. and one year's imprisonment; for the second, forfeiture of all goods and chattels, and imprisonment for life.

§ 7. It is not improper, under the title of this chapter, to consider crimes relative to marriage; which, though a civil institution, is stamped with the seal of religion.

[c] 9 Geo. II. c. 5.

Incest

Inceſt[d], and adultery[e], are vices ſo contrary to the well-being of a great and poliſhed ſtate, that one may wonder at the ſupineneſs of the Engliſh Law, which hath not ſubjected either as crimes, in any inſtance, or in any degree, to the temporal cognizance. Adultery is perhaps puniſhable by indictment[f], as a ſcandalous and public indecency; but in no caſe as the infraction of a ſacred tie, and tending to a general diſſoluteneſs of manners.

This offence among the Saxons was puniſhed by a fine, called Lecherwite, and Legergeldum. And we find in the Domeſday book, "*quod adulterium faciens 8s 4d emendabit homo, et fœmina tantundem: Rex habeat hominem adulterum, Archiepiſcopus fœminam.*" The Julian law of the Romans puniſhed it alſo by fine;

[d] Tune ſoror nati, genetrixque vocabere fratris,
Nec quot *confundas et jura et nomina ſentis?*
Ovid. Metam.

The crime of inceſt was puniſhed with great ſeverity by the Roman Law. See Dig. xlviii. 5. 38. 2. And this ſeverity was even extended to the mode of proſecution. "De ſervis nulla quæſtio eſt in dominos, niſi de inceſtu. Cic. Orat. pro Milone, c. 22.

[e] Oppida cœperunt munire et condere leges,
Ne quis fur eſſet, *neu latro*, *neu quis adulter*. Horat.

[f] Comberbatch, 377. Tremaine's Pleas of the Crown, p. 209, and p. 215. State Trials, vol. iii. p. 52.

the law of Moses[g] with death. Women committing adultery were by the Egyptians deprived of their noses, that they might not again allure men to wantonness; but I cannot learn that male offenders were liable to any corporal penalty. The wife's transgression in this respect is certainly more repugnant to the end of marriage, than the husband's; yet the sex of lawgivers influences the modes of punishment. A female Legislature, however inclinable to eradicate this offence, would hardly have had recourse to mutilation, as the most eligible expedient for that purpose.

§ 8. Polygamy is in our Law a felonious offence[h], but entitled to the benefit of Clergy: by the laws both of ancient and modern Sweden, as also by the laws of Denmark and of Spain, it is punished with death. It certainly

[g] Levit. xx. 10.

[h] 1 Ja. I. c. 11. But it is provided by the third section, "that if any person, divorced by any sentence of the ecclesiastical court, shall marry again, the former husband or wife being alive, he or she shall not for such marriage be liable to the penalties of the statute." Yet such sentence of the ecclesiastical court is no dissolution à vinculo matrimonii; the second marriage is merely void, and the bigamy is in its effects as offensive to the interest of society in this case as in any other. The reason of this lenity is obvious, but unsatisfactory. For instances, see Sel. p. 27. 1 Cro. p. 461.

is a groſs ſpecies of adultery, aggravated by the profanation of a religious rite; yet the law, which ought to look upon the individuals of the community with the eyes of a mother upon her children, ought to be very ſparing of the higheſt ſeverities, when the milder claſs of reſtrictions may ſuffice. In France it is puniſhed by ſentence to the gallies, or by temporary baniſhment.

By the ancient law of England, Chriſtians marrying Jews were *burnt* [i] alive.

§ 9. It is made a felony by a late ſtatute to ſolemnize clandeſtine marriages [k]. The crime is indeed prejudicial in its conſequences to the public police and œconomy: yet it might perhaps have been ſufficient to have made all ſuch marriages void, or to have ſubjected the offender to pecuniary forfeitures, or civil diſabilities.

§ 10. Sacrilege formed a very extenſive article in the Roman law, and was accounted

[i] I have tranſcribed this expreſſion from Sir Edw. Coke, 3 Inſt. 89. but it is evidently a miſtake. "*Contrahentes cum Judæis, Judæabus, pecorantes, ſodomitæ, vivi* confodiantur." *Fleta*, l. i. c. 35.

[k] 26 Geo. II. c. 33.

more odious than treaſon [l].—The Engliſh ſtatute-book draws no diſtinction of guilt from the holineſs of the place, or perſons offended; except in the crime of robbing a church, or chapel, which is excluded from the benefit of clergy by an act of Henry the Eighth; the fact however muſt be accompanied by an actual breaking [m]. By an Athenian law [n], a man committing this offence was baniſhed with all his children. It was alſo a maxim of the civil law, *quod delicta capiunt incrementa a loco, ſive ratione loci in quo committuntur* [o]. By the laws of King Canute [p], "if murder be committed in a church, a full compenſation ſhall be paid to Jeſus Chriſt, another full compenſation to the king, and a third to the relations of the deceaſed."

[l] *Proximum ſacrilegio eſt quod Majeſtatis dicitur.* L. i. ff. Leg. Jul.

Yet we are told that in the temple of Diana at Aricia near Rome, whoever killed the chief prieſt was entitled to become his ſucceſſor; a moſt unaccountable privilege!

Fanum in luco eſt, et perfuga, ſacerdos ibi conſtituitur, qui ſacerdotem ſuâ trucidaverit manu; ſtrictoque ſemper gladio paratus ad inſultus propulſandos circumſpicit.

Strabon. Geogr. l. v. p. 366.

Ecce ſuburbanæ templum nemorale Dianæ
Partaque per gladios regna nocente manu!

Ovid. Art. Am. i. 159.

[m] 2 Hawk. 351. [n] Meurſius, l. ii. c. 2.

[o] ff. l. xvi. § 5. [p] Lambard's Collection, Law 2.

deceafed." And in the 8th year of Edw. IV, it was attempted [q] to make facrilege high-treafon, fubjecting the offender to be burnt. A petition, the common method of tendering bills for the royal affent, was prefented to the king for that purpofe by both houfes. To this extraordinary requeft the king returned an anfwer, becoming the royal majefty of the crown, "*Le Roy s'avifera* [r]."

CHAP. XIII.

Of Crimes relative to the Law of Nations.

§ 1. THE law of nations is founded partly on the fuggeftions of natural equity, partly on pofitive ftipulations. It is univerfal in its extent and operation through the civilized world; and fupported by the general confcioufnefs of its general Utility.

Individuals are required to give their acquiefcence to this law, not as a matter of

[q] Cotton, 684. [r] Fofter, p. 192.

choice,

choice, but of obligation; and it is the province of legiſlators to force that acquieſcence, if kept back or neglected. For the faith of nations in their collective capacities would be of little avail, if private ſubjects were allowed to uſe hoſtilities and treachery towards each other; mutual diſtruſt, inſecurity, diſcord, and war, would follow. *Vim volumus extingui? jus valeat neceſſe eſt*[s]. If the views of each individual were permitted to terminate in ſelfiſhneſs, the miſery of all would be the conſequence; the ſtability of a building depends on the united ſupport of its correſponding parts.

This law becomes preciſe and definitive, in proportion to the continued intercourſe of nations[t], and the complication of their mutual connections. I am not however to conſider thoſe multifarious rules of equity, which have been tacitly eſtabliſhed in the conduct of war and commerce; ſuch as, declarations previous to hoſtilities, the prohibition of poiſoned weapons, capitulations, ſafety of hoſtages, ſuſpenſions of arms, maintenance of

[s] Orat. pro Sext. c. 42.

[t] *Quam legem exteri nobis poſuerunt, eandem illis ponemus.* Steirnhook, de jure Sueonum, l. iii. c. 4.

truces,

truces, the privileges, regulations, and reſtrictions of merchants. I confine myſelf merely to the penal cognizance of ſtates internally reſpecting the rapaciouſneſs and malice of Natives in their conduct towards Aliens. The crimes founded thereon are reducible to a ſmall compaſs.

§ 2. Offenders againſt the rights and privileges of Embaſſadors, by arreſting their perſons, or diſtraining their effects, are deemed violators of the Law of Nations; and, by a modern act [u], made liable to ſuch penalties, or corporal puniſhment, *as the Chancellor and the two Chief Juſtices ſhall think fit* [w]: a ſtrange, and unlimited diſcretionary power! abhorrent from the principles of a free government; unlikely indeed to be abuſed, but improper to be given. It would be eaſy to eſtabliſh a leſs exceptionable ſanction to that reverence which is due to the repreſentatives of kings. This Act is ſaid to have

[u] Stat. 7 Ann. c. 12.

[w] The ſame indefinite legiſlative Authority, as to military puniſhment, is annually given to the King, by the Mutiny Act, which empowers "his Majeſty, to form Articles of War, and conſtitute Courts-martial, to try any crimes by articles, and inflict ſuch penalties as the articles direct." But this cannot be extended to affect life or limb. Commentaries, B. i. 415.

been

been made under mortifying circumſtances, as a kind of public ſatisfaction to the Czar Peter; whoſe embaſſador, Mateof, had been arreſted in London for debt, and obliged to have recourſe to the other foreign miniſters to give bail for him. It ſeems hardly credible, that the characters of embaſſadors ſhould have wanted this ſanction in England in the 18th century. Mr. Whitworth was alſo ſent with a ſolemn apology to the Czar, in which he told him, ſays Voltaire [x], "that the Queen had impriſoned the perſons, who had preſumed to arreſt his embaſſador, and that the delinquents had been rendered infamous;" aſſurances, which, if they ever exiſted, had certainly no foundation in fact.

§ 3. Truce-breakers, and violators of ſafe conduct, are by a ſtatute of Henry the Fifth declared guilty of high-treaſon againſt the King's crown, and dignity [y]. It ſeems to be the better opinion [z], that this was repealed by the ſubſequent ſtatutes of Edward Sixth, and of Mary. The puniſhment was certainly extravagant; but the milder law of Henry the Sixth relative to the ſame crime [a], which

[x] Hiſt. de Ruſſ. c. 19. [y] 2 Hen. V. c. 6.
[z] Commentaries, B. iv. p. 70. [a] 31 H.VI. c. 4.

ſtill

ſtill remains in force, is too vague and indeterminate.

Commercial countries naturally ſhew a peculiar tenderneſs to the perſons and property of foreigners. " It is a beautiful circumſtance, ſays Monteſquieu, that the Engliſh nation made the protection of merchant ſtrangers a principal article in the great charter of her liberties [b]: the moſt benevolent indulgence was alſo ſhewn by our law to the proprietors of diſtreſſed and wrecked veſſels, at a very early period, when it was permitted

[b] There was a degree of national wiſdom in the clauſe to which Monteſquieu alludes, and which may be found in 9 H. III. c. 30. It muſt however be acknowledged, that the internal Hoſpitality of England doth not appear to be of great Antiquity. I ſhall tranſcribe a part of the oath, which Bracton records, as neceſſary to be taken by all perſons above fifteen years of age: " *Jurabunt etiam, quod nullum de nocte recipient in domum ſuam ad hoſpitandum, niſi bene notus ſit: et ſi forte ignotum aliquem hoſpitaverint, quod non permittent eum in craſtino recedere ante clarum diem, et hoc ſub teſtimonio trium vel quatuor virorum.*" L. iii. c. 3.

At the ſame time, it ſhould be obſerved, that the latter part of this tranſcript relates merely to the police of the kingdom, which in the early periods of our hiſtory was extremely ſtrict.

The hoſpitality of the ancient Germans was remarkable. " Quemcumque mortalium arcere tecto nefas habetur. Notum ignotumque, quantum ad jus hoſpitii, nemo diſcernit." Tacit. de M. G. c. 21.

It

mitted to other nations, *in naufragorum miſeriâ, et calamitate tanquam vultures ad prædam currere* [c]. This ſubject is certainly connected with the law of nations; but I ſhall only obſerve further upon it, that it hath been thought neceſſary by a very modern act, to make all plunderers of diſtreſſed or ſtranded ſhips guilty of felony without benefit of clergy [d]. This act was indeed eſſentially neceſſary to infer criminality on the plunderer; ſince Larceny could not at common law be committed of treaſure trove or wreck, till ſeized by the King, or him who hath the franchiſe; for till ſuch ſeizure [e] no one hath a determinate property therein.

If ſtealing furniture, above the value of twelve-pence, from lodgings, required the puniſhment of death [f]; the plundering of wrecks, aggravated as it is by the unfeeling

It is ſaid in the "Obſervations on the ancient ſtatutes," p. 22, that the Welſh Laws gave no protection to the Stranger. "*Tres ſunt homines quibus multa non debetur pro injuriâ eis illatâ: 1. Furioſus, 2. Alienigena, 3. et Leproſus:*" But I apprehend that the ſubſequent ſection had eſcaped the learned Writer's notice. "*Pretium legitimum unicuique eorum competit, et is qui injuriam illis intulerit multæ publicæ obnoxius erit.*" Leges Wall. p. 330.

[c] Stiernhook, l. iii. c. 5.

[d] 26 Geo. II. c. 19. [e] Comment. B. iv. 234.

[f] 3 and 4 W. and M. c. 9.

neglect of that sacred respect which is due to the unfortunate, certainly is not entitled to mercy. But arguments from analogy lead to bloody consequences in the framing of penal laws. By the code of the Visigoths, he, who took the opportunity of fire or shipwreck to steal goods, was obliged to restore fourfold [g].

The above-mentioned act hath made it a capital offence to put out false lights, with intention to bring any ship into danger. The crime is undoubtedly heinous in its nature, and may be dreadful in its consequences; but the punishment of death should be inflicted rarely, and with great caution, upon the Intention, where it is not followed by its Effect. It was thought sufficient to punish the destroyer of stated sea-marks with a penalty of 100 l. or outlawry [h].

§ 4. Piracy is a species of robbery, or unauthorized depredation on the seas. The wars of nations are in all cases unhappy, but often legitimate, even when offensive, being founded in the principles of self-preservation. For the life of nations resembles the life of

[g] L. vii. tit. 2. § 18. [h] 8 Eliz. c. 13. § 4.

man, and the right of ſelf-preſervation frequently induces the neceſſity of beginning the attack. It is not ſo with freebooters and pirates, who are to be conſidered as unprovoked enemies, or rather as beaſts of prey, to be hunted down by the univerſal concurrence of mankind.

This offence, by the common law of England, was a ſpecies of Treaſon, except when committed by aliens; but puniſhable only as ſuch, when the act, if committed on land, would have amounted to a capital crime. The ſtatute of treaſons left it a Capital felony only. The deſcriptions of it have been much extended by modern acts of parliament[i]; and it may be doubted, whether ſome offences are not deſcribed therein, and puniſhable as piracies, which have no connection with our ideas of that offence. " Any commander or other ſeafaring perſon, betraying his truſt, and running away with any ſhip, boat, ordnance, ammunition, or goods, ſhall be adjudged a pirate: and the trading with pirates, or in any wiſe correſponding with them, and the forcibly boarding any merchant veſſel: though without ſeizing and carrying her off,

[i] 11 and 12 W. III. c. 7. and 8 Geo. I. c. 24.

and

and deſtroying or throwing any of the goods overboard," are all under theſe acts deemed proofs of Piracy.

The miſapplication of terms in the framing of penal Laws is dangerous to liberty. And this conſideration reminds me of another modern ſtatute [k], which infers the guilt of high-treaſon on all thoſe, who ſhall knowingly make, or mend, or ſhall have in poſſeſſion, any inſtrument *proper only* for the coinage of money.

The Laws of Henry the Eighth were not more prepoſterous, when they gave the appellation of treaſon, to the ſtealing of cattle by Welſhmen, to the deflowering of his Majeſty's Aunts and Nieces, and to the bare ſolicitation of the chaſtity of his Daughter; nor the ancient law of Edmund, which made mere Fornication with a Nun puniſhable as homicide [l].

[k] 8 and 9 W. III. c. 26. made perpetual by 7 Ann. c. 25.

[l] "Auxi je trouva inter les leis de St. Edmond quondam roy deins ceſt realme, ceſt ley; ſ. Qui cum nunnâ vel ſanctimoniali fornicetur, emendetur ſicut homicida."
Staundfort, p. 23. B.

It was well obſerved by Tacitus in regard to Auguſtus, " *Quod culpam inter viros ac fœminas vulgatam, gravi nomine læſarum religionum ac violatæ majeſtatis appellando, clementiam majorum, ſuaſque ipſe leges egrediebatur.*"

CHAP. XIV.

Of Treaſons.

§ 1. MAJESTY hath no prerogative againſt the arm of fate. But the perſonal protection of Majeſty againſt the efforts of diſloyalty is within the province of human foreſight, and ſhould be within the firſt ſanctions of poſitive law.

Many are the ſleepleſs hours which the Sovereign muſt undergo, infinite is the heart-eaſe which he muſt neglect, for the ſake of his ſubjects. His preſervation becomes in return the primary object of their care. And thus it is, that the reciprocal duties of protection and allegiance form the foundation, and ſupport of the political union.—Juſtice watches, like a guardian angel over the reſt-

leſs

leſs pillow of her defender; for every blow, levelled at him, is, in its conſequences, levelled at the whole civil eſtabliſhment. The general welfare of the people is blended in the ſafety of their common father, and repreſentative; nor can his life fall a ſacrifice to conſpiracy or faction, without involving the whole realm in popular inveteracies, blood, and deſolation.

Hence it follows, that high treaſon, which, in every inſtance, ſtrikes ultimately at the well-being of ſovereignty, is the fouleſt crime that can be committed; becauſe it is of all crimes the moſt audacious in its nature, and the moſt extenſively pernicious in its conſequences. But the fouleſt inſtance of this crime is that, which aims directly at the royal perſon; becauſe it is the moſt fatal and moſt entire renunciation, of faith, duty, ſubjection, and allegiance.

The peculiar jealouſy of mankind on this point is ſuch, that, in every known ſyſtem of laws, the mere imagination of the traitor, when evidenced by any external action, is ranked in the ſame degree of guilt, and ſubjected to the ſame degree of puniſhment, as the actual completion of the Treaſon; not becaufe the idea is deemed equivalent to the perpetration of the fact; but becaufe the fevereft chaftifement, within the poffible difpenfation of the lawgiver, is thought due to the malignity of the intent—"*Eâdem feveritate voluntatem hujus fceleris, quâ effectum puniri jura voluerunt* [m]:" Such were the words of the Roman Law, which did not fuffer the crime of high treafon to be extinguifhed even by the death of the criminal [n]; but with an unjuftifiable fingularity extended the profecution to his corpfe, and the forfeitures to his reprefentatives and heirs.

The

[m] Cod. ad leg. Jul. l. ix. t. 8. l. 5.

[n] *Extinguitur crimen mortalitate, nifi forte quis majeftatis fit reus: nam hoc crimine, nifi fucceffloribus purgetur, Hereditas fifco vindicatur.* ff. ad Leg. Jul. Maj. l. xi.

Alienationes, quas fraude vel jure aliquis fecerit, ex eo tempore quo de ineundâ factione cogitaverit, nullius effe momenti ftatuimus. Cod. ix. 8. 5.

Nam ex eo tempore quo hanc cogitationem fubiit, propter cogitationem dignus eft pœnâ. Cod. ad L. J. vi.

In England a perfon flain in open undoubted rebellion is not liable to any forfeiture; for the benevolence of our law always prefumes the poffibility of a defence known only to the criminal: and on the fame principle, if even after conviction and judgement the offender fhould become infane, his execution fhall be ftayed; for, were he of found mind, he might perhaps alledge fomething in ftay of the proceeding. The 33d of Henry the VIII. c. 20. directed, in cafes of treafon, the Lunatic to be tried and executed, "*his lunacy and madnefs notwithftanding*:" but this act was repealed.

The old laws of the Lombards puniſhed as a Traitor "any Man, who ſhould conceive a thought againſt the ſoul of the King[o]:" the ſame Laws[p] puniſhed the marriage of any woman, that had taken a religious habit, "every ſuch woman being precontracted *as the ſpouſe* of God." The pruriency of a figurative imagination ought not to be indulged in the compoſition of penal laws; poetical licenſe in the deſcription of crimes leads to ſanguinary conſequences.

The laſt obſervation is in ſome degree applicable to the ſtatute of Edward the third, which is at this day the ſtandard meaſure to the people of their duty to the Sovereign. The firſt clauſe of that ſtatute is in the following words, "When a man doth compaſs or imagine the death of our Lord the King, of Madam his Companion (conſort), or of their eldeſt ſon and heir." This was declaratory of the Common Law of the realm,

repealed. There is good ſenſe on this point in the Grand Couſtumier: "*Si aliquis extra mentem conſtitutam ſuâ dementiâ aliquem interfecerit aut mehaigmaverit, perpetuo carceri eſt mancipandum.*" fol. 13.

[o] *Siquis contra animam regis cogitaverit.*

[p] Book ii. tit. 57.

which might have been copied with better precision from the words of Bracton [q]; "*Si quis ausu temerario machinatus sit in mortem domini regis.*" The word "compasseth" in the statute was probably borrowed from Britton [r], or from the editor of the Myrror, who wrote in the time of Edward the First, about forty years after Bracton. The other word "imagineth" seems first to have inadvertently received this harsh application from the Parliament of Edward the Third; but it was not the temper of that excellent parliament, to leave the construction of such words vague, and indeterminate; and it accordingly required, that "the criminal should be attainted, *upon full proof* [s] *of an open deed, by people of his own condition.*"

It

[q] L. iii. c. 2.

[r] "Grand treson est de compasser notre mort." Brit. c. 3. "Peche de Majesty est vers le Roy de la terre en trois manieres. 1. per ceux que occident le roy ou compassent de faire. 2. per ceux que luy desheritent del royalme per trahissent un host, ou compassent de le faire. 3. per ceux avowterors que spargissent le femme le roy, le file le roy eignesse legitime, avant ceo que elle soit mary, en la garde le roy; ou la neece le etant le heire le roy." Mirror, c. 1. § 4.

It should be observed, that, in this account of the several species of treason, Coining is not mentioned.

[s] "*Provablement*," this word is by the editors of the statutes inadvertently rendered "*probably*," notwithstanding the

It is then, and it hath ever been, the law of England, to punifh a mere intention to kill the king, more feverely than the actual and moft wilful murder of a private fubject; but the guilt commences only, when *fome meafure* [t] fhall appear to have been taken to effectuate the guilty purpofe. A mere concealment of a traiterous confederacy will not with us, as among the Romans [u], amount to treafon. There muft be alledged, and proved, fome act declaratory of the intention, fome pofitive participation in the guilt, fome confultation, perfuafion, or means of incitement. Advice given in a treafon merely inchoate, and never executed, will make the advifer a principal in the treafon [w]. A fending of letters, or a

the caution of Sir Edw. Coke. "The adverb "*provably*" "(faith he) hath a great force, and fignifieth a direct and "plain proof: which word the King, Lords, and Com-"mons did ufe, for that the Offence was fo heinous, and "was fo heavily and feverely punifhed, as none other the "like. Note, the word is not "*probably*," for then "commune argumentum might have ferved." 3 Inft. 12.

[t] Fofter, p. 195. 1 Hale's, P.C. 119. Kel. 17.

[u] "Id quod de prædictis reis majeftatis, etiam de fatellitibus, *confciis*, ac miniftris eorum eadem feveritate dicimus." L. vi. Cod. ad Leg. Jul. Even the wife on this point was obliged to betray her hufband. Nov. cxvii. c. 8.

[w] But it feems to be an indefinite and therefore dangerous pofition, that "if any one do *any thing by which he fhew-*"*eth his liking* and approbation to the traiterous defign, "this is in him High Treafon." Kelyng, p. 12.

prepa-

preparation of weapons, or poiſon, in contemplation of the crime; treaſonable printing or writing with publication; or unpubliſhed writings, if relative to the practices charged in the indictment; words explanatory of an act, or ſpoken *in proſecution* [x] of a traiterous purpoſe; are all matters of proper, and competent evidence, to be offered in proof. But the open deed, to be ſhewn at the trial, muſt be ſpecifically, and correctly charged in the indictment, that the perſon accuſed may be prepared to refute, explain, or defend it. And an open deed, not ſo charged, cannot be given in evidence, unleſs it conduce to prove one that is [y] ſo. This rule, in caſes of treaſon, is founded on a poſitive proviſion; but it hath ever been the wiſe and equitable practice of our courts, in other criminal proſecutions, to reject all manner of evidence, unconnected with the point in iſſue. A multiplicity of diſtinct and independent facts, however tending to the ſame inference, might inſenſibly confound the attention of the perſon accuſed, baffle the plan of his defence, and influence the diſpoſition of his judges.

[x] Foſter, p. 200.

[y] State Trials, vol. v. p. 22.

But there are other open deeds of a more explicit kind, which come within the idea of compaſſing the King's death, though in themſelves (and under expreſs ſtatutes ſo deſcribed) diſtinct ſpecies of treaſon, and liable, as ſuch, to be charged and proved. Thus, levying of war; and, under certain limitations[z], conſpiring to levy war; concerting with foreigners and others in order to an invaſion of the kingdom[a]; entering into meaſures for depoſing the Sovereign; may always, and in ſome caſes muſt[b], be charged, as overt acts of compaſſing. Again, the actual murder of the King operates in legal evidence, only as an overt act to prove the compaſſing of his death[c]. To the ſame purpoſe may be ſhewn an overt act of conſpiracy to impriſon the King, or to reſtrain his perſon by force. Here the law preſumes, that when reſpect is ſo far forgotten, the more ſacred duties of allegiance will ſoon be obliterated in blood;

[z] Foſter, p. 213.

[a] This was the caſe of Cardinal Pole, who was ſaid to have written a book for that purpoſe to the Emperor Charles. Co. P. C. p. 19.

[b] For example, a combination with foreigners in amity with the kingdom, cannot poſſibly be brought within any other clauſe of the ſtatute; nor will a mere conſpiracy to levy war amount to treaſon, unleſs particularly pointed againſt the perſon of the King, or *his* government.

[c] Kelyng, p. 8; The caſe of the Regicides. 1 Hawk. 34.

and

and hiſtory proves, that priſons are generally the ſlaughter-houſes of Princes. The inſtance of a Monarch, conducted to the ſcaffold after all the ſolemnity of a trial and judgement, in the open day, in the preſence of his people, with all the apparatus and formalities of a penal execution, is without a parallel.

§ 2. The ſecond ſpecies of treaſon in this ſtatute is, "*when a man doth violate the King's* "*conſort, or his eldeſt daughter unmarried; or* "*the wife of his eldeſt ſon and heir.*" Violation[d] here implies a carnal knowledge by whatever means obtained, and is made a treaſonable act for very ſolid, ſatisfactory, and evident reaſons. There are certainly inaccuracies[e] in the wording of the clauſe; but perhaps they are immaterial. The wife of the ſecond ſon is not within the ſtatute, though her iſſue is inheritable in preference to the eldeſt daughter; neither doth it ſeem treaſon to violate the eldeſt daughter, that hath been married, ſuch violation not being

[d] This offence committed by a tenant with the wife of his lord, was in the feudal law ſubjected to a forfeiture. "*Si vaſallus fecerit feloniam dominum forte cucurbitando.*" Feud. l. ii. t. 38. Brit. l. i. c. 22.

[e] Hale's Hiſt. P. C. i. 129.

within

within the letter of the ſtatute, though within the reaſon. The common law extended the ſame ſanction to *all* the daughters.

In the conſtruction of the laſt-mentioned clauſe, it hath been the unanimous inference of all the writers on the Engliſh law [f], that " if both the parties be conſenting, they are " equally guilty of treaſon ;" conſequently, that a Queen conſort committing adultery committeth treaſon ; and the caſes of Queen Anne Boleyne, and of Catharine Howard, are referred to, as the grounds of this opinion.

I ſubmit with great diffidence, that a different concluſion ought to have reſulted from each of thoſe caſes. Anne Boleyne's judges would very chearfully have given the appel-

[f] Coke, Inſt. iii. 2. Hale's Hiſt. P. C. i. 124. Commentaries, B. iv. 81.

This idea, which certainly is not warranted by the words " if a *man* doth violate," *&c.* ſeems to have ariſen from the manuſcript report of Judge Spelman " of " matters relative to the trial of Anne Boleyne," which, I believe, is now loſt. Sir E. Coke profeſſedly founds his opinion thereon ; and Biſhop Burnet, who wrote his account from Spelman, obſerves, that " there would have " been no need of ſtretching the other ſtatute, if they " could have proved the violating the Queen ; *for then* the " known ſtatute 25 Ed. III. would have been ſufficient."

 lation

lation of burglary, piracy, or horſe-ſtealing, to the crime of which ſhe was accuſed; but, in fact, ſhe was executed under the ſtrained conſtruction of an inadvertent expreſſion [g]. She was proved to have ſaid to her ſervants, "that the King never had her heart," which was charged to be ſlanderous to the iſſue begotten between the King and her. She was convicted therefore on a ſtatute made two years before, declaring it treaſon to throw ſlander on the King, Queen, or their iſſue. "So that, ſaith Biſhop Burnet, the law that "was made for her, and the iſſue of her "marriage, was now made uſe of to de-"ſtroy her [h]." An act of parliament was ſoon

[g] 25 H. VIII. c. 22. § 8. Biſhop Burnet, vol. i. p. 202. And Hume's Hiſt. vol. iii. p. 207. Stow 557. Hall 227.

[h] "In her, ſaith Lord Herbert, were eminent the moſt "attractive perfections. Beauty indeed is not always "the beſt keeper of itſelf; yet ſhe was thought both mo-"derate in her deſires, and of diſcretion enough, to make "her capable of being truſted with her own perfections. "I do reject all thoſe therefore that would ſpeak againſt "her honour, in thoſe times they ſtaid in France; but I "ſhall as little accuſe her in this particular of her affairs "in this time; it is enough that the law hath condemn-"ed her. No cauſe hereof is related yet, unleſs that at "a tournament ſhe let fall a handkerchief, wherewith "ſome one, ſuppoſed to be her favourite, wiped his face; "and that this was perceived by the King. But ſuſpicion "in great minds is like a tempeſt, which, though it ſcarce ſtir

ſoon afterwards made to declare her marriage to have been unlawful, "for that his Highneſs had choſen to wife the virtuous and excellent Lady Jane; who, for her convenient years, excellent beautye, and pureneſſe of fleſhe and bloude, would be apt, God willinge, to conceive iſſue by his Highneſſe." As to Catharine Howard, ſhe was beheaded under an expreſs ſtatute of attainder [i], upon petition of both houſes of parliament to the King, "that he would not vex himſelf, but give his royal aſſent to what they ſhould do." Her grandmother the Ducheſs of Norfolk, with twelve perſons more, was at the ſame time attainted of miſpriſion, for having concealed her vicious life, which they were ſuppoſed to have known previous to her marriage. The ſame act required [k] all, who hereafter ſhould know, or vehe-

"ſtir low and ſhallow waters, when it meets with a ſea, both vexes it, and makes it toſs all that come thereon. The Archbiſhop of Canterbury, in a conſolatory letter to the King, wrote as much in her behalf as he durſt. The King ſolemnized his intended marriage three days after her death, *not thinking it fit to mourn long for one the law had declared criminal.*" Hiſt. of Hen. VIII. p. 285, and 440.

[i] Stat. 33 H. VIII. c. 21. Herbert, p. 538.

[k] But not under the pains of high treaſon, as miſconceived by Mr. Hume, vol. iii. p. 248; or under any other penalty:

vehemently preſume, any condition of lightneſs of body in her which ſhould be Queen, to diſcloſe it to the King, or Council; at the ſame time "prohibiting every one to blow "it abroad, or whiſper it to others."

The ingenuity of this parliament went further; for they not only made it treaſon in the Queen to have committed an act of incontinency, prior to the marriage, without previouſly revealing it; but they extended the ſame guilt to all concealers of that incontinency; and alſo[1] made it treaſon in the Queen to make advances of gallantry after marriage, by writing, words, tokens, or otherwiſe, though not followed by any effect.

It is ſomewhere well obſerved in regard to Henry the Eighth, that he never ſpared man in his wrath, nor woman in his luſt. To the impulſe of ſuch motives we muſt attribute, that endleſs variety of ſanguinary laws which

penalty: the clauſe was merely a permiſſive protection to the informer, againſt the words of the ſtatute, under which Anne Boleyne had ſuffered.

[1] All theſe proviſions are in the ſame ſtatute; the enactors cannot be preſumed to have retained any remains of ſhame; yet it is obſervable, that it was not entered on the roll.

were

were framed during his reign in opposition to all the influences of natural affection, the ties of confidence, and the sentiments of shame and decency.

The passive pliability of parliaments in that age was wonderful. Henry was hardly cold in his grave, when the Protector, Somerset, in order to engage the short-lived approbation of the people, obtained the repealing stat. 1 Edw. VI. c. 12. which recites in the preamble, "that it had been necessary in the "time of the late King to make many laws, "which might appear to men of exteriour "realms, and to many of his Majesty's sub-"jects, very strait, sore, extreme, and ter-"rible; though they had not been without "great consideration, and policy, moved and "established. But, as in tempest, or winter, "one course and garment is convenient, in "calmer warm weather a more liberal case, "or lighter garment, so &c."

In like manner the 1 Mary, c. 1. recites, "that *many laws had been made*, *by which even learned and expert people*, *minding honesty*, *are oftentimes trapped and snared*; therefore &c."

Thus all theſe forced, and ſtrange effects of Henry's invention were abrogated by the firſt acts of his children; and the doctrine of treaſons was once more reduced to the ſtandard of the 25 Edw. III.

§ 3. The next treaſon, mentioned in that ſtatute, is of a more outrageous nature, and tending more immediately to break all the bands of government; I mean "the levying "of war againſt the King in his realm." Under this deſcription, a mere conſpiracy to levy war, unleſs directly againſt the King, is not treaſon; but in a conſpiracy for more remote purpoſes, if war be actually levied by ſome of the conſpirators, they are all conſidered as principal traitors.

The words of the ſtatute ſeem to imply a military aſſemblage, or armed inſurrection; not upon a private quarrel between powerful individuals; not in maintenance of a perſonal claim, or in purſuit of a particular redreſs; but ſuch a riſing, as may, in judgement of law, be intended to have been againſt the perſon of the King, to ſeize, dethrone, or impriſon him; or to oblige him *by violence*, to alter the meaſures of his government; or to

compel

compel a change in the religion ſettled by law; or to withhold caſtles or fortreſſes by weapons offenſive and invaſive; or, laſtly, a wilful joining with open rebels, in which caſe force is no excuſe, unleſs applied immediately againſt the perſon, or exciting *inſtant* fear of death. For if the fear of having houſes burnt, or goods ſpoiled, or of other collateral injury, were a ſufficient plea, it might be in the power of any leader to indemnify all his followers [m]. And this pretext of perſonal apprehenſion is moſt ſtrictly conſtrued: for at the trial of Axtel, who commanded the guards at the execution of King Charles, when he alledged in juſtification, "that he had acted only as a ſoldier and under the command of his ſuperior officer, whom he muſt obey or die;" it was anſwered by the court, that "where the command is traiterous, there the obedience to that command is alſo traiterous [n]."

It is not for private ſubjects, miſguided perhaps by ignorance, and heated by faction, to determine the proper moment of reſiſtance againſt ſupoſed violations of fundamental

[m] Macgrowther's caſe. State Trials, vol. viii. p. 56.
[n] Kelyng, p. 13.

laws, subversions of the constitution, and breaches of the original contract:

For never yet did Insurrection want
Such water-colours to impaint her cause;
Nor moody beggars, starving for a time
Of pell-mell havock and confusion [o].

The infatuated misconduct of princes may certainly induce a crisis, in which the rising of the nation, as one man, is not only justifiable, but laudable, and glorious; but such a crisis is to be decided by the united voice of the Society at large, not by the partial dissonance of clamorous Individuals. One may admire the courage, but it would be difficult to justify the conduct, of Flavius the Tribune, so finely recorded by Tacitus [p]; *Dein postquam urgebatur, confessionis gloriam amplexus, interrogatusque de Nerone, quibus causis ad oblivionem sacramenti processisset: "Oderam te, inquit; nec quisquam tibi fidelior "militum fuit, dum amari meruisti. Odisse "cœpi, postquam parricida matris et uxoris, "auriga, et histrio, et incendiarius, extitisti."* Had the attempt of Flavius succeeded, he would have deserved to be treated as a trai-

[o] Shakespeare. [p] Tacit. Annal. l. xv. c. 67.

terous

terous aſſaſſin. For though the character of Nero was undoubtedly moſt deteſtable; yet the perſon of the prince is in no caſe liable to chaſtiſement from the hand of a private ſubject. Dreadful indeed would be the condition of Sovereignty, if a contrary doctrine were tolerated.

It ſeems, on the whole, to have been the ſole object of this clauſe, to ſuppreſs, and puniſh the daring efforts of *poſitive rebellion* againſt the adminiſtration of government, or the perſon of majeſty; and this deſcription might, in ſtrictneſs, be thought to comprize every poſſible caſe, within this ſpecies of treaſon. But the idea hath, in the courſe of years, been extended with great liberality of interpretation.

A riſing with intention to kill one of the privy council[q]; a tumultuary combination[r] to compel the King to put away his miniſters; an armed force with a *general purport* to deſtroy incloſures, to deliver priſons[s], or to demoliſh bawdy houſes[t], or to pull down meeting houſes of diſſenters, (in which caſes the uni-

[q] Talbot's caſe, 17 R. II. [r] Earl of Eſſex's caſe.
[s] Old Bailey Trials, 1688. [t] Hale's Hiſt. P. C. i. 134.

 verſality

verſality of the deſign is conſtrued into rebellion); laſtly, inſurrections to effect redreſs or innovation of public and general concern, in which the inſurgents have no ſpecial intereſt [v]; "or forcibly to render ineffectual any act of "parliament, or law of the realm;" are all ſeverally adjudged to be a levying of war within the ſtatute.

The recital of this laſt very general head of conſtruction will naturally bring to the reader's recollection one of the articles of the mutiny act; which receives the annual ſanction of parliament, and makes "the diſobedience of legal orders puniſhable by death." *Such precarious, indefineable claſſes of crimes, have a neceſſary tendency to deſtroy the confidence of the ſubject, and to give an arbitrary power to the Judge.*

As to the other enormities abovementioned, the conſtitution hath certainly intruſted the firſt, and proper exertion for the redreſs of grievances to the high court of parliament; yet to the eye of humanity it will appear doubtful, whether certain offences have not

[v] Foſter, 213.

occa-

occaſionally received the hard denomination of rebellion, which might more properly have been puniſhed as treſpaſſes, miſdemeanors, and riots.

It is by no means the temper of modern Judges to encourage arguments of implication to the extenſion of penal laws; I ſhall tranſcribe the concurring ſentiment of the learned and benevolent Sir M. Hale, with particular regret in this inſtance, that his manuſcript [w] remained ſo long unpubliſhed.

" We muſt acquieſce in reſolutions when
" made and ſettled: but in my opinion, if
" new caſes happen for the future, *that have*
" *not an expreſs reſolution in point, nor are ex-*
" *preſſly within the words of the* 25 E. III.
" though they may ſeem to have a parity of
" reaſon, it is the ſafeſt way, and moſt
" agreeable to the wiſdom of that great act,
" firſt to conſult the parliament, and have
" their declaration; and to be very wary
" in multiplying conſtructive, and interpre-
" tative treaſons; *for we know not where it*
" *may end.*"

[w] Hiſt. P. C.

§ 4. The ſtatute proceeds to deſcribe that fourth ſpecies of treaſon, which conſiſts in "adherence to the kings enemies." The deſcription of this offence had been in the ſame words near 200 years before, whenever any Norman quitted for France the allegiance due to England; and the ſtyle of forfeitures under King John was, "*quia adhæſit inimicis noſtris in Normanniâ.*"

By "enemies" are meant "all aliens in notorious hoſtility." The ſolemnity of a previous denunciation of war is not always neceſſary [x], as in the inſtance of general letters of marque and repriſals; and ſometimes it is impoſſible, as in the emergency of a ſudden invaſion. That the perſons adhered to were enemies, is a matter of fact proper to be averred, and evidenced by its public notoriety.

Furniſhing money, arms, ammunition, and proviſions, or ſending intelligence to the king's enemies, are all in reaſon, and conſequently in law, acts of adherence; even though they ſhould be intercepted in their

[x] Bynkerſhoek, Quæſt. Juris Publici, p. 1. et ſeq.

paſ-

passage [y]; for the treason, though ineffective, is complete on the part of the traitor.

A subject of the enemy-country, continuing under the protection of England, and practising, whilst in England, to the aid and assistance of that enemy-country, comes under the words of the statute; but mere residence in a hostile kingdom is not in itself an adherence, though a refusal to return to the mother country upon proclamation may be evidence thereof.

Other acts of adherence are, actual war against the king's allies, the treacherous surrendering in collusion with the enemy of a place of defence, a voluntary oath of fealty to the enemy king, or cruizing under his commission, though without any absolute act of hostility [z].

§ 5. To a speculative mind, unbiassed by the habitual warpings of positive law, I may now appear to have considered all the treasons, which can exist, as mediately or immediately

[y] Gregg's case, A. D. 1707.—See Burnet's History.—and Dr. Hensy's case in B. R. 31 Geo. II.—Foster, 218.

[z] State Trials, vol. v. p. 22. 8 W. III. Trial of Capt. Vaughan, who was executed for this offence.

relative

relative to the perſon of Majeſty, and the ſafety of the realm. But, diſguſting as the taſk is, it ſeems neceſſary to make ſome mention of a great variety of other delinquencies, which, by the ſtatute of Edward the Third, and by ſubſequent acts of parliament, have been branded with the hard denomination and heavy penalties of high-treaſon.

It was conſiſtent with the ſcholaſtic ſubtlety of ſome, and the credulity of others of our anceſtors, to argue and to believe, that a miſapplication of the royal prerogative by a ſubject amounted in guilt to an uſurpation of ſovereignty; and that an abuſe of the king's image, though merely with a view to private gain, ought to be conſidered as the moſt traiterous diſaffection to the perſon of Majeſty [a].

On theſe principles the ſtatute proceeded to make it treaſon "to counterfeit the king's great or privy ſeal, or the king's money; or to bring counterfeit money into the realm, knowing it to be falſe." Nor doth this proviſion

[a] The extravagance of this idea among the Romans was ſuch, that Severus and Antoninus found it neceſſary by Reſcript to declare, "that if a Perſon in throwing a ſtone ſhould by chance ſtrike one of the Emperor's Statues, he ſhould not, on that account, be liable to proſecution for Treaſon." ff. l. v. ad Leg. Jul.

vision appear to have lain dormant; for we find frequent mention of its effects in the writers of that age; and on one occasion [b] in the subsequent reign, before Belknap, Skipwith, and others, apud Lincoln, "*Septem falsarii monetæ tracti fuerunt, et suspensi; et quidam Vicarius de Wintringham obmutescens adjudicatus erat ad pœnam Mutorum.*"

But still the offences of clipping, filing, lightening, and impairing, were not expressly described; yet they were found equally pernicious to trade, and equally affronts to the image of sovereignty, though not such immediate usurpations of its attributes. *To settle the doubt therefore, and not merely as a new law*, all such diminutions were declared to be high-treason [c]. And indeed clipping seems to have been a crime of a very serious nature, prior even to the statute of treasons; for we find the following remark, so early as the year 1728, "*Judæi pro tonsurâ mo-*

[b] Knyghton's Hist. A. D. 1389.

[c] 3 Hen. V. c. 6. which statute hath not been remarked by modern writers, who date the penalty of treason for the offence of impairing the coin from stat. 5 Eliz. 8.—The Answer on the Rolls given by Henry the Fifth is, "Quant a le loture, tonsure, et fillage, soit il declaré pur treson."

netæ

netæ in magnâ multitudine ubique per Angliam ſuſpenduntur [d]."

This, with other intermediate treaſons, was repealed, and revived alternately, during a long courſe of years. At preſent, by the aid of many modern ſtatutes, in which the accuracy and ingenuity of deſcription ſeem to have engaged all the anxiety of the enactors, it forms a very conſiderable article in our laws; and frequently puzzles all the efforts of mercy to ſave the wretches, who become liable to its penalties.

It is now high-treaſon, to have in poſſeſſion any inſtrument, or tool, "not of common uſe in any trade," but proper only for Coining [e]. With almoſt equal propriety it might be called homicide to be in poſſeſſion of a Piſtol.

It is alſo high-treaſon, "to make, or mend, or have in poſſeſſion, any inſtrument," or cutting-engine, for cutting round blanks by force of a ſcrew, out of flatted bars of gold, ſilver, or other metal: I have copied the words of the

[d] Thom. Walſingham, Hypodigm. Neuſt. p. 69.
[e] 8 and 9 Will. III. c. 26.

ſtatute.

ſtatute. It may be proper to obſerve here, that there are alſo many offences, relative to the coin, in the nature of felonies and miſdemeanors; and it is much to be regretted, that the ſeveral ſtatutes on this ſubject are not all reduced into one act.

I ſhall only add, that, by the laſt act on this ſubject [f], "*the alteration of a farthing with intention to make it paſs for a ſixpence, is high-treaſon in the offender, his aiders, and abettors.*"

The idea, of what Bodin affectedly calls, the harmonious proportion of puniſhments, ſhould never be forgotten in acts of penal legiſlation. It is mercileſs and abſurd, to impute the ſame guilt, and give the ſame chaſtiſement, to the leader of a rebellion, and the diminiſher of a piece of money.

This extravagant idea ſeems to have exiſted in the common law of England; and probably derived its origin from the law of the Romans. "*Cudendæ pecuniæ obnoxii Majeſtatis crimen admittunt, et omni dilatione remotâ Flammarum exuſtionibus mancipentur* [g]:" and

[f] 16 Geo. II. [g] Cod. ix. 24. 2.

again,

again, "*Quicunque nummos aureos partim tinxerint, partim finxerint, vel raserint, si quidem liberi sunt, ad bestias dari; si servi, summo supplicio affici debent.*" Such were the expressions of Theodosius and Justinian; but no early authority can justify the consequences of their import, which will be best described in the words of an eloquent and humane modern writer. "This confounds "the distinction and proportion of offences; "and by affixing the same ideas of guilt "upon the man who coins a leaden groat, "and him who assassinates his sovereign, "takes off from that horror, which ought to "attend the very mention of the crime of "high-treason, and makes it familiar to the "subject."

In France also this crime is considered as a species of treason, and subjected to Capital punishment by an edict, A. D. 1726; it was formerly treated with greater mildness, as we learn by the following law promulgated by Childebert III, A. D. 744[h]; "*de falsâ monetâ jubemus, ut qui eam percussisse comprobatus fuerit, manus ei amputetur; et qui hoc consensit, si liber*

[h] Baluze, t. i. c. 20. p. 154.

eſt, ſexaginta ſolidos componat; ſi ſervus, ſexaginta ictus accipiat."

§ 6. The laſt kind of treaſon, declared in ſtat. 25 Edw. III, relates to the actual killing of certain magiſtrates in the execution of their offices. Reverence and ſecurity are certainly due to the diſpenſers of public juſtice; but it may be doubted, whether they are ſo immediately the repreſentatives of ſovereignty, as to make the crime of killing them, however aggravated in its nature, loſe its proper name of murder.

§ 7. All the treaſons created between this ſtatute, and the firſt of Mary, were repealed in the commencement of her reign; together with all felonies and præmunires enacted under Henry the Eighth.

But the ſtruggles and jealouſies attending the firſt progreſs of the Reformation, introduced under Q. Elizabeth a new ſpecies of treaſons; of which, after various alterations, many exceptionable inſtances are ſtill exiſting.

The

The ſecond offence of extolling the Pope's power is at this day treaſon [i]; upon which it is obvious to obſerve, that the idea of a treaſon, ariſing from a repetition of the offence, is in itſelf an abſurdity. It is alſo treaſon, to obtain, or publiſh, or put in execution, within the Britiſh dominions, a Popiſh Bull of abſolution, or reconciliation [k]; or to withdraw, *or be willingly withdrawn*, to the Popiſh religion; or to receive Popiſh orders; or to refuſe a ſecond tender of the oath. I have already obſerved, how repugnant it is to reaſon, religion, and humanity, to extend the infliction of death to the irreſiſtible dictates of conſcience, and belief.

§ 8. It will be ſufficient to refer to our ſtatute books for the particulars of another modern ſpecies of high-treaſon, the poſſibility of which ſeems ſoon likely to expire; and the neceſſity of which, as a civil ſanction, is already ſunk, in the united and affectionate attachment of the whole realm to the illuſtrious family of its preſent Sovereign. But the miſdirected, and dangerous zeal of political enthuſiaſts, made it expedient, in the eſta-

[i] 5 Eliz. ſtat. 2. Sav. 46. [k] 13 Eliz. c. 2.

bliſhment of the Proteſtant ſucceſſion, to affix the higheſt civil guilt to every overt act; by writing, or otherwiſe, in oppoſition to that eſtabliſhment; to every denial of the power of parliament to limit the ſucceſſion; and to every mode of correſpondence with the abdicated prince, or his children[1].

To theſe wiſe ſeverities of our anceſtors we are in ſome degree indebted for the inheritance of thoſe rights, of which we boaſt the preſent enjoyment. The imitation of their venerable example, in the unimpaired tranſmiſſion of thoſe rights to our poſterity, is a duty, to which we are called by the united voice of civil and religious liberty.

§ 9. Having now, upon the principles of juſtice and neceſſity, examined the crime of high-treaſon, both as actually conſidered by the poſitive laws of different countries, and as it ought to have been conſidered by thoſe laws; I ſhall endeavour to purſue the ſame method as to the degrees of puniſhment, which have been, and which ought to be, adapted to it.

[1] See 1 Ann. ſtat. 2. c. 17. and ſtat. 6 Ann. c. 7.

Here we have a melancholy inſtance, how much the recollection of humanity may be inſenſibly ſtifled in the warmth and reſentments of ſelf-love. The crime, being perſonally and immediately againſt lawgivers and legiſlation, hath engaged the full exertion of ingenuity and power, to make its puniſhment as immoderate, and as complicated as poſſible.

It would be a painful taſk, to deſcribe the executions of Ravaillac, and of Damiens; neither is it neceſſary to refer to the executive juſtice of foreign nations. I ſhall confine myſelf on this point to the practice of England, which cannot be ſtated better, than by an extract from the authoritative, and nervous deſcription of Sir Edward Coke; who, with great profuſion of learning, and a total want of common benevolence [m], enters into the following diſcuſſion in the preſence and hearing of ſeven unhappy men,

[m] Thoſe, who are anxious to apologize for Sir E. Coke, will ſay, that the crime, of which thoſe men ſtood accuſed, was perhaps the moſt horrid that ever entered into the heart of man: this apology might have ſome weight, if his harrangue had been rather *after* conviction, than *before*.

who were about to undergo this ſentence full of horrors [n].

" Theſe traitors have exceeded all others " their predeceſſors in miſchief; yet his " majeſty in his admirable clemency and " moderation will not invent any new tor- " tures or torments for them; but hath been " graciouſly pleaſed to afford them as well " an ordinary courſe of trial, as an ordinary " puniſhment much inferior to their offence. " And ſurely worthy of obſervation is the " treatment by law provided and appointed " for high-treaſon.

" For firſt, the traitor ſhall be drawn to " the place of execution, as not being wor- " thy any more to tread upon the face of " the earth, whereof he was made; and with " his head declining downwards, and as " near the ground as may be, being thought " unfit to take the benefit of the common " air.

" He ſhall next be hanged up by the neck " between heaven and earth, as deemed un- " worthy of both or either, as likewiſe that

[n] State Trials, vol. i. p. 235.

"the eyes of men may behold, and their "hearts contemn him. Then is he to be "cut down alive, and to have his parts of "generation cut off, and burnt before his "face, as being unworthily begotten, and "unfit to leave any race after him. His "inlayed parts ſhall be alſo taken out, and "burnt; for it was his heart, which har-"boured ſuch horrible treaſon. His head "ſhall be cut off, which imagined the miſ-"chief; and laſtly, his body ſhall be quar-"tered, and the quarters ſet up in ſome "high and eminent place, to the view "and deteſtation of men, and to become "a prey for the fowls of the air. And this "is the reward due to traitors; for it is the "phyſic of government, to let out corrupt "blood."

It hath been affirmed both with reſpect to nations and individuals, that the ſentiments of benevolence bear a general proportion to the progreſs of ſcience; but the name of Sir Edward Coke will not be cited in ſupport of this obſervation. With great acuteneſs and depth of learning, he retained through life a hard, unpitying nature; that brutal inſolence which is ſo often produced in narrow minds, by by undeserved or unexpected prosperity, marked all his actions. His learning, indeed, was not of that kind which we call *literæ humaniores*; but it would be an inference, highly injurious to the profession, to suppose, that the practice of law blunts the sensibility of the mind.

As to the punishment inflicted by our law on high-treason, which occasioned this digression; it appears formerly to have been a part of the judgement [o], that the convict should be drawn upon a hurdle; but an instance is recorded [p], in which Shard, Justice, ordered, that nothing should be brought, whereupon he should be drawn, "*mes que sans cley, ou autre chose a desouth lui, soit tray de chivaux, hors de la sale, ou il avoit judgment, tanque a les furcs, &c.*" It was also a part of the ancient judgement [q], "*que les privies membres scient excises de son corps, et comburés deins son vieu:*" but this was omitted by Lord Hardwick in the judge-

[o] Staunford, l. iii. c. 19. p. 182. It is remarkable, however, that before the time of Henry VII. there were hardly two judgements, of which the form was the same. See Carthew's Reports, p. 349. Walcot's case.
[p] Ass. xxxiii. 7. Hale's Hist. P. C. i. 382.
[q] Staunford, iii. 19.

ments paſſed upon the four Lords in the year 1746 [r]; and in a former caſe had been thought unneceſſary [s]. Still, however, the criminal muſt be ordered to be cut down alive. For upon a writ [t] of error, to reverſe an attainder in the 8th of W. III. it was aſſigned for error, that the court had only directed, "*quod interiora ſua extra ventrem ſuum capiantur, et in ignem ponantur,*" omitting, "*ipſo vivente,*" or, "*in conſpectu ejus*;" and it was ſaid by Lord Chief Juſtice Holt, that "though this omiſſion be for the benefit of the party attainted, yet ſtill it is error; *for the judgement in all capital caſes is ſtated and ſettled by the common law, which no court can alter.*" The attainder was thereupon reverſed, and the reverſal was affirmed in parliament [u].

It is certain, that the crime of high-treaſon is often of ſuch a tendency, as to require the *ultimum ſupplicium*, or, in other words, the extirpation of the criminal.

But when we are conſtrained to have recourſe to that fatal extremity, it ſhould always

[r] State Trials, vol. ix. [s] Lord Raymond, p. 1.
[t] Walcot's caſe, 12 Mod. 95, 96.
[u] Mich. 11 W. III. Shower's Parl. Caſes, p. 127.

be

be obſerved, that whatever exceeds ſimple death is mere cruelty. Every ſtep beyond is a trace of ancient barbarity, tending only to diſtract the attention of the ſpectators, and to leſſen the ſolemnity of the example. There is no ſuch thing as vindictive juſtice; the idea is ſhocking. Public utility is the meaſure of human puniſhments; and that utility is proportionate to the efficacy of the example. But whenever the horror of the crime is loſt in ſympathy with the ſuperfluous ſufferings of the criminal, the example loſes its efficacy, and the law its reverence.

A nation, familiarized and reconciled to the execution of the Engliſh ſentence in caſes of high-treaſon, would probably conſiſt of a puſillanimous and deſpicable people; cruelty and cowardice are inſeparable.

CHAP. XV.

A Digreſſion relative to the Engliſh Trials in Caſes of High-Treaſon.

§ 1. I Ought not to diſmiſs this ſubject, without remarking a very pleaſing part of Engliſh law relative to high-treaſon; as as founded in humanity, animated by the ſpirit of freedom, and perfected by all the powers of limited wiſdom.

From the affectionate temper of the nation, great warmth hath been ſhewn againſt the crime of diſloyalty, both in the liberality of its conſtruction, and in the ſeverity of its puniſhment; but the whole attention of the legiſlature hath at the ſame time been exerted, to obviate all poſſibility of oppreſſion in the proſecution, and all defect of certainty in the proof. Infinitely various have been the amendments, refinements, and alterations to this purpoſe; and, upon the whole, the following cautionary proviſions have been thought ſufficient, and are at this day in force.

No perſon ſhall be proſecuted for high-treaſon, except on a charge of [w] aſſaſſination deſigned or attempted on the body of the King, unleſs he be indicted thereof within three years after the offence committed. It had been obſerved by Sir Ed. Coke, near a century before this proviſion took place, " that there wanted nothing to the perfec-

[w] 7 W. III. c. 3. § 6.

tion

tion of the ſtatute of the 25th Ed. III. but a limitation of ſome certain time, wherein the offender ſhould be accuſed." And ſuch had been the idea of Bracton: "*Poſt intervallum temporis accuſator non erit audiendus, niſi docere poſſit, ſe fuiſſe juſtis rationibus impeditum* [x]."

Nor ſhall any perſon be indicted, except upon the teſtimony of two lawful witneſſes, either both to the ſame overt act, or the one of them to one, and the other to another overt act of the ſame treaſon [y].

And now, ſince the deceaſe of the late pretender, a copy of the indictment, with a liſt of the witneſſes to be produced at the trial, and of the jurors impanelled, with the profeſſions, and places of abode of the ſaid witneſſes, and jurors, ſhall be delivered to the perſon indicted, ten days before the trial [z]; and it ſeems, that this would be conſtrued excluſively of the day of delivery, and the day of arraignment.

[x] 3 Inſt. c. 2. Bracton, l. iii. fol. 118. b.
[y] 7 W. III. c. 3. § 2. which clauſe is founded on 1 Edw. VI. and 5 Edw. VI. And 1, 2, Phil. & M.
[z] 7 Ann. c. 22. and 20 Geo. II. c. 30.

Further,

Further, the ſame proceſs is given to compel perſons to appear for the perſon accuſed, as is uſed to compel them to appear againſt him; and laſtly, they ſhall be upon oath, which was not the uſage heretofore.

I ſhould have obſerved, that theſe privileges, except the laſt, are not extended to certain offences concerning the papal ſupremacy; nor to thoſe againſt the coin; nor indeed to any treaſon, wherein the corruption of blood is ſaved by ſtatute.

The jurors muſt, by the common law, be of the ſame county wherein the offence was committed. When the trial comes on, the priſoner is allowed to object peremptorily to thirty-five, on mere caprice, prejudice, or private knowledge of their characters or prepoſſeſſions; and to any indefinite number, upon the aſſignment of a legal objection to each.

In this, and in the whole courſe of the proſecution, he ſhall alſo be allowed to make his defence, as well in points of fact, as in legal queſtions, by Counſel learned in the law, not exceeding two in number, to be named by himſelf, and aſſigned by the court; and his

Counſel

Counsel shall have free access to him at all seasonable hours [a].

The trials of Sir William Freind, Sir William Parkyns, and others, on the assassination plot, came on after this provision had received the royal assent, but before the commencement of its operation [b]. "I intreat," said the last of these gentlemen, "that I may have "the allowance of Counsel; I have no skill "in indictments; I do not understand these "matters, nor what advantages may be pro-"per for me to take. The new statute wants "but one day. What is just and reasonable "to-morrow, surely is just and reasonable "to-day; and your Lordship may indulge "me in this case."

Holt, Chief Justice, was too good a judge to suffer the stubborn principles of law to yield to the milder inferences of equity. "*We "cannot* (he replied) *alter the law, till law-*

[a] 7 W. III. c. 3. § 1. But this did not extend to any prosecution by impeachment till stat. 20 Geo. II. c. 30. which allowed Counsel in that case also. "And with great reason (saith Mr. J. Foster) since the Defendant is struggling under the whole weight of the Commons of Great-Britain."

[b] State Trials.

"*makers direct us; we must conform to the law,*
"*as it is at present, not what it will be to-*
"*morrow; we are upon our oaths so to do.*"

It is remarkable, that this indulgence is not yet allowed, except in points of mere legal disquisition, in any other capital crime; a deficiency, which hath given rise to the very benevolent adage, "That the judge shall always be counsel for the prisoner." And indeed, the probity of the English judges, assisted by their experience and humanity, would generally afford ample security to persons accused, if counsel had not full permission to be employed against them. This permission, in good times, was never exerted without great discretion and tenderness; still however it was not always ineffective in its consequences. But surely it is contradictory to the first principles of justice, that a prisoner, labouring under the weight of a capital charge, weakened by long confinement, distracted by apprehensions though perhaps innocent, distressed by the tears of his family, checked by conscious ignorance, and disconcerted by the awful novelty of his situation; that, in such a state of mind, a prisoner should be singly exposed to the united, and unrestrained prosecution of learned men, habituated to public ſpeaking, and (in the words of a very ancient author) "ſkilled in the arts of forwarding, "and defending a cauſe by the rules of law, "and cuſtoms of the realm [c]." The judge may be anxious to expoſe, and refute the prevarication of the witneſſes; but he is ignorant of the minute circumſtances of the fact in queſtion; he knows not the characters of the men, and cannot ſtop the trial to receive private inſtructions from the priſoner. The jurors are honeſt, and inclinable to mercy; his equals, and his neighbours; choſen in ſome meaſure by himſelf; and ſuperior to all ſuſpicion: but perhaps they are illiterate; at all events they are men; and therefore liable to be hurried away by the eloquence and abilities of advocates.

Both the Romans [d], and Athenians, appear to have given full ſcope to the exertion of oratory

[c] Gents ne ſachent my comunement touts les exceptions que valent en reſponſe; ſont countors neceſſaires, que ſachent les cauſes avancer et defendre; per les Rules del Ley, & les uſages del Realme.

Myrror, c. 3. de Exceptions.

[d] "*Non ſolum autem dicendo, ſed etiam faciendo quædam, lacrymas movemus: unde et producere ipſos, qui periclitentur, ſqualidos atque deformes, et liberos eorum ac parentes, inſtitutum;*

oratory in criminal cases, both for and against the defendant. Among the Athenians indeed there was a law of Solon's, forbidding advocates to use either *exordia* or *perorations*; or to circumvent the passions of the judges by artifices, either of commiseration or amplification. Yet we are told by Cicero, that, when Demosthenes was expected to plead, the fame of his eloquence brought a general concourse of strangers to Athens from the most remote parts of Greece, as to the most celebrated spectacle in the world; and those of his orations, which have reached our time, are undoubtedly powerful examples of that pathetic and personifying species of eloquence, which is calculated to intoxicate the imagination of an audience, and communicate the successive emotions of anger, indignation, and pity. There is a very remarkable anecdote recorded by Athenæus [e], relative to the trial of Phrynè, the Athenian Courtezan. She was the same, from whom Apelles drew his picture of Venus rising from the

institutum; *& ab accusatoribus ostendi cruentum gladium, et lecta e vulneribus ossa*; *et vestes sanguine perfusas videmus, et vulnera resolvi, ac verberata corpora nudari*, quarum rerum ingens plerumque vis est, velut in rem præsentem animos hominum ducentium. *Et populum Romanum egit in furorem prætexta Caii Cæsaris prolata in foro cruenta.*" Quinctil. vi. 1.

[e] Athenæus, l. xiii.

the waves, and who ſerved alſo as a model for the famous ſtatue of Praxiteles; two circumſtances, not immaterial in ſupport of the following fact. "*Phrynæ cum in capitali* "*noxâ patrocinaretur Hyperides, et jam mani-* "*feſtum eſſet calculis judicum condemnatum iri;* "*in apertum eam produxit, et diſciſſis tuniculis,* "*pectoreque nudato, poſtremâ orationis parte,* "*illius conſpectâ pulchritudine, ita peroravit,* "*ut, tanquam miniſtram ſacerdotemque Veneris,* "*judices* religione tacti, *et miſericordiâ com-* "*moti, necandam minime cenſuerunt.*" To this ſudden ſenſibility of the Areopagites, one may fairly apply Quinctilian's obſervation, "*quod harum rerum ingens plerumque vis eſt,* "*velut in rem præſentem animos hominum du-* "*centium.*"

It is a conſequence of that wiſdom which characterizes the Engliſh, as a people, in the whole ſyſtem and adminiſtration of their Laws, that all the artifices of ſpeech are baniſhed from the Bar. The paſſions ought not to be addreſſed in appeals to the reaſon. The unſubſtantial harmony of declamation may be well adapted to the ears of an arbitrary tribunal: but the deciſions of Engliſh Judges are founded on the argumentative in-

ferences

ferences of ſtrict ſtatutes, and recorded precedents. Our courts have furniſhed proofs indeed, that the ſtrains of ancient eloquence are neither inimitable, nor unattainable; but a nobler and more proper theatre hath been found for the exertion of that talent. Plain ſenſe, delivered in accurate expreſſion, with a warm and graceful articulation, is the true eloquence of law.

But to return to my inquiry, how far Counſel ought to be admitted, either for, or againſt the defendant, in criminal proſecutions. Upon the whole, perhaps it might be the beſt medium, in all caſes, to confine the diſcuſſion of the fact to the artleſs unguided tale of the witneſſes; with a full permiſſion to Counſel, on both ſides indifferently, to ſuggeſt, ſupport, or refute queſtions, or objections of law, and to undertake the management at large, when the iſſue turns not upon the general queſtion of "Guilty" or "Not Guilty," but upon collateral facts [f]. It

[f] In which caſe, from inſtances ſo early as the firſt year of Hen. VII. the defendant appears to have been always entitled to the full aſſiſtance of Counſel, and indeed without ſuch aſſiſtance it would be impoſſible for him to know either when to hazard his defence upon collateral allegations, or how properly to enfore thoſe allegations. See Foſter, p. 232. Stra. 824.

might

might be proper at the ſame time to declare, how far trivial miſtakes, in matters of mere form, ſhould continue fatal to the whole proceſs; and whether any exceptions of counſel ſhould be heard or allowed[g], but what tend in ſome degree to affect the merits of the caſe.

§ 2. The admiſſibility and ſufficiency of evidence in trials for high-treaſon is alſo ſubjected to very peculiar limitations.

No evidence can be received of any overt act, not charged in the indictment; except, as in ſupport only of one which is charged. Two witneſſes are requiſite to the conviction, in the ſame manner as to the indictment; and they ſhall in giving their evidence be confronted with the perſon accuſed, which is now indeed the practice in all caſes. If two diſtinct treaſons be charged, one witneſs to each ſhall not be two within the meaning of the ſtatute; but one witneſs is ſufficient to prove any fact, on which the criminality of the charge is ultimately and not immediately founded; I ſhall cite an inſtance[h].

[g] Hale's Hiſt. P. C. ii. 193. Mr. Emlyn's note.
[h] State Trials, vol. v. p. 38.

When, in the trial of Captain Vaughan for adhering to the King's enemies, it was neceſſary in the outſet to prove him a ſubject of England; it was objected by his counſel, that one witneſs only had been called for that purpoſe; and the objection was over-ruled by Holt, Chief Juſtice, "for that is "no *overt* act; if there be one witneſs to "prove that, it is ſufficient." In like manner, writing, being a deliberate act, certainly may [i] under ſome circumſtances *with publication* be an overt act of treaſon; and when ſo laid in the indictment, muſt be proved by the teſtimony of two witneſſes. But the teſtimony of one is competent to prove writings, offered only as collateral evidence; and ſuch papers, though not of the hand-writing of the priſoner, may be read as evidence, if found in his cuſtody [k]; and papers under certain deſcriptions may be in the legal cuſtody of a perſon, though not actually found upon him [l].

"*Unius reſponſio teſtis omnino non audiatur*," were the words of the Civil Law, which did not allow the teſtimony of one witneſs

[i] Foſter 198. caſe of Layer, State Trials, vol. vi. p. 321.
[k] State Trials, vol. vi. p. 281.
[l] Lord Preſton's caſe, State Trials, vol. iv. p. 431.

to

to be conclusive in any case[m]. And Baron Montesquieu seems to have adopted this idea in its fullest latitude. "*Les Loix (dit il) qui sont périr un homme sur la déposition d'un seul témoin, sont fatales à la liberté. La raison en exige deux; parce qu'un témoin qui affirme, et un accusé qui nie, sont un partage; et il faut un tiers pour le vuider. Les Grecs, et les Romains exigeoient une voix de plus pour condamner. Nos loix Françoises en demandent deux. Les Grecs prétendoient, que leur usage avoit été établi par les Dieux; mais c'est le nôtre*[n]."

It may be doubted, whether the plea of the prisoner, which is dictated by the sentiment of self-preservation[o], can with any propriety be said to counterbalance the solemn oath of his disinterested accuser. Yet such were the sentiments of the president Montes-

[m] Cod. iv. 20. 9. "Vox unius vox nullius est." Harmonius, l i. c. 6. See the Commentaries on the Law of England, B. iv. 351.

[n] L'Esprit des Loix, l. xii. c. 3.

[o] It is not unusual, even at this day, upon the Continent, to administer an oath to the supposed criminal, in order to extort the truth from him; reducing him (says the Marquis Beccaria) to this terrible alternative, either of offending God, or of contributing to his own immediate destruction; and leaving him only the choice of becoming a bad Christian or a Martyr.

 quieu,

quieu, and ſuch hath been the uſage of many great and learned nations. The law of England hath ſeen reaſon to reject an idea, which, if ſtrictly adhered to, would give the privilege of impunity to every crime, however flagrant in its nature, if committed in the preſence of one perſon only. Except therefore in caſes of treaſon, in which the principles of our conſtitution demand peculiar ſtrictneſs of proof, one witneſs, if credited, is with us ſufficient to eſtabliſh the conviction of any capital crime, and indeed of any offence whatever. I ought perhaps to except alſo the caſe of perjury, in which, a ſingle unſupported witneſs would be adjudged inſufficient; for the oath of the accuſer being placed in oppoſition to the oath of the accuſed, truth remains ſuſpended. In ſuch a ſituation, the ſcale of innocence ſhould be preſumed to preponderate.

The nature of my deſign will not permit me to extend this digreſſion upon criminal proceſs in caſes of treaſon, to an enquiry into the general principles of evidence. It is however a field ſtill open to inveſtigation. For the conſiderations of ſome very ingenious writers on this ſubject, have been too much influenced

influenced by their acquiefcence in practical authority; and we are furnifhed, rather with ufeful and fenfible hiftories of what the law of evidence actually is, than with any free and fpeculative difquifition of what it ought to be.

§ 3. By ftatute 7 W. III. c. 3. the above-mentioned requifites towards conviction can only be fupplied by "the confeffion of the party, made in open court, willingly and without violence."

The words "in open court" were not inferted in the ftatute of Edward VI, which contained the reft of this provifo; and confeffions, taken out of court upon the examination of the party, had been holden fufficient [p]. But now, it fhould feem, that fuch confeffions, though proved by two witneffes, cannot in any cafe operate to conviction; and that there muft ftill be two witneffes to the treafonable fact.

But another doubt hath arifen, how far fuch confeffions can be admiffible, even as

[p] Cafe of Tonge. Hale's Hift. P. C. i. 304. Kel. 18. Anderfon, ii. 67.

collateral evidence; and it ſeems to be the better opinion [q], "that a confeſſion out of "court may be proper to be ſubmitted to the "jury, in corroboration of the other evi-"dence of the overt acts," only "when "made during the ſolemnity of an examina-"tion before a Magiſtrate, or perſon having "authority to take it; when the party may "be preſumed to be properly on his guard, "and apprized of his danger." However, a greater and more exceptionable latitude of conſtruction, on this ſubject, appears in ſome inſtances [r] to have been admitted.

The

[q] Foſter, p. 242, 243.

[r] At a meeting of the Judges in January, 1707, to conſider ſome matters relative to the intended trial of Gregg for treaſon Holt, Ch. Juſtice, Powel, Powis, and Dormer Juſtices, Smith, and Bury Barons, were all clearly of opinion, "that the priſoner's confeſſion, though not in court, might, "if proved by two witneſſes to have been voluntarily made, "notwithſtanding what is contained in the 7 W. III. c. 3. "§ 2. be read as evidence againſt him. But Trevor, "Chief Juſtice, was of a contrary opinion, and Tracy, "Juſtice, doubted." I ſhould obſerve, that this caſe is not in any reporter, but copied from Bacon's Abridgement, vol. v. p. 146.

The two learned Judges, who diſſented, had no doubts on a future occaſion, as to the admiſſibility of confeſſions on matters merely collateral; and in this diſtinction they ſeem to have proceeded on very ſolid grounds. For, in the caſe of Smith, who was indicted in June, 1709, for adhering to the Queen's enemies, "Alienage was the defence;

and

The confeffion of a criminal, when taken even before a magiftrate, can rarely be turned againft him, without obviating the end for which he muft be fuppofed to have made it. Befides, we have known inftances of murders avowed, which never were committed; of things confeffed to have been ftolen, which never had quitted the poffeffion of the owner.

It is both ungenerous therefore, and unjuft, to fuffer the diftractions of fear, or the mifdirected hopes of mercy to preclude that negative evidence of difproof, which may poffibly, on recollection, be in the power of the party; *we fhould never admit, when it may be avoided, even the poffibility of driving the innocent to deftruction.* Nothing was more common in the beginning of the laft century than confeffions of witchcraft. Sir James Melville

and his confeffion that he was an Englifhman born, was allowed to be admiffible Evidence, by Trevor, Powel, Powis, Tracy, and Bury, though his counfel infifted on the act of the 7th of King William." Fofter's Rep. 243.

It is faid, however, that Evidence of confeffion was, without any fuch diftinction, holden fufficient by the Judges, who fat upon the commiffion in the North in 1746. But the inftances are not, I believe, in print; and "it is dangerous (faith Sir Edward Coke) to report a cafe by the ear, efpecially concerning treafon."

mentions ſeveral inſtances in the proſecution of Earl Bothwell; and, though rather a ſceptical man, was candid enough to believe them. The poor women were accordingly burnt; and poſterity was furniſhed with a very accurate deſcription of the devil; who is ſaid to have appeared "in a black gown, with "a black hat on his head, in the attitude of "preaching, and with poſteriors as cold as "ice [s]."

The evidence of words, alledged to have been ſpoken by the perſon accuſed, and connected with the criminality of the charge, ought alſo to be received with great diſtruſt. Such words are either ſpoken in the zeal of unſuſpicious confidence, and cannot be repeated without a breach of private faith, which detracts much from the credibility of the witneſs; or in the unguarded hours of boaſting diſſipation, in which caſe they are not unlikely to be falſe in themſelves, and very likely to be falſely repeated. Beſides, words may be very innocent when ſpoken, and highly criminal when related; for their determinate ſignification depends much on the

[s] Melvill's Memoirs, fol. p. 194.

tone

tone in which they are uttered. "It often "happens too, that, in repeating the ſame "words, a different meaning is conveyed, "which depends on their connection with "other things; and ſometimes more is ſig-"nified by ſilence, than by any expreſſion "whatever [t]."

§ 4. Such are the principal rules, limitations, and reſtrictions, to which the Engliſh proſecutions of high treaſon are ſubjected in every ſtage of the proceſs.

Laſtly, the poſitive teſtimony of a thouſand witneſſes to the poſitive allegation of the indictment is not concluſive, in any caſe, as to the verdict of the jurors. But they will ſtill retain an indiſputable, unqueſtionable right to acquit the perſon accuſed [u], if, in

[t] L'Eſprit des Loix, l. xii. c. 12.

[u] "In the Caſe of 7 R. II. Tit. Coronæ Fitz H. 108. "upon Acquittal of *a common thief*, the Judge ſaid, the "Jurors ought to be bound to their good behaviour during "their lives; but, ſaith the book, quære per quel Ley? "But that was only gratis dictum by the Judge, for no "ſuch thing was done." Vaughan's Reports.

It muſt be confeſſed, that in later times the Judges, in their diſagreements with Jurors, did not confine themſelves to threats; and it would be uncandid to ſuppreſs the following inſtance, becauſe it is connected with the matter in queſtion.

Kelyng's

in their private opinions, they disbelieve the accusers; or if, in their consciences, they think, however erroneously, that the fact partakes not of that degree, or species of criminality, with which it is charged in the indictment. They may, if they find doubts or difficulties in the case, require the direction of the court; but whether they be in any case *compellable*, either to have recourse to that direction, or to submit to it when voluntarily given, are questions, on which a very important diversity of opinion hath appeared in the minds of great and good men.

" It is the privilege of Englishmen, say those who support the negative, to be tried

Kelyng's Rep. 50. " Memorandum, Lent Circuit, Winchester, 18 C. II. one Henry Hood was indicted for the murder of J. Newen, and upon the evidence it appeared, that he killed him without any provocation. And thereupon I directed the Jury that it was murder; for the law in that case intended malice; and I told them they were judges of the matter of fact, *viz.* whether Newen died by the hand of Hood: *But whether it was murder, or manslaughter, that was matter of law, in which they were to observe the direction of the Court.* But notwithstanding they would find it only manslaughter. Whereupon I took the verdict, and fined the jury 5 l. apiece, and committed them to jail, till they found sureties to appear at the next assizes, and in the mean time to be of the good behaviour. But after, upon their petition, I lowered their fines to 40s. a-piece, which they all paid, and entered into recognizances.

by

by their equals; and that privilege will become *vox et prætereà nihil*, whenever it ceaſes to be the duty of thoſe equals, to infer and conclude their verdict from the teſtimony of witneſſes, by the act and force of their own underſtanding.

Would it not, they continue, be a moſt prepoſterous doctrine, that they, who, under the obligation of a ſolemn oath, are choſen to try a fellow citizen for a crime, and as a criminal, and bounden by that oath to give a true verdict between the public and the priſoner according to the evidence; that, in this predicament, they ſhould be told, that the criminality or innocence of the intention, the legality or illegality of the fact, are matters of indifference, not ſubjected to their enquiry; and that their verdict ought not to be influenced by any ſuch conſiderations?

"To what end (ſaid Lord Chief Juſtice "Vaughan), are the Jurors challenged ſo "ſcrupulouſly to the array and poll? to "what end muſt they have ſuch a certain "freehold, and be *probi et legales homines*, "and not of affinity with the parties con- "cerned? to what end muſt they have in

"many

" many cases the view, for their exacter in-
" formation chiefly? to what end must
" they undergo the heavy punishment of the
" villainous judgement? if, after all this,
" they implicitly must give a verdict by the
" dictates and authority of another man,
" when sworn to do it, according to the best
" of their own knowledge? *A man cannot see*
" *by another's eye, nor hear by another's ear;*
" *no more can a man conclude, or infer the thing*
" *to be resolved by another's understanding or rea-*
" *soning*; and though the verdict be right, which
" the jury give, yet they, being not assured
" it is so from their own understanding, are
" forsworn, at least *in foro conscientiæ*. That
" *decantatum* in our books, *ad quæstionem facti*
" *non respondent judices, ad quæstionem legis non*
" *respondent juratores*, literally taken, is true;
" for if it be demanded, what is the fact? the
" Judge cannot answer it; if it be asked,
" what is the law in the case? the Jury can-
" not answer it. But upon all general issues,
" though it be a matter of law, whether the
" defendant be a trespassor, a debtor, disseisor,
" or disturber, in the particular cases in issue;
" yet the jury find not, as in a special ver-
" dict, the fact of every case by itself, leaving
" the law to the court: but find for the
" plaintiff

" plaintiff or defendant upon the iſſue to be " tried, wherein they reſolve both law and " fact complicately, and not the fact by itſelf: " ſo as though they anſwer not ſingly to the " queſtion, what is the law; *yet they determine the law in all matters, where iſſue is* " *joined and tried in the principal caſe*, except " when the verdict is ſpecial [u]."

" Special verdicts," ſay the Commentaries on the Law of England, " ariſe, when the " jurors *doubt* the matter of law, and there- " fore *chuſe* to leave it to the determination " of the court [x]."

" And it is (ſaith Sir Matthew Hale) the " conſcience of the jury, that muſt pronounce " the priſoner guilty, or not guilty; for to " ſay the truth, it were the moſt unhappy " caſe, that could be, to the judge, if he, at " his peril, muſt take upon him the guilt or " innocence of the priſoner; unhappy alſo " for the priſoner: for, if the judge's opinion " muſt rule the verdict, the trial by jury " would be uſeleſs [y]."

[u] Vaughan's Reports, p. 148—151.
[x] Commentaries, B. iv. p. 354.
[y] Hale's Hiſt. P. C. ii. 313.

But

But, a contrary opinion hath been given by a learned and worthy Judge in very decisive language. "In every case (saith Mr. Justice "Foster, p. 255) where the point turneth "upon the question, whether the homi-"cide was committed, willfully and ma-"liciously, or under circumstances justify-"ing, excusing, or alleviating the matter "of fact, *viz.* whether the facts alledged by "way of justification, excuse, or alleviation "be true; *is the proper and* only *province of "the jury.* But whether, upon a supposition "of the truth of the facts, such homicide be "justified, excused, or alleviated, must be "submitted to the judgement of the court." Again, p. 256, "When the law maketh use "of the term, *malice aforethought*, as de-"scriptive of the crime of murder, it mean-"eth, that the fact hath been attended with "such circumstances as are the ordinary sym-"ptoms of a wicked, depraved, malignant "spirit." And, p. 257 [z], "the *malus animus*, "which is to be collected from all circum-

[z] It is an obvious remark on these passages, that the learned writer hath rested his position on the mere authority of an assertion, unsupported by argument or reference; and, in a subsequent chapter, I shall have occasion to cite another passage from the same work, but of a very contradictory import.

"stances, *and of which*, as I before said, *the* "*court, and not the jury*[a], *is to judge*, is what "bringeth the offence within the denomina-"tion of wilful malicious murder, whatever "might be the immediate motive to it, whe-"ther it be done as the old writers express "themselves, *irâ, vel odio, vel causâ lucri*, or "from any other wicked or mischievous in-"centive."

When wise and good men differ upon points of great constitutional importance; it is the duty of their humbler fellow citizens, to

[a] In the trial of Coke and Woodburne for disfiguring Mr. Crispe, it was much urged by the former, that his intent to kill, and not to maim, was a point of law, proper only for the decision of the court. But the Lord chief justice King, after stating the Evidence, thus addressed the jury.

"Now, gentlemen, what the intent of these persons "was, in slitting Mr. Crispe's nose, you are to try; *this is* "*a matter of fact* for your consideration and determina-"tion: it is the same in other felonies, where the intent "of the party makes the crime. Burglary is breaking "open an house in the night-time, with an intent to "commit a felony; though no felony be committed, yet "if there were an intent to do it, it is burglary. So in "the case of larceny, the intent, with which another "man's goods have been taken away, is a matter of fact "to be enquired into and determined by the jury. So "that *in this case you are to try no other matter than what* "*is tried in other felonies, viz. the intent of the parties.*" State Trials, vol. vi. p. 222.

wait the reſult of that diſpaſſionate and candid difference, with a ſilent prayer, "*ne quid* "*detrimenti capiat reſpublica.*" To which however this may be added as a certain truth, that the political liberty of every individual bears a proportion to the ſecurity given by the laws to the innocency of his conduct; which ſecurity decreaſes, in proportion to the multiplication of penalties, the uncertainty of penal laws, and the irregularity of trials.

CHAP. XVI.

A further Digreſſion relative to the gradual Improvements of criminal Proceſs.

§ 1. IN the ſixth century, Clotarius, King of France, made a law, that nobody ſhould be condemned to death without a hearing [b]. Prohibitory laws may generally be preſumed to have a retroſpect to a contrary uſage; it ſeems ſtrange therefore, that this, which I have mentioned, ſhould have been

[b] L'Eſprit des Loix, l. xii. c. 12.

neceſſary in ſupport of the moſt obvious principle of juſtice. But the efforts of human wiſdom are ſlow in their progreſs, and limited in their extent; political ſyſtems therefore are, in all inſtances, though in different degrees, imperfect, and conſequently beſt underſtood by compariſon.

In this point of view, a ſhort ſtate of criminal proceſs by the common law of England will form a ſtriking illuſtration of the foregoing chapter, and may have a more eſſential effect; for it will be found, that in proſecutions of felony, and in other particulars, we ſtill retain ſome veſtiges of that oppreſſive barbariſm which I am about to deſcribe.

I ſpeak not of thoſe proceedings, which were founded in the groſs ſuperſtitions of our fore-fathers; ſuch as the preſumptuous purgation of ordeal, either by fire or by water[c]; in

[c] We find in the Welſh laws a third ſpecies of ordeal, unknown probably in all other countries. *Fœmina matura viro, quæ cum aliquo clandeſtino abiverit, et vel in agris, vel in domo ſtuprum paſſa ſit, et ab illo poſtea repudiata fuerit, et querelam contra illum inſtituerit, apud gentiles ſuos et in curiâ, hoc modo dotabitur. Si tauri trimi caudam detonſam, et ſebo inunctam, per januam vimineam immiſſam, mulier intra domum, pedibus limini innixis, manibus prehendens detinere po-*

in which it was impoſſible for innocence to eſcape, without a miracle from Heaven [d]: nor yet of that more unchriſtian, impious mode of trial by battle; which, when the defendant was innocent, often ended in his murder; and when guilty, in his triumphal acquittal, with the additional ſtain of the appellant's blood upon his head. My obſervations ſhall be confined to the boaſted, and venerable inſtitution of trial by jury, its preparatory proceſs, conduct, and conſequences.

§ 2. The ancient *Juſticiarii in itinere* made their circuit round the kingdom, for the purpoſe of trying cauſes and criminals, only once in ſeven years; in which interval, by the common calculation of lives, it is probable, that, excluſive of the diſtreſſes, and conſequent depopulation of families, one half of of the wretches under ſuſpicion, and in cuſtody, died in the dungeon. At all events, the crime had generally eſcaped the memory of mankind, before the execution of the crimi-

tuerit, licet taurus a duobus hominibus utrinque ſtimulis urgeatur; pro ſuo habebit in compenſationem, ob infamiam violatæ pudicitiæ: ſin aliter, habebit tantum ſibi, quantum manibus adhæſerit. Leges Wallicæ, fol. p. 82.

[d] Murat. Diſſertatio de judiciis Dei. Antiquit. Italic. vol. iii. p. 612.

tral. But this was remedied ſo early as A. D. 1285, by ſtat. 13 Ed. I. c. 30. whence the preſent Juſtices of aſſiſe and *Niſi prius* are derived; an inſtitution, which bears ſome reſemblance to one of the cuſtoms aſcribed by Tacitus to the ancient Germans; *eliguntur in iiſdem conciliis et principes, qui jura per pagos vicoſque reddunt. Centeni ſingulis ex plebe comites, conſilium ſimul et auctoritas, adſunt* [e].

§ 3. The temporary releaſe of the priſoner, previous to the trial, when the criminal charge was apparently unjuſt, or ill founded; or when the crime was of ſo inferior a nature, as to admit his enlargement on pledges for his future appearance, ſeems, in the earlieſt periods of our conſtitution, to have been a matter of right; but the courtly pliability of ſome judges had involved this doctrine in very oppreſſive difficulties. Theſe were at length happily, and totally removed , in 31 C. II.

[e] Tacit. de Mor. Germ. c. 12.

[f] Stat. 31. C. II. c. 2. "This act was carried by an "odd artifice in the Houſe of Lords; Lord Grey and "Lord Norris were named to be the Tellers; Lord Norris, "being a man ſubject to vapours, was not at all times at-"tentive to what was paſſing; ſo a very fat Lord coming "in, Lord Grey counted him for ten, as a jeſt at firſt, but "ſeeing

C. II. whoſe reign, though in its conſequences happy to this kingdom, was a ſtrange medley of liberty and tyranny, honour and profligacy, religion and impiety, benevolence and bloodſhed.

In every ſtage both of civil and criminal ſuits, the laws, like the prayers[g], were adminiſtered in an unknown language; and this continued, as to matters of record, indictments, pleas, verdicts, judgements, &c. until the ſtat. 12 Geo. II. c. 26. They were alſo written in a ſtrange hand with technical abbreviations. In this there was real danger; for though the indictment was always read to the priſoner in Engliſh; yet if there were any objections, recourſe was had to the Latin original to ſupport its inſufficiencies: *contra formam ſtatut. in hujuſm. caſ. edit. et proviſ.* (ſays Lord Hale) ſhall be conſtrued either ſingularly or plurally. We cannot wonder then at the recital of the above-mentioned ſtatute[h], that "many and great miſchiefs do frequently

" ſeeing that Lord Norris had not obſerved it, he went on
" with this miſreckoning of ten, and by theſe means the
" bill paſſed, though the majority was indeed on the other
" ſide." Biſhop Burnet, vol. ii. 8vo. p. 121.

[g] Commentaries, B. iv. 412.

[h] 12 G. II. c. 26.

"accrue

"accrue to the ſubjects of the kingdom, "from the proceedings in courts of juſtice "being in an unknown language; thoſe "who are impleaded having no knowledge "or underſtanding of what is alledged for "or againſt them, in the pleadings of their "lawyers and attorneys, who uſe a charac-"ter not legible to any but perſons practiſ-"ing the law." But we may reaſonably wonder, that the remedy was deferred to the eighteenth century.

§ 4. The chriſtian name, and ſurname of the defendant, with his addition of ſtate and degree, were firſt required to be ſet forth in the indictment, by an act of Henry the Fifth[i]. One may infer, that, previous to this act, there was a great want of preciſion, in the formal parts of proceſs; but the inclination of ſucceeding Judges, in favour of life, hath carried this matter to the oppoſite extreme of ſcrupulous, and over-grown nicety. Numberleſs are the inſtances, in which the ſubſtance of juſtice hath been loſt in the purſuit of the ſhadow of mercy[k].

The

[i] 1 H. V. c. 5.

[k] For inſtance, *murdredavit* for *murdravit*, *felonitei* for *felonice*, have been adjudged to vitiate the indictment; *bur-*

The discontinuance of Latin indictments hath rendered such instances less common; but there is still sufficient reason to apply the observation of Sir Matthew Hale: "for the "truth is, that it is grown to be a blemish, "and inconvenience in the law, and the ad- "ministration thereof; more offenders escap- "ing by the over-easy ear given to exceptions "in indictments, than by their own inno- "cence; and many times gross murders, "burglaries, robberies, and other heinous and "crying offences, go unpunished by these un- "seemly niceties, to the reproach of the

burgariter for *burglariter* hath been a fatal objection, but *burgulariter* hath been holden good. Yet these exceptions were allowed on the idea of uncertainty, not from an inclination to classical accuracy; for *præfato reginæ* did not vitiate.

31 Eliz. J. Webster was indicted for murder, and the stroke being laid *sinistro bracio* instead of *brachio*, he was dismissed. In Leke's case, 34 Eliz. "A. B. *alius dictus* A. C. butcher" was deemed insufficient; it ought to have been "A. B. butcher, *alias dictus* A. C. butcher." An indictment of poisoning, wherein it is alledged, that J. S. *fidem adhibens* to the prisoner, *et nesciens potum prædictum cum veneno fore intoxicatum accepit et bibit*, without saying *venenum prædictum*, is not good, and shall not be supplied by the implication of other parts of the indictment. So *gladium in dextrâ suâ*, without "*manu*," &c. 5 Co. Rep. 121. Dyer 46. 4 Co. Rep. 39.

"law

"law, to the shame of government, to the "encouragement of villainy, and to the dishonour of God[l]."

§ 5. At the common law[m], no prisoner, in capital cases, was entitled to a copy of the indictment, pannel, or any other of the proceedings. It was refused to Sir Harry Vane, and Colonel Sidney. It was again much urged in the trial of Lord Preston, A. D. 1690, who desired to have it argued by counsel; which the court unanimously refused, "it being a point, that would not "bear a debate."

§ 6. It appears to have been a common practice so late[n] as the reign of Charles II. for the Judges in their circuits to impose arbitrary fines on Grand Juries for supposed concealments and non-presentments; a dangerous exertion of power, tending to the encouragement of ill-founded accusations, and not warrantable by law!

§ 7. There were several means at common law of bringing felons to trial, without

[l] Hale's Hist. P. C. ii. 124.
[m] Foster, p. 228. State Trials, vol. iv. p. 411.
[n] Vaughan's Rep. p. 153. Hale's H. P. C. ii. 160.

any previous indictment; ſuch as, upon the Mainouvre, when the thief was detected with the thing ſtolen *in manu*, and upon appeals.

The latter mode, *of appeals*, is ſtill ſubſiſting; and, though conſidered as odious by ſome, doth not appear in any inſtance to have occaſioned injuſtice. Perhaps it ought to be regarded as an old branch of the law, which by poſſibility may become an eſſential ſafeguard to the rights of the people. It muſt however be admitted to have ariſen from that ancient barbarous principle of legiſlation, which exacted the puniſhment of the criminal merely as civil damages to the party injured[o]; and accordingly I find, that in the ancient Salic laws murder was puniſhed with death, and no compoſition admitted, unleſs with the conſent of the neareſt friend of the deceaſed. From a ſimilar reaſoning, it continues at this day the law of Saxony, that, if a thief ſuffer death, his heir is not compellable to reſtore the ſtolen goods[p].

[o] Kaim's Hiſt. Law Tracts, p. 40. See alſo Robertſon's Hiſt. of Charles the Fifth, vol. 1.

[p] Carpzovius, iv. 32, 23.

The

The conviction or acquittal upon an indictment of murder or manslaughter, was at common law a good plea in bar to the appeal; but this privilege tended only to prolong the imprisonment and procrastinate the delivery of persons accused; for, before the statute 3 Hen. VII, the court was obliged by law not to proceed upon any indictment of murder within the year and a day; and it was usual in other cases to allow a similar interval, because of the interest of the appellant; who, being thought entitled *ex debito justitiæ* to the gratification of his revenge, might in an appeal of death have execution upon the judgement notwithstanding any pardon; and who, in case of robbery ought to have restitution, which upon an indictment before statute 21 H. VIII. he could not have [q].

Appeals in parliament by private persons, which, especially in matters of treason, were in frequent use [r], were abolished by statute 1 H. IV.

[q] See the case of Armstrong *v.* Lisle, reported by Lord Chief Justice Holt, (Kelyng, p. 96.) which contains much information on this subject.

[r] 3 Inst. 31. 132. 1 Mod. 148. "All petitions against great persons, and the prince's officers, were heard before the *barones majores*. And this court became a place of original jurisdiction for impeachments, which were preferred

1 H. IV. c. 14. "for the many great in-"conveniences and mifchiefs, which had often happened thereby." A cuftom of this kind is obferved by Tacitus, to have prevailed among the Germans; "*licet apud concilium accufare quemque, et difcrimen capitis*[s] *intendere.*"

§ 8. I now proceed to the arraignment of the Prifoner; in which ftate of the procefs, as he muft be prefumed to be free from guilt, he ought not to be required to hold up his hand at the bar[t]. It is a fort of infult offered to innocence; nor is the ceremony of kneeling at the bar, as if juftice were the confequence of intreaty, lefs liable to objection. In the former practice, though difpenfable (for any criminal may refufe to hold up his hand) we ftill purfue the fteps of our ancef-

preferred either by private perfons or by the whole commons of England: and likewife the dernier refort to correct the errors of inferior judicatures; and when any matter of fact was to be tried, it was ufual to iffue writs to the Jufticcs in Eyre, to fummon the parties before them, and to try the fact according to the command of the writ, as may be feen in *Ryley* 74, 75." Gilbert's Forum Romanum, p. 8.

[s] De Mor. Germ. c. 12.

[t] Lord Bacon mentions a Welfhman, who, when fummoned to comply with this ceremony, conceived the judge to be a fortune-teller.

tors;

tors; the latter doth not appear to have been anciently used[u].

It is the law of the land, and certainly ever hath been so, that a prisoner ought not at any time to be charged with fetters[w]; unless the Jailer be constrained to have recourse to them by the actual necessity of safe custody. In the trial of the regicides it was determined by all the judges[x], "that when prisoners "come to the bar to be tried, their irons "ought to be taken off, be their crimes ever "so great." And this agreed with Fleta[y], "*Cum autem capti in judicio produci debeant,* "*non producantur armati, sed ut judicium re-* "*cepturi; nec ligati, ne videantur respondere* "*coacti.*"—Yet Pratt, Chief Justice, in the trial of Layer[z], ventured to make a distinction

[u] State Trials, vol. i. p. 83. D. of Norfolk's Trial, A. D. 1571. And p. 157. Earl of Arundel's Trial.

[w] Grand abusion est, que prisonner soit charge de ferres, ou mise en peine, avant ceo que soit attaint de felony. Myrror, c. 5. § i. 54.

[x] Kelyng's Reports.

[y] L. i. c. i.

[z] "My Lord (said Layer) I have been used more like "an Algerine captive, than a freeborn Englishman; I "have been dragged through the streets by the hands of "Jailers, and have been made a shew, and spectacle. *I* "*now hope to have these chains taken off, that I may have* "*the free use of that reason and understanding which God* "*hath given me; they have brought the strangury upon me*

tion between the time of arraignment and the time of trial, and would not allow the chains to be taken off. His Lordſhip did not conſider, that the diſtraction of the mind, in ſo painful and important a criſis, ought not to be aggravated by the tortures of the body. *The rights of the unhappy have been rarely violated in modern times.*

It is thought by a very learned writer [a], that the dreadful puniſhment, inflicted on a refuſal to plead, (even when the offender, if convicted, would be entitled to the Benefit of Clergy), was unknown to the common law, and derived from a ſtatute of Edward I. Be this as it may, it ſtill exiſts in full force; though repugnant to the ſpirit of our conſtitution, and nearly allied to torture, which was always illegal, though ſometimes practiſed [b]. The Commentaries on the Laws of England

" *to a very painful degree; and I am told your Lordſhip is* " *afflicted with that diſtemper.*" This was *argumentum ad hominem*; but it was ineffectual.

[a] Obſervations on the ancient ſtatutes, p. 62.

[b] Foſter, 244. Ruſhw. i. 638. " *The Judge* (ſaith Sir Ed. Coke, 3 Inſt. p. 25.) is never preſent at any torture; neither, *upon the arraignment* of the priſoner is any torture ever offered." Theſe words ſeem to admit the uſe, but the ſubſequent paſſage in the ſame volume, p. 35, denies

England have, in very pathetic terms [c], called for the legiſlative abolition of this cruel proceſs; and ſurely it would be eaſy in felonies, as in the caſe of treaſon, to conſider an obſtinate refuſal to plead, as a confeſſion, and conviction of the charge; or even as a plea of Not Guilty, which is the practice of the Scotch courts, and probably derived from the civil law [d].

But alteratives, though preferable to abſolute neglect, are an inſufficient ſpecies of medicine, when the cauſe of the diſeaſe is ſuffered to remain. If the forfeitures [e], annexed to the conviction of the crime, were in all caſes equally extended to the contumacy

denies the legality. "There is no law to warrant tortures in this land, nor can they be juſtified by any preſcription being ſo lateley brought in."

[c] B. iv. p. 323.

[d] *Nihil intereſt neget quis an taceat interrogatus; an obſcure reſpondeat ut incertum dimittat interrogatorem.* Dig. ii. 1. 11. 7.

It was not unuſual in England, ſo late as in the reign of Charles the Second, to force criminals to plead, by tying their thumbs together with compreſſed whipcord. See Kelyng, p. 28. And there were even in the reign of Q. Anne, occaſional inſtances of this practice; which was certainly a ſpecies of torture in the worſt ſenſe of the word, though calculated to ſave the priſoner from the *peine forté et dure.*

[e] See Mr. Emlyn's Preface to the State Trials.

of

of ſtanding mute, there would be no temptation to commit the offence; which, in the preſent ſtate of the law, is generally founded on the becoming principle of parental tenderneſs.

§ 9. It was formerly uſual for the priſoner, if he thought the charge indefenſible, to confeſs the indictment, and be admitted, on his own requeſt, to become an approver againſt others of the ſame felony; upon the conviction of whom, he was entitled to his pardon. This practice never was prohibited by law, but gradually diſcouraged and diſuſed; "for "the truth is (ſaith Sir M. Hale) that more "miſchief hath come thereof by falſe accu-"ſations of deſperate villains, than benefit to "the public by the diſcovery and convic-"tion of real offenders." Yet I obſerve with reluctance, that certain modern acts of parliament[f] have in ſome degree unwarily revived this dangerous doctrine, by the frequent offers of rewards and pardons to capital felons, on diſcovery and conviction of

[f] 4 and 5 W. and M. c. 18. 10 and 11 W. III. c. 3. 5 Ann. c. 31. 29 Geo. II. c. 30. 6 and 7 W. III. c. 17. § 9. 6 Geo. I. c. 23. 8 Geo. II. c. 20.

 their

their accomplices; and in ſome inſtances [g], it is expreſsly provided, that the ſums of money to be given to the apprehenders, and convictors of felons, ſhall not incapacitate their teſtimony. The price of blood ſhould in no caſe receive the legiſlative ſanction.

In Italy (ſays Pufendorff) pardons are ſometimes promiſed by public edict to any of the banditti, that ſhall bring with him the head of another of the ſame gang. It may be good policy to raiſe mutual jealouſies among villains; but there is ſomething horrid in the idea of murder, by law eſtabliſhed.

§ 10. But, if the defendant thought it adviſable to plead, he was entitled firſt to pleas declinatory of his trial; namely the plea of ſanctuary, which was followed by attainder, and forfeiture of land and goods [h]; and the plea of clergy, which ſoon ceaſed to be pleaded, until after conviction; it being more beneficial to the party, to take the chances of an acquittal in the courſe of the trial.

[g] 8 Geo. II. c. 16. § 9.

[h] Upon the actual abjuration, 2 Hawk. 52. Finch, 389. 3 Inſt. 217.

Of

Of the former of these pleas I have already given a short account; and I feel little inclination to enter more largely on the latter. Mr. Justice Foster has very forcibly observed, that "it was an absurd distinction "between subject and subject, originally owing to downright impudence on the one "part, and to mere fanaticism, or amazing "pusillanimity on the other [i]." During a long course of years, it exempted convicted offenders, if qualified for holy orders, from the punishment of offences of the most atrocious kind, murders not excepted. And in many cases a conviction, and having clergy, conduced more to the safety of the prisoner than an acquittal. For he was thereby, until stat. 8 Eliz. discharged of *all* crimes committed before clergy had; but if he had been acquitted, he was liable to answer for any others committed prior to his acquittal [k]. The reading of a scrap of Latin, "*Miserere mei, Deus*," called with great propriety "the Neck verse," was the criterion of this senseless privilege. Women, and all persons unable to read, were exposed without mercy to the literal rigour of the law. It

[i] Foster, p. 306.

[k] Kelyng, 103. Dyer, 214. 1 And. 112.

was a great offence in jailers to teach criminals to read during their impriſonment, previous to their trial; "*Per cauſe de ſalvation* "*de leur vie, et deſturbation de la common ley, en* "*deceit del roy*[1]." Many illiterate perſons were actually executed for clergyable felonies; and Lord Chief Juſtice Kelyng informs us, that he, in the year 1665, fined a biſhop's chaplain, for having reproached his ſacred function, and abuſed the court, by anſwering "*legit*" upon the demand of "*legit aut non legit?*" Whereas in truth the priſoner, when examined by his Lordſhip himſelf, could not read, *and was thereupon not admitted to his clergy.*

Women, in caſes of grand larceny to the value of ten ſhillings, were admitted to clergy by the 21 James I. The wall of partition was at laſt entirely removed by the ſtatute of 3 & 4 W. & M.; which entitles women to the *privilegium clericale*, equally with men; and by the Fifth of Queen Anne, which aboliſhed the whole ceremony of reading.

[1] Liber Aſſiſ. p. 138. Obſerv. on the ancient ſtat. p. 351.

Here it is to be wiſhed, that the legiſlature had advanced one ſtep further, to an open declaration, that all offences, proper in the firſt inſtance to be exempted from capital puniſhment, and now called clergyable, ſhould hereafter, in that firſt inſtance, either be ſubjected to ſome inferior ſpecies of chaſtiſement, or be conſidered as pardonable, with a power to the Judges to tranſport the convicts, whenever the dangerous nature of their crime and character ſhould make it expedient [m]. At preſent, ſuch offenders, upon conviction, being made to kneel, they know not why; and to pronounce an expreſſion, which they do not underſtand; find themſelves, in the height of their amazement at this cabaliſtical ceremony, once more upon the wide world in perfect liberty. *It is wonderful, how much the exemplary ſolemnity of juſtice may be diſgraced by trivial abſurdities.* Beſides, from the rule that this privilege cannot be pleaded more than once (except by clerks in orders, in regard to whom it is

[m] As was enacted in the caſes of great and petty larceny, by ſtatutes 4 Geo. I. c. 11. and 6 Geo. I. c. 23. which proviſions however do not extend to Clerks in Orders.

ſtill

ſtill unlimited) it follows, that, when a man commits two offences, both clergyable in their claſs, but totally different in their kind, as manſlaughter and larceny, he muſt ſuffer death for the ſecond, though in the eye of reaſon it hath no perceptible connection with the firſt.

§ 11. But to return to the ancient mode of proſecution. Let us ſuppoſe the priſoner to have pleaded, "Not guilty." Here began his trial; and in the progreſs of it he was expoſed to ſuch dangers, as left him but little ſecurity even in the ſtricteſt innocence.

The uſe of Counſel was permitted only on the part of the proſecution, "*becauſe* (ſaith Sir E. Coke) [n] *that the teſtimony and proof of the crime ought to be ſo clear and manifeſt, that there can be no defence of it.*" This humane reaſon exiſted in ſpeculation only; for the ideas of our anceſtors, as to the clearneſs and ſufficiency of teſtimony, and proof were extremely unſettled; and it may almoſt be aſſerted, that, ſo late as the whole ſixteenth, and part of the ſeventeenth Century, the firſt and moſt eſſential principles of evidence were

[n] 3 Inſt. 29.

either unknown, or totally disregarded. Depositions of witnesses, forthcoming if called, but not permitted to be confronted with the prisoners; written examinations of accomplices, living, and amenable; confessions of convicts°,

° The instances are infinite; I select the following on account of its collateral matter. " Then Mr. Attorney *(Sir Ed. Coke)* took in hand the evidence against Sir G. Merrick, and Mr. Cuffe. To Cuffe, Mr. Attorney said, that he was the arrantest traitor that ever came to that Bar.—And still following matters strongly against him, told him, that he would give him such a *Cuff* as should set him down: and thereupon called to have read the *(late)* Earl of Essex's confession, and also a part of Sir Henry Nevil's confession; which were both full and plain against him, as he had not to answer them." State Trials, vol. vii. p. 59.

But the trial of Throckmorton in the preceding reign, before many Judges of the first eminence in that age, was still more remarkable. The confession of Winter was read against him; and he was told, that if he should desire it, he should have Winter to justify it to his face; the confession of the Duke of Suffolk who had been executed on the same accusation was also read against him; the testimony of Vaughan then under sentence of death for the same fact was received in support of the prosecution; the testimony of Fitzwilliams offered in favour of the prisoner was rejected, and the prisoner acknowledged that it was unusual to examine witnesses *against the Crown*. A part of his own confession was read against him; and when he requested that the whole might be read, he was answered, " that it would be but loss of time, and would make nothing for him." Lastly, when he desired that an Act of Parliament might be read, he was answered, that it was not the business of the Court to find books for him, and that the Judges were to resolve all doubts in Law.

State Trials, Vol. i. p. 63.

lately hanged for the ſame offence; hearſays of thoſe convicts, repeated at ſecond hand from others; all theſe formed ſo many claſſes of competent evidence, and were received as ſuch, in moſt ſolemn trials, by very learned Judges.

It was ſometimes agreeable to the counſel for the Crown, and ſuitable to the nature of the caſe, to conduct the proofs by parole teſtimony; a circumſtance moſt unfavourable to the Defendant, as it tended to throw the whole weight of credibility into the adverſe ſcale. For the perſon accuſed was rarely permitted to call witneſſes to his exculpation; and, even when indulged ſo far, he was not in any caſe allowed to examine them upon oath. At the ſame time, there was frequent practiſing on the hopes and fears of the witneſſes by the alternate encouragements and menaces of the counſel for the proſecution: and juries were reminded, that, for verdicts contrary to the inclination of the court, they were liable to unlimited fines and impriſonments. This indeed they had learnt by fatal and re-iterated experience; but they were rarely in want of any memento; for it was a common, and very lucrative practice with the sheriffs, to return juries so prejudiced, and partial, that, as Cardinal Wolsey observed, "they would find Abel "guilty of the murder of Cain [p]."

The Judge held his office, and income, during the pleasure of the prosecutor [q]; and was often actuated by an intemperate zeal in the support of the charge; as if his indignation at the offence had stifled all tenderness towards the supposed offender.

Thus, ignorant of the forms and language of the whole process, unassisted by counsel, unsupported by witnesses, discountenanced by the court, and baited by crown-lawyers, the poor bewildered prisoner found an eligible

[p] Observations on the ancient statutes, p. 360.

[q] It may safely be affirmed, that the present independence of our Judges is the best safeguard of our constitutional liberties. The stat. 1 Geo. III. c. 23. engrafted on 13 W. III. c. 12. hath completed that independence, in regard to the King, his Ministers, and Successors; and in the security of the full salaries during the continuance of the commissions. Yet it deserves serious consideration, whether those salaries, amidst the general opulence of the kingdom, be more than barely sufficient to support the state and dignity of the offices to which they are annexed. It is of essential importance to every individual in the nation, that the seats of Justice should continue to be filled by men the most eminent in their profession for Wisdom, Learning, Experience, Benevolence and Integrity.

gible refuge in the dreadful moment of conviction.

§ 12. This ſhort ſketch of the adminiſtration of criminal juſtice in the ſixteenth century diminiſhes the ſurprize, which we ſhould otherwiſe feel, when we are told[r], that in the reign of Henry VIII, ſeventy-two thouſand criminals were executed; which, upon an average, is nearly equal to ſix every day, Sundays included. The ſame authority aſſures us, that executions were reduced to about one fifth of this proportion in the latter end of Queen Elizabeth's reign. The annual number is at preſent eſtimated at one hundred.

Thus "when people of all ranks and conditions had, in their turn, been taught "moderation in the ſchool of[s] adverſity," Reaſon and Mercy gradually prevailed; but an ample field is ſtill open to the exertion of their influence.

The peruſal of the firſt volume of the Engliſh State Trials is a moſt diſguſtful

[r] Holingſhed. See Obſervations on the ancient ſtatutes, p. 402.

[s] Foſter, 235.

drudgery; but it is impoſſible to ſurvey that chaos of oppreſſions, ſo long exiſtent, and ſo patiently born, without being aſtoniſhed at the foundation, on which the beautiful fabric of our preſent liberties is raiſed.

CHAP. XVII.

Of other Crimes immediately relative to the State.

§ 1. UNDER this head are proper to be conſidered all offences, below the degree of treaſon, which amount to violations of the prerogative, or infractions of the public peace; and, in ſhort, all the inferior offences, which directly affect the King, and his government.

It is ſaid, that in Japan, every breach of any law of a public nature, and every diſobedience to the miniſters of juſtice, is conſidered as a perſonal affront to the Emperor, and puniſhed as a capital crime [t]. The conſequence

[t] A ſimilar account is given of the courſe of juſtice in Peru, where every crime is conſidered as a breach of the com-

ſequence is evident: the Emperor's authority is univerſal and unlimited. An authority ſo unnatural is not likely, if it be allowed poſſible, to be ſupported, without a conſtant violation of the rights of nature.

The human mind is delighted with the exerciſe of power, and at the ſame time incapable of indulging an extreme eagerneſs in any purſuit, without running into abſurdity. Hence it follows, that the penal laws of deſpotic ſtates are both wanton and ſanguinary; adapting the puniſhment of death, like the bed of Procruſtes, to offences of all ſizes and denominations. Very different ſhould be the ſentiments and practice of that envied nation, which hath diſcovered, and eſtabliſhed, a permanent ſyſtem of government, in the happy medium between lawleſs liberty, and abſolute deſpotiſm.

§ 2. An accurate examination of this ſpecies of crimes would lead me into a tireſome detail; I ſhall confine myſelf to ſome of the moſt ſtriking inſtances.

commands of the Ynca, who is reverenced as ſomething more than human. Garcilaſſo de la Vega, Com. Reg. l. ii. c. 12, 13.

The

The mere knowledge and concealment of treaſon, without any degree of aſſent thereto, is called in our law, a miſpriſion of treaſon; and is puniſhed with the loſs of the profits of lands during life, forfeiture of goods, and *imprisonment during life*[u]. It is alſo by 14 Eliz. c. 3. a miſpriſion of treaſon to forge any foreign coin, though not made current by proclamation. By ſtatute 9 Ed. III. ſtat. 2. no ſterling money ſhall be melted down, upon pain of forfeiture thereof. This law is written in a very different ſpirit from the ſtatute 8 and 9 W. III. c. 26. which enacts, that, if any perſon ſhall receive, or pay any counterfeit, or diminiſhed money of this kingdom, at a leſs rate than it ſhall import to be of, he ſhall be guilty of felony.

By 9 Geo. II. c. 30. enforced by 29 Geo. II. c. 17. if any ſubject of Great Britain ſhall enliſt himſelf, or if any perſon ſhall procure him to be enliſted, in any foreign ſervice, or detain or embark him for that purpoſe, without licence under the King's ſign manual, he ſhall be guilty of felony without benefit of clergy—*a very ſevere law!*

[u] Ph. and M. c. 10. Previous to which ſtatute, every concealment, under the conſtruction of aiding and abetting, ſeems to have been conſidered as treaſon.

Deſertion

Desertion from the King's armies in time of war, is also made a capital felony by 3 Edw. VI. stat. 2, *and the offence is made triable by the justices of every shire.* This offence was subjected by the laws of Canute to the loss of life and lands [w].

Prison-breaking by the offender, when lawfully committed, was at the common law a felony in every case; but by stat. 1 Edw. II. no person shall for breaking prison have judgement of life or member, except the cause for which he was imprisoned would

[w] "*Servus etiam aufugiens a domino suo vel a socio suo per segnitiem suam, sive sit in navali expeditione, sive in terrestri, perdat omne quod habet, et propriam vitam, et capiat dominus possessionem illam ac terram ejus quam ipsi prius dedit. Et si propriam terram habeat, regis manibus ea tradatur.*" Leges Cnuti 75.

It was anciently the custom in France to cut off the ears, or slit the nose, of the deserter; "and it was absurd, says Montesquieu, to relinquish this practice for the punishment of death. Soldiers are habituated to the contempt of death, and the dread of shame; so that the terrors of the penalty were diminished, while they were intended to be increased." L'Esprit des Loix, l. vi. c. 12.

Charondas, the lawgiver of the Thurians, enacted that deserters should be compelled to sit three days in the market-place cloathed in female dresses; and this law, says the Historian, excelled the provisions of other lawgivers on the same subject both in humanity and wisdom. Κρεῖττον γάρ ἐστιν ἀποθανεῖν, ἢ τοιαύτης ὕβρεως ἐν τῇ πατρίδι πειραθῆναι. Diod. Sic. l. xii. c. 16.

have

have had ſuch judgment, if he had been duly tried and convicted.

Our law, even with this mitigated ſeverity, ſeems to bear, with ſome degree of harſhneſs, againſt the natural impulſe of ſelf-preſervation [x].

The reſcue or forcible freeing of another from an arreſt, or impriſonment, is alſo, in many caſes, a felony without benefit of clergy,

The unlawful aſſembling, to the diſturbance of the peace, by any twelve perſons, who, being ſo aſſembled, ſhall continue together for one hour, after proclamation made to diſperſe, is capitally puniſhed by ſtatute, 1 Geo. I. c. 5.

All forcible acts of ſmuggling, carried on in defiance of the laws, are by ſtat. 19 Geo. II.

[x] I ſhall tranſcribe the words of a very ancient writer on this ſubject:

"Abuſion eſt a tenir eſcape del priſon, ou de bruſerie de gaole, per peche mortelle, car cell uſage n'eſt garrant per nul ley; ne en nul partie eſt uſe, forſque en ceſt realme et en France; *eins eſt len garrantie de ceo faire per ley de nature.* Myrror, p. 283.

c. 34.

c. 34. made felonies without the benefit of Clergy.

In this branch of the penal ſyſtem, lawgivers ſhould be extremely cautious, not to confound atrocious breaches of the civil contract, with ſimple violations of the police.

CHAP. XVIII.

Of Murder.

§ 1. AN Engliſh gentleman, ignorant of Engliſh law, (in which predicament there are ſome) would probably confine his ideas of homicide to the two diviſions, of " murder" and " excuſable killing;" and, when informed, that the law of England comprehends ſeveral other claſſes, both in name and puniſhment, would profeſs himſelf unable to diſcover any ground of further diſtinction.

" The act of homicide (he would ſay) is " either murder, or it is not ſo. The intention of the killer is the criterion; and the " malignity

" malignity of that intention is in the nature
" of a ſingle, controverted fact, ſubjected to
" enquiry, and capable of ſtrict proof. If
" that malignity be not ſuggeſted, or if on
" ſuggeſtion it be diſproved, the act of kill-
" ing becomes, as to civil guilt, negative,
" and excuſable."

There is ſomething in the firſt view of this poſition very plauſible. An Engliſh lawyer would give the following anſwer to it.

" The act of homicide is either occaſioned
" by mere accident, or founded in the diſ-
" penſations of public juſtice, or in ſelf-pre-
" ſervation, or in a ſudden tranſport of paſſion,
" or in malice; and, in theſe different views,
" it is capable of a great variety of gradations,
" from abſolute innocence to the moſt aggra-
" vated guilt.

" True (it would be replied); every crime
" hath its proper degree of enormity, variable
" as the mind of the criminal; but you miſ-
" apply the property of the crime to the act
" on which the crime is founded. That act,
" in itſelf, and abſtractedly conſidered, is a
ſimple

"simple consequence of the attributes of "matter; unfortunate indeed and pitiable; "but neither culpable nor punishable, until it "be proved to have co-operated with a mis- "chievous intent. When that proof is given, "then, and not before, it becomes criminal, "under the appellation of murder."

Here then we are reduced to state the law as we find it; and to leave its doctrines to their own support and defence.

§ 2. I begin with that class to which our laws annex no idea of guilt; and which is called justifiable homicide. It is founded on necessity, and, in some instances, on the positive precept of law.

Such is the case of the Judge who passes sentence of death upon a convicted criminal, and gives the warrant for his execution; and such, more immediately, is the case of the Sheriff, who causes that warrant to be executed. On this point it hath been holden [y], that, "if the execution vary from the judge-

[y] Hale's Hist. P. C. ii. 411. And Bracton, l. iii. p. 104. "*non alio modo puniatur quis, quam secundum quod se habeat condemnatio.*"

"ment, it will be murder in the Sheriff." But this muſt be underſtood [z] of ſuch a varying only, as tends to aggravate the puniſhment beyond the intention of the law; not of any mitigation, in regard to the pain, or infamy of the ſentence, at the ſame time conſiſtent with the ſubſtantial juſtice of the caſe.

Women, convicted of either high or petty treaſon, are directed by judgment of law *to be burnt in the fire, till they be dead*; yet Sheriffs have generally had humanity enough to direct them to be ſtrangled before the fire can affect them. It is the ſentence of traitors, to be hanged by the neck, *but not till they be dead*; yet it is now the practice [a], and very properly, not to ſuffer them to be cut down, in order to the ſubſequent mangling of their bodies, whilſt any appearance of life remains.

[z] Foſter, p. 269.

[a] Aſhton, Jan. 19, 1690, at the Old Bailey; and Mathews the printer, Oct. 32, 1719, at the ſame place, were ſentenced for high-treaſon; and were hanged until they were dead, without even any ſubſequent quartering or beheading. State Trials.

Upon

Upon the ſame principle of mercy, a curious doubt hath ariſen on this ſentence of treaſon; whether, if the King ſhould in any caſe remit all but the hanging, it would not be murder in the Sheriff, to hang the criminal until he be dead.

But I proceed to that homicide, which is juſtifiable by permiſſion of law; and ſuch it is, when any man reſiſteth perſons in the due courſe of juſtice [b], having authority to take, or impriſon him, though perhaps he may be innocent, and is killed in the ſtruggle. This rule is founded on reaſon and public utility; *but there ſhould be an apparent neceſſity on the ſide of the officer.*

The ſame benignity of conſtruction is extended to homicide, committed by any perſon, interpoſing to preſerve the public peace, and prevent miſchief; for ſuch interpoſal is a branch of ſocial duty.

[b] The ancient expreſſion, in the caſe either of flight, or of reſiſtance, was, "quod juſticiari ſe non permiſit."
Paſch. 16 Ed. III. coram rege, Rot. Norff. "*Vicecomes domini regis, qui interfecit duos latrones non permittentes ſe juſticiari, acquictatur.*"

In like manner, officers, endeavouring to disperse a riotous or rebellious assembly, are justifiable, both by the common law and by statute[c], though death should ensue. *But here also there should be an actual, existent necessity*, otherwise it will be murder; and of this necessity the law will exact a rigorous proof. And though it hath been adjudged, that those who attend the Justices, in order to suppress a riot, have power to take with them such weapons, as shall enable them *effectually*[d] to do it; yet the misapplication of that power to wanton or tyrannical purposes, will be most severely construed. It is indeed a power dangerous to the constitution, and to be guarded with jealousy against all abuse.

Lastly, homicide is justifiable in the resistance of any capital crime, attempted and accompanied by violence. As[e], in the case of

[c] Hale, H. P. C. i. 465. Hawk. P. C. i. 161. Popham, 121, 122. And stat. 1 Mary, c. 12. 1 Eliz. c. 16, which were both temporary acts. And 1 Geo. I. c. 5. to the same purport; which is perpetual.

[d] Hawk. P. C. i. 161. § 21.

[e] "*Hadrianus rescripsit eum, qui stuprum sibi, vel suis, per vim inferentem occidit, dimittendum.*" Dig. l. xlviii. t. 8. § 1.

any

any woman, who kills a raviſher in defence of her chaſtity; or of any traveller, who, in the immediate defence of his property, ſhoots a highwayman; or of any perſon who kills another in an attempt to commit burglary. The ſame idea prevailed in the civil law. *Furem nocturnum ſi quis occiderit, id impune feret, ſi parcere ei ſine periculo ſuo non potuit.* And again, *ſi quis percuſſorem ad ſe venientem gladio repulerit, non ut homicida tenetur; quia defenſor propriæ ſalutis in nullo peccâſſe videtur* [f].

But here it is obſervable, "that our law "will not ſuffer any crime to be prevented "by death, unleſs the ſame, if committed, "would have been capitally puniſhable." Hence it hath followed, that, though it be lawful for a man to kill another, whom he detecteth in the night-time, in the act of carrying away his property; yet if he take another in the act of adultery with his wife, and kill him, it will be manſlaughter and felony. Such is the law, though in fact it hath been executed with great benignity [h]. And ſurely, if

[f] Domat. l. ii. p. 638.

[g] Commentaries, B. iv. 102.

[h] John Maddy was (23 C. II. in B. R.) indicted for murder, and the jury gave a ſpecial verdict; "that he coming

if the former caſe be juſtifiable, the latter, though it ſavour more of ſudden revenge, than of ſelf-preſervation, ought to be ſo *a fortiori*; for adultery is the higheſt invaſion of property. The Athenians [i] comprehended both theſe caſes

coming into his houſe, found the deceaſed in the act of adultery with his wife, and immediately ſtruck him with a joint ſtool on the head, ſo that he died; they alſo found that there was no precedent malice, and the court were all of opinion, that it was *but* man-ſlaughter, the provocation being exceeding great; and the executioner was directed to burn him gently." But Twiſden, Juſtice, remembered a caſe, in which the priſoner, being informed of the adulterer's familiarity with his wife, ſaid, that he would be revenged on him, and afterwards, finding him in the act, killed him, *which was held by Jones to be murder.* Ventris i. 159. Raymond 212.

[i] A fine comment on this Law of the Athenians may be found in the Oration of Demoſthenes, Κατὰ Αριςοκράτυς.

The Athenians not only gave the conſtruction of juſtifiable homicide to the death of the adulterer; the injured huſband was, by another law, permitted to exerciſe his vengeance in whatever manner he might prefer. "Si "quis adulterum in ipſâ turpitudine deprehenderit, de eo, "quod libuerit, ſtatuito."

Ουκ ἔςι μοιχῦ πρᾶγμα τιμιώτερον,
Θανάτυ γάρ ἐςιν ὤνιον.

Menandri Fragm.

Py. *Ille ubi reſcivit factum, frater violentiſſimus.*
Pa. *Quidnam fecit?* Py. *Colligavit eum miſeris modis.*
Pa. *Colligavit?* Py. *Atque equidem orante, ut ne id faceret, Thaide.*
Pa. *Quid ais?* Py. *Nunc minatur porro, ſeſe id, quod mœchis ſolet:*
Quod ego nunquam vidi fieri, neque velim.

Ter. Eunuch. V. 5. 11.

Necat

cases in the same law, and permitted no degree of punishment in either of them. If it be true, that *positive laws, contradictory to natural sentiment, are cruel and dangerous*; it is an imperfection in our system, that it hath not adopted the same regulation.

§ 3. The next species is Excusable Homicide; and first, *per infortunium*: as when a man doing an act, not unlawful, and without a mischievous intention, and using proper, that is, usual, or ordinary circumspection, happeneth to kill.

If however the act, on which death ensueth, be unlawful only as *malum prohibitum*; if (for instance) it should consist in shooting at game without a statutable qualification, it

Necat hic ferro, secat ille cruentis
Verberibus, quosdam mœchos et mugilis intrat.
Juv. x. 315.

Ah tum te miserum, malique fati,
Quem attractis pedibus, patente portâ
Percurrent raphanique, mugilesque.
Catull. xv. 17.

See also Aristoph. Plut. ver. 168.

The Roman Law, in some degree, permitted the killing of the adulteress. *Is, qui uxorem in adulterio deprehensam occidit, humiliore loco positus, in exilium perpetuum dandus; in aliqua dignitate positus, ad tempus relegandus.* Inst. l. i. § 5.

is not under that description to be considered as an unlawful act.

Secondly, by self-defence; as when a person, in the course of a sudden and dangerous affray, which leaves no power, consistently with security, to wait for the intervention of the law, retreats as far as he can with safety, and, urged by mere necessity, and to avoid his own death, killeth his adversary.

This idea is finely expressed by Cicero in his oration for Milo. "*Est igitur, Judices,* "*haec non scripta, sed nata lex; quam non di-* "*dicimus, accepimus, legimus, verum ex naturâ* "*ipsâ arripuimus, hausimus, expressimus: ad* "*quam non docti, sed facti; non instituti, sed im-* "*buti sumus; ut si vita nostra in aliquas insidias,* "*si in vim, si in tela aut latronum, aut inimi-* "*corum incidisset, omnis honesta ratio esset expe-* "*diendae salutis: silent enim leges inter arma;* "*nec se expectari jubent, cum ei, qui expectare* "*velit, ante injusta poena luenda sit, quam justa* "*repetenda.*"

But in both these cases of homicide, by mere accident, and by self-defence, it must appear, that there was no deliberation previous

vious to the act; and even then, they are by our law [k] subjected to forfeitures, not only of the thing, or instrument, which was the immediate cause of the death, but of the goods or chattels of the party. The latter have long been remitted in both cases, upon a pardon under the great seal, and a writ of restitution; and to prevent such expence, in the case of homicide *per infortunium* it is usual for the judges to recommend a verdict of acquittal.

And here it is well observed by Mr. Justice Foster [l], that "Judges are ministers, appointed by the crown for the ends of public justice, and should have written on their hearts the solemn engagement of their king in his coronation-oath, to *cause law and justice in mercy, to be executed in all his judgements*; that it is not therefore the part of judges to be perpetually hunting after forfeitures, where the heart is free from guilt; to heap afflictions on the head of the afflicted, and to wound a heart already wounded past cure." And surely, it may be added, that it cannot be the part

[k] Ever since the statute of Gloucester, 6 Edw. I. A. D. 1278.

[l] Foster, p. 264.

of lawgivers to *permit* forfeitures in ſuch caſes.

A great writer apologizes for ſuch forfeitures [m], by ſuppoſing the law to ſet ſo high a value upon the life of a man, that it always *intends* ſome miſbehaviour in the perſon who by any means takes it away; *preſuming* a faulty negligence in the caſe of miſadventure, and an unknown wrong or provocation, in homicide by ſelf-defence. But it is difficult to conceive a mixture of criminality in mere accident, or that there can be "*neceſſitas culpabilis*," in ſelf-preſervation. The law ſhould be an indulgent parent, not an ungenerous ſtep-mother.

It is indeed the duty of law, if I may be allowed the expreſſion, to look with a very jealous eye on every action which hath a tendency to bloodſhed; and it may by ſome, perhaps, be thought the wiſdom of law, to affix ſome mark of diſapprobation on every actual inſtance of bloodſhed, however caſual or blameleſs: but it is repugnant both to the duty and wiſdom of law, to ſeek any ends by

[m] Commentaries, B. iv. 186.

the harsh and unseemly intervention of subterfuges and fictions. *The candor of legislation should ever be inviolable.*

The true cause of forfeiture, in cases of excusable homicide, was well known to our Saxon and Norman Kings; who did not seek any refinements of reasoning to support this very considerable branch of their royal revenue. They believed themselves to possess a valuable, ascertainable property in the lives and limbs of their subjects. Fines therefore were imposed in all cases of death and mayhem, and proportioned to the degree of the person killed or hurt. In the earlier periods of our history, a fine, or composition, was given to the relations of the deceased also [n]. But when judges, properly so called, were established; and when individuals had given up the right of avenging their own

[n] "*Si mulier occidatur prægnans, et puer in eâ fuerit vivus, uterque plenâ werâ* (Vir-gelt, the price of a Man) *reddatur; si nondum vivus sit, dimidia wera solvatur parentibus ex parte patris.*" Vide Leges Henrici I. c. 70. which contain many curious particulars on the subject of compositions.

The same notions prevailed among the ancient Germans; "*Equorum, pecorumque numero convicti multantur; pars multæ regi vel civitati, pars ipsi, qui vindicatur, vel propinquis ejus exsolvitur.*" Tacit. de M. G. c. 12.

wrongs;

wrongs; the whole of this traffick was gradually transferred from private hands to the public treaſury. The innocence of the intention, ſays a law of Henry the firſt, ſhall make no difference [o] as to the compoſition; *ſive ſponte, aut non ſponte fiunt hæc, nihilominus tamen emendetur: Quæ enim per inſcientiam peccamus, per induſtriam corrigamus.* Such reaſoning tended to annihilate all diſtinction between voluntary and involuntary acts; compoſitions for crimes became as common in the courts, as compoſitions for ſins in the churches; and they were extended even to the moſt atrocious murders, in the ſame manner as to accidental deaths. Earl Godwin was adjudged by the Wittenagemot, to pay twelve handfuls of gold to Edward the confeſſor for having killed his brother; and the hundred of Boctone [p] was fined two marks for the default of a certain maid ſervant, *who was preſent*, when a horſe ſtruck a man, and killed him.

[o] Yet there ſeems ſome reaſon to collect from Bracton, that, by the common law, there were no fines on death per Infortunium; except in places where a contrary uſage had particularly prevailed. "*Item, de iis, qui Mortui ſunt per Infortunium, nullum erit Murdrum, licet in quibuſdam partibus de conſuetudine aliter obſervetur.*" De Coron. c. 15. § 6.

[p] Madox, Hiſt. Excheq. c. 14. § 15.

It seems however to be the better [q] opinion, that in the cases of homicide *per infortunium*, or *se defendendo*, the forfeiture of the whole never was incurred at common law. For it was not unusual, to pay the mulct or fine [r] in horses, hounds, hawks, honey, &c.; and if the person who had committed the Homi-

[q] Foster, p. 287.

[r] This fine was called *Murdrum*.

"Vicecomes reddit compotum de x Marcis pro uno murdro in hundredo de Hereford."

"Liulfus de Alstredaga reddit compotum de cc Marcis argenti et x fugatoribus, et x accipitribus pro morte Gamel, in thesauro XL Marcas Argenti; et debet CLX Marcas Argenti, et x fugatores et x accipitres."

"Stephanus filius Erchem-baldi reddit compotum de x marcis argenti pro interfectione hominis Willelmi filii Odonis."

"Odo filius Alsi *debet* LX*s pro occisione filiorum Jochi.*

Oliver de Cail and others fine *pro eâdem occisione.*"

I have selected these instances from the reign of King Stephen. See Madox, c. 14. 6.

In the same sense the word is used in the 26th chapter of the Stat. of Marlbridge. "Murdrum de cætero non adjudicetur, ubi infortunium tantummodo adjudicatum est, sed locum habeat murdrum de interfectis per feloniam tantum."

Fines, as a composition in cases of wilful Murder, are at this day common in Mahometan countries, and are established on a positive precept of the Koran. See b. i. chapter of the Cow; (and Chardin, Voyage de Perse, t. ii. p. 299) "If any one forgive the blood of his brother, he may pursue the malefactor for damages and interest; but he who shall injure the wicked after having received satisfaction, shall in the day of judgement suffer the most grievous torments."

cide

cide were too poor to pay it, or had fled, or could not be discovered; the Vill, wherein it was committed, or, if that were too poor, the whole hundred was subjected to a fine.

The same ideas seem to have prevailed in all the cotemporary governments of Europe; and the principle, on which they were founded, appears to have retained a very lasting influence in our laws.

" *Vita et membra sunt in manu regis*, says
" Sir Edward Coke[s]; nay, the Lord of the
" Villeine, for this cause, cannot mayheme
" the Villeine, but the King shall punish
" him for mayheming of his subject; for that
" hereby he hath disabled him to do the
" King's service, by fine, ransome, and im-
" prisonment until the fine be paid." " And
" in my circuit in Anno 11 Jacobi, in the
" county of Leicester, one Wright, a young,
" strong, and lusty rogue, to make himself
" impotent, thereby to have more colour to
" beg, or to be relieved without putting him-
" self to to any labour, caused his companion
" to strike off his left hand, and both of

[s] Co. Litt. 127. B.

" them

"them were indicted, fined and ransomed "therefore [t], and that by the opinion of the "rest of the Judges."

The law of Spain, far from allowing forfeitures in homicide by self-defence, gravely observes [u], "that it is better for a man to "defend himself, when alive, than to leave "it to others to avenge him, when he is "dead."

As to homicide *per infortunium*, it is true, that it was subjected by the Athenians to banishment for a year; but it should be observed, that this was not in the nature of a punishment, but rather a protection [w] to the unfortunate person from the impetuosity of revenge; for if, previous to his departure

[t] By a declaration of Lewis XIV, A. D. 1677, "les criminelles condamnés à servir sur nos Galeres, comme forçats, lesquels aprés leurs jugemens auront mutilé ou fait mutiler leur membres, soient punis de mort pour reparation de leur crime." Code penal. p. 139.

[u] See the Observations on the ancient statutes, p. 55.

[w] See Euripid. Orest. ver. 511—518. and the Iliad, l. xxiii. ver. 85. and Petit. Leg. Att. p. 609. "Qui alium casu fortuito necâsset, in annum deportator, *donec aliquem e cognatis occisi placâsset*; revertitor vero peractis sacris et lustrationibus."

A full comment on this Law may be found in the latter part of the Oration of Demosthenes against Nausimachus.

or

or during his absence, he were able to satisfy the relations of the deceased, the exile ceased from that moment. And indeed, the Athenians[x], as well as the Romans, seem to have formed very clear distinctions upon the different instances of homicide.

§ 4. The English law describes a third species of homicide under the name of manslaughter. This, though in the first instance within the benefit of clergy, is made highly criminal and felonious; and the offender shall be burnt in the hand, and forfeit all his goods and chattels. And if for any previous felony,

[x] The ingenious writer of the "Historical Law Tracts" seems (p. 33.) rather inadvertently to have made a different assertion. The words of Solon's Law are very remarkable, *φόνου καὶ τραύματος ἐκ προνοίας*. Again, the punishment of death was annexed to *wilful* murder, *Τὸν ἐκ προνοίας ἀποκτείναντα θανάτῳ ζημιοῦσθαι*.—And if the Murderer withdrew before conviction into banishment, he was subjected to a total forfeiture; but the other instances of homicide were not liable either to corporal punishment or forfeiture.

The Roman Law proceeded expressly on the same principles; *In Maleficiis voluntas spectatur.* And Hadrian declared by Rescript, "*Eum, qui hominem occidit, si non occidendi animo hoc admisit, absolvi posse: leniendam pœnam ejus, qui in rixâ, casu magis quam voluntate homicidium admisit.*" And by another Rescript of one of the Emperors, "*Infans vel furiosus, si hominem occiderint, lege Corneliâ non tenentur: cum alterum innocentia consilii tuetur, alterum fati infelicitas excusat.*"

as for sending live sheep out of the realm, or for harbouring offenders against the law of customs, or for having solemnized a clandestine marrriage, or for any other fact of the most foreign nature, he should have used his plea of clergy, *not being a clergyman*, he is then in the first instance of manslaughter subjected to the pains of death.

I have stated the punishment previous to the definition of the offence; because many most ingenious and learned writers have, on this subject, as on many others, expatiated, with more liberality than reason, on the merciful disposition of the English government; as if it were their object rather to write the panegyric, than to make known the imperfections, of the constitution.

We are told[y], "that the benignity of our "law imputeth manslaughter to an infir-"mity, which is incident to the human "frame;" yet manslaughter is a capital offence. We are told[z], "that our law pays "such respect to human frailty, as not to "put a hasty, and a deliberate act upon the "same level of guilt;" yet it will appear,

[y] Foster, p. 290. [z] Commentaries, B. iv. p. 191.

that

that both manslaughter and murder may be committed, without any intent to do personal mischief, and without any mixture of deliberation whatever.

Manslaughter is agreed to be, the killing of another without malice, express, or implied; either voluntarily, upon a sudden heat; or involuntarily, in the commission of an unlawful act.

Voluntary manslaughter, (which, being an act of homicide without either a legal or a personal necessity, is therefore neither justifiable nor excusable,) ensueth most frequently upon some provocation given, or supposed to be given. But words of reproach, and contemptuous gestures, are in no case sufficient to free the party killing from the guilt of murder[a]; *unless* the killing be in consequence of a blow given in a manner, and with a weapon, not likely to kill[b]; or unless, upon the immediate quarrel of the parties, they proceed to blows or fighting; so as to make the whole transaction one continued act of

[a] Hale, 473. 3 Cro. 779. "In the assembly of the Judges, 18 Car. II. this point (says Lord Chief Justice Holt) was positively resolved." Kel. p. 130.

[b] See the case of John Grey. Kel. p, 64.

passion

passion or sudden affray, in which no undue advantage is taken on either side.

There must be some actual assault upon the person killing, to soften, what would otherwise be an act of murder, into manslaughter. But even this indulgence is confined to that sudden impulse of passion, which is supposed to be irresistible; *for, if there should appear to have been a sufficient interval for the voice of reason to be once heard*, the act of homicide will then be attributed to the malignant principle of deliberate revenge, and will receive the name and punishment of murder.

It was enacted in the reign of Hen. II. that if any were killed at any just or tournament it should be no felony; "for that in friendly manner the parties contended to try their strength, and to be able to do the King service in that kind as occasion should be offered [c]."

Involuntary manslaughter happeneth in the case of accidental death, ensuing upon an act

[c] Mirror, c. 1. § 13. *des Adventures.*

unlawful as *malum in ſe*, but in the nature only of a treſpaſs. But, if the homicide be in conſequence of an act felonious in itſelf, or in proſecution of a felonious intent, it will be murder.

It is not difficult to illuſtrate this diſtinction by an example; though I purpoſely avoid any mention of adjudged precedents, that I may not be led into a long, and weariſome labyrinth of facts. It is extremely dangerous to give any extract from caſes of homicide, where *every circumſtance weigheth* " *ſomething in the ſcale of juſtice*," and where imperfect reports have the moſt fatal tendency.

A man ſhooting at a bird, and uſing proper and ordinary caution to prevent danger, unfortunately happeneth to kill his neighbour. The guilt of this man in the eye of our law, and conſequently the proportion of his puniſhment, will depend, partly on the nature, ſhape, and ſize of the bird; and partly on the intention of the man with reſpect to the bird; but will have no connection whatever with the act of homicide.

If the bird chanceth in evidence to prove a wild pigeon [d], *feræ naturæ et nullius in bonis*, it will be excusable homicide; if a tame fowl, and shot at for the amusement or improvement of the marksman, it will be felonious, and manslaughter, because an unlawful trespass on the property of another; lastly, if the bird were private property and intended to be stolen, which must be collected from the circumstances, it will be murder, by reason of that felonious intent [e].

Such on this point is the doctrine of our law; and infinite is the variety of constructive crimes, which have been established thereon: the instance, which I have selected, is no exaggeration.

That external, unconnected [f] circumstances should regulate the nature and enormity of crimes,

[d] Kelyng, 117. State Trials, vol. vi. p. 222. Foster, p. 258.

[e] On the same principle, when a man, endeavouring to kill another, and missing his blow, happeneth to kill himself; it is in judgement of our Law *wilful and deliberate self-murder*. See Hale, H. P. C. i. 413.

[f] In all such instances, the intent of the prisoner, which *can only* be collected from the circumstances, is evidently and necessarily subject to the sole determination of the Jury: "that A. shot at the poultry of B. and by accident killed a man,"

crimes, that the intention ſhould be transferred to the accident which reſults from it, are poſitions, which, in their preſent extent, have ever ſeemed to me moſt prepoſterous and unnatural. They bear however the venerable ſtamp of antiquity; and the errors derived from them, if indeed they be errors, are the accumulation of many centuries.

I proceed therefore with diffident and trembling ſteps on this hitherto untrodden ground; fearful, though in the purſuit of truth and the defence of natural rights, of wandering into the mazes of abſurdity, or

man," would be an inſufficient verdict, on which no judgement could be given. The intent of A. with regard to the poultry ought alſo to have been found. "If an action unlawful in itſelf be done deliberately, and *with intention of miſchief*, or great bodily harm to particulars, or of miſchief indiſcriminately, fall it where it may, and death enſue againſt or beſide the original intention of the party, it will be murder. But if *ſuch miſchievous intention* doth not appear, which *is matter of fact* and *to be collected from circumſtances*, and the act was done heedleſsly and incautiouſly, it will be manſlaughter: not accidental death, becauſe the act upon which death enſued was unlawful."

But quære, How this can be reconciled with another paſſage in the ſame book, which ſaith, "*that the court, and not the jury, is to judge the malus animus, which is to be collected from all circumſtances*, and bringeth the offence within the denomination of wilful malicious murder, whatever might be the immediate motive to it." Foſter, p. 261. and p. 257.

ſtriking

ſtriking at the fundamental principles of Government.

It is true, that crimes are to be eſtimated, in ſome degree, by the actual miſchief done to ſociety; becauſe the internal malignity of mankind is not within the cognizance of human tribunals.

But, if this poſition were received in its fulleſt latitude, it would prove too much; it would prove that every act of homicide is equally criminal, and that the intention is in no caſe to be conſidered. The following reſtriction ſhould then be obſerved, as inviolably connected with the principle. *Every member of ſociety hath a right to do any act without the apprehenſion of other inconveniences, than thoſe which are the proper conſequences of the act itſelf*; for it is the right of every member of ſociety to know, not only when he is criminal, but in what degree he is ſo. This is the great boundary of political liberty; which gives way to inſecurity and danger, whenever the arbitrary inferences of magiſtracy are admitted within its confines. Can it be ſaid, conſiſtently with this principle, that the caſual conſequence of an intended larceny ſhall be liable to receive the appellation and puniſhment of wilful murder? This may be reconciled to the philoſophy of ſlaves; but it is ſurely repugnant to that noble and active confidence, which a free people ought to poſſeſs in the laws of their conſtitution, the rule of their actions.

Yet there are ſome caſes in which it may be reaſonable to carry over the felonious intent to commit one act, to a different act enſuing in proſecution thereof. As when a potion is given to the mother to deſtroy the child of which ſhe is pregnant, and it kills the mother; this is murder, and hath been ſo adjudged [g]. In like manner, "if a man lay "poiſon with an intent that B. ſhould take it, "and C. by miſtake takes it, and is poiſoned "to death; this is murder, though it were "not intended for him [h]." So, "when a "man intending to burn one houſe, in exe-"cution thereof happens to burn another "houſe, this is a malicious and felonious "burning, for it ſprings out of a malicious

[g] By Sir M. Hale, at Bury, A. D. 1670. Hale's Hiſt. P. C. i. 429.

[h] See Agnes Gore's caſe, Plowden, i. 474. and Hale's Hiſt. P. C. i. 431.

"and felonious intent[i]." *But* in all theſe caſes it ſhould be obſerved, that the conſequence participates the nature of the original crime, and that the general malice of the intention is followed by a fact of the ſame degree and kind.

When it was ſaid, that involuntary manſlaughter happens in the caſe of accidental death enſuing upon unlawful acts; I ought to have added, that acts lawful in themſelves, but done without due care and circumſpection, are to be conſidered as unlawful, and even as felonious in their conſtruction, if done with a negligence ſo notorious as to imply malice againſt all mankind. And on this diſtinction, a killing, in conſequence of a piece of timber or ſtone thrown from the top of a houſe into the ſtreet, is always cited in our books as an inſtance of homicide, which may be miſadventure, manſlaughter, or murder, according to the circumſtances of the caſe.

§ 5. The offence of mortally ſtabbing another upon ſudden provocation, not then having a weapon drawn, nor having firſt ſtricken

[i] State Trials, vol. vi. p. 222. 3 Inſt. p. 67. "*the Event ſhall be coupled to the Cauſe.*"

at the party killing, is a peculiar ſpecies of manſlaughter, which is puniſhed as murder by a ſtatute made in the firſt year of James the Firſt, upon a ſpecial occaſion :—"The of-"fence (ſays Lord Raymond) conſiſted in the "manner of doing it; becauſe the Scots car-"ried ſhort daggers, and frequently, upon "differences ariſing at table, ſtabbed others "unprovided."

The particular grievance between the nations hath long expired; and the particular remedy provided for it ought not to have ſurvived.

The ingenuity and benignity of the judges have gone hand in hand in the conſtruction and mitigation of this ſtatute [k]; yet it hath proved fatal to many unfortunate perſons, who have ſuffered, not merely becauſe they had killed, but becauſe they had adopted a mode

[k] Of this the following ſolemn determination in the caſe of Page and Harwood is a curious inſtance. "Though in judgement of law every one preſent, and aiding, is a principal; yet in the conſtruction of this ſtatute, which is ſo penal, it ſhall be extended *only to ſuch as really and actually made the thruſt; not to thoſe who in conſtruction of law only may be ſaid to make it.*" Hale i. 468. Allen, 43. Stiles, 86.

of killing, to which the law expreſſes a partial antipathy.

§ 6. The diffuſe manner in which I have now conſidered the inferior inſtances of homicide, hath almoſt exhauſted the ſubject; and it might perhaps be ſufficient to add, that every remaining inſtance amounts to the crime of murder [l], that crime at which our nature ſhudders.

Murder is the killing of another with malice aforethought, either expreſs, or implied. No homicide, *publicly* committed, amounted to murder by the common law; for murder, according to the ancient definition of Bracton, *eſt* occulta *hominum extraneorum et notorum occiſio manu hominum nequiter perpetrata.* This was remedied by ſtat. 13 Richard II. which gives a deſcription of murder according to common underſtanding [m].

The act then is not complete without the death of the party; but if the party ſhould not die ſpeedily after the blow, yet if he die within a year and a day, and if the wound

[l] Commentaries, B. iv. 194.

[m] Kel. p. 125.

be

be the ultimate, though not the immediate caufe of death, it is murder[n].

And fuch murder is not confined to direct attacks upon life, but may be the confequence of indecifive acts, or wilful neglects, or cruelties, from which death was likely to enfue. This was the cafe of the woman who left her infant in an orchard covered only with leaves, in which condition it was ftruck by a kite, and died.

Exprefs malice is that deliberate intention to take away the life of a fellow-creature, which is manifefted by external circumftances, capable of proof. It has indeed been extended to that head of conftructions which I have already mentioned. As when two or more meet together to do an unlawful act, the probable confequence of which may be blood-fhed, and one of them kills a man;

[n] It feems however to be a harfh refolution in Kelyng's Reports, p. 26, that " If one gives wounds to another, " who neglects the cure of them, or is diforderly, and " doth not keep that rule which a perfon wounded fhould " do; yet if he die, it is murder, or manflaughter, ac- " cording as the cafe is in the perfon who gave the " wounds: *becaufe if the wounds had not been, the man had* " *not died.*" Newgate Seffions, 14 Oct. 14 Car. II.

ſuch killing is adjudged to involve the whole company in the guilt of murder, they being preſumed to have proceeded on a general and malicious reſolution againſt all oppoſers. The fact, however, muſt appear to have been committed *ſtrictly in proſecution of the purpoſe for which the party was aſſembled*; and this diſtinction probably governed the caſe of Lord Dacres [o], in which indeed there is an apparent hardſhip. The park-keeper was killed without his knowledge, and far out of his ſight and hearing; yet in the eye of the law he was preſent, being at that inſtant engaged, though in a different part of the park, in the encouragement, protection, and ſupport of the common enterprize. It is eaſy to illuſtrate this poſition by another inſtance: it hath been adjudged, that "If divers per- "ſons be engaged in an unlawful act, and "one of them, with malice prepenſe againſt "one of his companions, finding an oppor- "tunity, kills him; the reſt are not con- "cerned in the guilt of that act [p]," becauſe it hath no connection with the crime in contemplation.

[o] Hale's Hiſt. P. C. i. 534. Moore, 86. Foſter, 354.
[p] Kel. p. 112.

Implied

Implied malice is that inference which arifes from the nature of the act, though no particular malice can be proved. As when a man fuddenly kills another without any apparent provocation; when he gives poifon to another without any known inducement; when he wilfully fuffers a beaft, notorioufly mifchievous, to wander abroad, and it kills a man. The laft inftance is certainly a moft grofs mifdemeanour; and Lord Chief Juftice Hale thinks it a murder, as by the Jewifh law [q], and mentions a report of a perfon being actually executed thereon.

A peculiar protection is, in conftruction of law, given to minifters of juftice executing the ordinary procefs; and alfo to private perfons endeavouring in certain cafes to arreft or imprifon: the killing of fuch perfons, though in the exertion of perfonal violence, is homicide committed in defiance of the juftice of the kingdom, and is therefore deemed murder of malice prepenfe.

[q] Exodus xxi. 29. "But if the ox were wont to pufh with his horn in time paft, and it hath been teftified to the owner, and he hath not kept him in, but that he hath killed a man or a woman, the ox fhall be ftoned, and his owner alfo fhall be put to death."

And

And here it hath been much debated, how far acts of oppreſſion towards individuals may authorize them, or the bye-ſtanders in their behalf, to attempt a reſcue; and how far the party, whoſe perſon or property is invaded under colour of law and juſtice, or others interpoſing in his defence, and committing homicide, may be thought to have acted on a provocation ſufficient to acquit them of the guilt of murder.

The juſtification of reſiſtance to magiſtracy, attended with ſuch conſequences, muſt principally depend on the circumſtances of each particular caſe; and ſuch reſiſtance is generally founded rather in deliberate intention, than in the venial infirmity of paſſion.

Yet a worthy Judge [r] ſeems to have made an unpleaſing diſtinction on this ſubject, between the ſtability of government, and the private rights of the people. "Let us (ſays "he) ſuppoſe the caſe of an upright and de-"ſerving man, univerſally beloved and eſ-"teemed, ſtanding at the place of execution "under a ſentence of death, *manifeſtly unjuſt*.

[r] Foſter, p. 316.

"This

"This is a caſe that may well rouze the in-
" dignation, and excite the compaſſion, of the
" wiſeſt and beſt of men: but wiſe and good
" men know [s], that it is the duty of private
" ſubjects to leave the innocent man to his
" lot, how hard ſoever it may be, without
" attempting a reſcue; for otherwiſe, all
" government would be unhinged."

The ſtating of the caſe now before us, ſuppoſes abſolute certainty as to the injury, and excludes all poſſibility of popular miſconception. It is difficult to perſuade oneſelf, that in ſuch a caſe the reſiſtance of the bye-ſtanders would be unjuſtifiable [t].

Drunkenneſs, voluntarily contracted, though it be a temporary frenzy, is no excuſe for murder in the law of England; which proceeds in this inſtance on an idea, that one crime ought not to be privileged by another. I have ſome-where read, that a beautiful ſtatue having killed a man by its fall, was by a

[s] Socrates carried this idea to a great Extreme, when, doomed to death by an unjuſt ſentence, he refuſed to ſtir from his priſon, though the doors were opened to him.

[t] In the ſtory of Appius and Virginia, one cannot diſapprove the inſurrection of the Roman people againſt the Decemvirs.

ſolemn ſentence, founded on a law of Draco, thrown into the ſea. The Roman law ſhews great indulgence on this ſubject, "*per vinum* "*delapſis capitalis pœna remittitur*[u]."

§ 7. The crime of taking away the life of another by falſe teſtimony, deliberately given, ought not to paſs unnoticed. It is in its nature a moſt malignant ſpecies of aſſaſſination, contaminating with blood the ſacred ſtream of juſtice, and fatal to the lives, properties, and honours of the innocent.

By the laws of Egypt, perjury in general was capital[w]; for it was ſaid to involve in itſelf the two greateſt crimes, viz. impiety to the Gods, and violation of faith to man.

At Rome it was alſo a capital crime, but properly confined to thoſe "*qui falſum teſtimo-* "*nium dolo dixerint, quo quis publico judicio rei* "*capitalis damnaretur*[x]."

[u] ff. xlix. 16. 6.

[w] Diodorus Siculus, l. i. c. 6.

[x] Dig. l. xlviii. t. 8. § 1.; and under a ſimilar reaſoning, magiſtrates were ſubjected to capital puniſhment in caſes of bribery, if the bribe were received to put an innocent man to death. Dig. xlviii. 11. 7. 3.

In

In like manner, it is puniſhed with death in France, and with good reaſon; for in France the perſon accuſed [y] is not permitted to produce witneſſes in his defence, and his doom depends ſolely on the veracity of thoſe who give teſtimony on the part of the public.

This circumſtance brings credit to the aſſertion of our ancient writers [z], that perjury was capitally puniſhed by the common law. A milder doctrine however hath long prevailed; partly from an apprehenſion, that ſuch ſeverity might tend to intimidate witneſſes, who would often be induced to ſtifle their teſtimony [a], if it muſt be given at the peril of their lives; partly in conſideration of the nature of our trials, which furniſh the accuſed with a variety of reſources; inaſmuch as truth and mercy are admitted to combat falſhood and malevolence, and the whole examination is rather in the nature of a diſcuſſion between

[y] L'Eſprit des Loix, l. xxix. c. 11.

[z] Mirror, c. 1. § 9. Brit. c. 5. Bracton, l. iii. c. 4. Contra, Mr. Juſtice Foſter, p. 132.—In ſome inſtances, the tongue of the perjured perſon was cut out. "Aſcuns ſont punies per couper des langues, come ſoiloit eſtre de faux teſtmoignes." Mirror, c. 4. § de Peine.

[a] Commentaries, B. iv. 197.

the

the parties, than of a prosecution against an undefended oppressed individual.

False testimony is at present punished capitally in Scotland; but this severity doth not appear to be warranted, either by ancient custom or by statute, but rather to have been assumed upon the indignation of the people against an offence so prejudicial to society [b].

§ 8. There is another species of murder of most aggravated malignity, and known in our law by the name of petty treason; because it is a breach of that allegiance which the murderer oweth to the deceased, when the fact is committed [c].

Petty

[b] By stat. 26 Geo. II. c. 23. "It is made a felony without benefit of clergy, wilfully to destroy, or cause or procure to be destroyed, any register book of marriage, or any part of such register book, *with intent to subject any person to any of the penalties of that statute.*" An offence certainly more venial than the crime of perjury in a capital accusation! But I have already observed, that arguments of analogy, in the framing of penal laws, lead to sanguinary consequences.

[c] In England, women *(from a regard to decency,* say our books) are burnt alive for the crimes both of high and petty treason. In Russia, for the murder of their husbands, they suffer a sort of death, less terrible perhaps in idea, but certainly more painful to sense.

" Les femmes, qu'on enterroit toutes vives jusques aux epaules, pour avoir tué leurs maris, vivoient plusieurs jours

 dans

Petty treaſon, in our law, differs widely from other inſtances of murder, in certain privileges given to the defendant; ſuch are, the power of a peremptory challenge of thirty-five jurors, and the requiſition of two witneſſes to the indictment and at the trial [d].

It is certainly true, that *the credibility of a witneſs, or, in other words, the probability of the atteſted fact, decreaſes in proportion to the aggravated atrocioufneſs of the charge.* Cicero was aware of this principle, and made a fine application of it to the crime of parricide:

"*Extent oportet expreſſa ſceleris veſtigia, ubi,*
"*quâ ratione, per quos, quo tempore, maleficium ſit admiſſum. Quæ niſi multa et manifeſta ſunt, profectò res tam ſceleſta, tam atrox, tam nefaria credi non poteſt: pene dicam, reſperſas manus ſanguine paterno judices videant, oportet, ſi tantum facinus, tam immane, tam*

dans cette derniere ſituation." Voyage en Siberie, d'Auteroche.

[d] Yet it is thought, as petty treaſon comprehends murder, that, if two witneſſes cannot be produced at the trial, the evidence of one may be ſubmitted to the jury, who may thereupon find the defendant guilty of the murder, and acquit him of the treaſon. Foſter, p. 328. Contra, 2 Hawk. 258. § 144.

"*acerbum ſint credituri. Magna eſt enim vis*
"*humanitatis, multum valet communio ſangui-*
"*nis: reclamitat iſtiuſmodi ſuſpicionibus ipſa*
"*natura: portentum atque monſtrum certiſſi-*
"*mum, eſſe aliquem humanâ ſpecie et figurâ, qui*
"*tantum immanitate beſtias vicerit, ut propter*
"*quos hanc ſuaviſſimam lucem aſpexerit, eos in-*
"*digniſſime luce privârit*[e]!"

I am ſorry to add, that parricide is not comprehended within the claſs of petty treaſon, nor ſubjected by our laws to any degree of exemplary notice. Reiterated experience hath given a melancholy refutation to Solon's idea, "that it is impoſſible to commit ſo un-" natural a barbarity."

It ſeems proper, at the concluſion of this chapter, to mention a rule eſtabliſhed by Sir Matthew Hale, relative to trials in caſes of murder; "I would never (ſays he) con-" vict any perſon of murder, or manſlaugh-" ter, unleſs the fact were proved to be done, " or at leaſt the body found." He then mentions two extraordinary caſes, which ſhew this rule to be founded both in humanity and

[e] Orat. pro Sext. Roſc. Amerin. c. 22.

wiſdom; and we find the ſame maxim in the Roman law: *Item illud ſciendum eſt, niſi conſtet aliquem eſſe occiſum, non haberi de familiâ quæſtionem* [f].

§ 9. The proper judgement againſt deliberate murder. is death; and in the rigid infliction of this judgement both the ſafety and morality of mankind are greatly intereſted. It is the voice of nature, confirmed by the law of God, that "Whoſo ſheddeth man's "blood, by man ſhall his blood be ſhed;" and therefore, ſaith the Moſaical law, "Ye "ſhall take no ſatisfaction for the life of a "murderer, which is guilty of death; "but he ſhall ſurely be put to death, ſo "ye ſhall not pollute the land wherein ye "are."

[f] Dig. l. xxix t. 5. § 24.

CHAP.

CHAP. XIX.

Of Duelling.

§ 1. THE law of England hath assigned the punishment of murderers to Duellists and their Seconds [g]; and in this it is supported by the laws of Religion and Morality. But this crime, though prohibited

[g] It is very certain, that, in cases of Duelling in cold blood, or when there hath been a sufficient interval for the passions to subside, the Principal and his Second, if homicide should ensue, are, in our Law, both guilty of Murder. Some able writers have holden, that the Second of the person killed is equally guilty, in respect of that aid, and countenance, which he gives to the Principals in the execution of their mutual purpose; but it seems (says Serjeant Hawkins) too severe a construction to make a man by such reasoning the murderer of his friend, to whom he was so far from intending any mischief, that he was ready to hazard his own life in the quarrel. Hale, p. 443. Hawk. i. p. 82. Dalt. c. 93.

The reasoning faculties of men vary as much as their faces: it hath been impossible therefore for the law to fix any time in which the passions shall be supposed to become cool; this must depend on the circumstances of deliberation to be given in evidence; and in many cases it hath been adjudged, that death in consequence of an appointment and meeting a few hours subsequent to the provocation is murder. See Legg's case; Kelyng, 27.

ed by the legiſlature under pain of death and the laſting conſequences of an Attainder, is unhappily enjoined by the prejudices of mankind, and the fallible voice of popular eſtimation; and when ſhame is the conſequence of obedience to law, the ſword of Juſtice loſes its terrors. Hence the Duelliſt kills his friend, whom he loves [h]; and the Judge condemns the Duelliſt, whilſt he ſcarcely knows how in his own heart to diſapprove his behaviour.

It is in vain to ſay, that this unhappy cuſtom might be deſtroyed by puniſhing the aggreſſor, who firſt gives the affront; for the affront is often indeſcribable.

The infliction of extreme penalties on the act without regard to its conſequences might be more effectual; but is it not to be feared,

There is a degree of hardſhip in the caſe of John Barbot, who was executed at the Iſland of St. Chriſtopher, A. D. 1753. State Trials, vol. x. p. 182. But I have not found any caſe of an actual execution *in England*, in conſequence of a duel *fairly fought*. There were not however any ſuſpicions of a contrary kind in the caſe of Major Oneby, who would certainly have been executed, if he had not killed himſelf the night before. See Lord Raymond, p. 1485.

[h] Spectator, N° 84. Rouſſeau, la nouv. Heloiſe, t. i.

that

that the propenſity of our natures to revenge would ſubſtitute the more fatal, and more odious practice of aſſaſſination? I ſhall be anſwered perhaps, that the ſword and the ſtilleto were equally unknown, both at Rome and at Athens; but it ſhould be remembered, that ſoftneſs and refinement of manners were alſo unknown there[i].

Of little avail is it to object, that true honour depends not on the prejudices of the people, but hath its ſource in the heart; that it is more courageous to reſiſt the abſurd tyranny of cuſtom, than to ſubmit to it; that the defence of honour is not placed in occaſional appeals to the ſword and piſtol, but in a life of integrity and virtue; that, when a fencing-ſchool is made the court of juſtice, there is

[i] Gallantry, as well as Duelling, is of modern invention; and it is very obſervable, that they have been concomitants in their progreſs. The intercourſe of the ſexes hath been the ſchool of manners: and there even ſeems reaſon to ſuſpect that our fantaſtic notions of honour are derived from the influence of female ſenſibility. One of the courtiers of William the Third expreſſed this idea very naturally, when, being aſked by his friends, why one of his eſtabliſhed character for courage and good ſenſe would anſwer the challenge of a coxcomb; he confeſſed, "that for his *own* ſex, he could ſafely truſt their judgement: but how ſhould he appear at night before the *maids* of Honour?" See Shafteſbury, Adv. to an Author.

no law but violence, no argument but murder; that reputation is not cleared by cutting the throat of the calumniator; that there is no affinity between the manner of justifying, and a real justification; that benevolence is the basis of every virtue; and that *it is the frenzy of fashion which tempts us to decide petty animosities by the hazard of eternity.* All these assertions may be true; but the most solid reasoning is received as mere declamation, when opposed to the impetuosity of passion, or the fear of shame.

CHAP. XX.

Of Suicide.

PRoxima deinde tenent mœsti loca, qui sibi Lethum
Insontes peperere manu, lucemque perosi
Projecere animas [k].

The best argument of the ancient writers against suicide is to be found in Plato's

[k] Virgil, Æn. l. vi.

Phædo,

Phædo, in a part of the dialogue between Socrates and Cebes. The philoſopher indeed had no occaſion to exert his abilities on the oppoſite ſide of the queſtion, for he lived in hourly expectation of the executioner. "*Illa tanquam cycnea vox divini Hominis*[1]," had no effect on Cato, who is ſaid to have given a repeated reading to theſe ſpeculations on the very night that he deſtroyed himſelf. Robeck wrote a voluminous and diſpaſſionate apology for ſuicide, and, when he had finiſhed his book, put a period to his own exiſtence. Numerous alſo are the inſtances, credibly atteſted, of men, whoſe conduct in every other reſpect hath been blameleſs, who have quitted life, upon the ſuppoſed conviction of cool and deliberate reaſoning. "When all the ties, ſay they, of ſentiment and affection, which attach the heart to this world, are by a variety of misfortunes diſſolved, or forced aſunder, the idea is obvious; when exiſtence becomes a burden, death is the reſting-place of nature."

Such is the argument of thoſe gloomy ſophiſts, who loſe ſight of the final object of

[1] Cicero, de Oratore.

their

their exiſtence; who forget, that they are not created merely to exiſt, to ſuffer, and to die; and are weak enough to place a few years of miſery in competition with immortality.

Such men are deaf to the voice of God; it cannot be expected, that they will liſten to the comparative inſignificance of human edicts. Temporary conſiderations have no weight with thoſe, to whom the proſpect of eternity is become a ſubject of indifference.

The confiſcation therefore of property, inflicted by many governments on the crime of Suicide, is ineffectual and abſurd. It is cruel alſo and unjuſt thus to heap ſufferings on the head of innocence, by puniſhing the child for the loſs of its parent, or aggravating the diſtreſs of the widow, becauſe ſhe hath been deſerted by her huſband.

The ignominious burial of the ſelf-murderer is not liable to ſuch exceptions; *valeat, quantum valere poteſt.* Plutarch tells us, that the virgins of Miletum, being ſeized with an

epidemic

epidemic inclination to hang themſelves, perſiſted in that practice with great alacrity; till the magiſtrates ordered the bodies of all, who were found hanging, to be dragged naked by the ſame rope round all the ſtreets of the city. He adds, that it proved a very effectual remedy [m].

Tiberius is ſaid to have given encouragement to criminals, to become their own executioners. "*Damnati, publicatis bonis, ſepulturâ prohibebantur: eorum, qui de ſe ſtatuebant, humabantur corpora, manebant teſtamenta, pretium feſtinandi.*"—Tacit. Annal. l. vi.

[m] "Le Parlement de Paris condamne les cadavres des homicides d' euxmémes, à être traînés ſur une claie, conduits à la voirie, enſuite pendus par les pieds et leurs biens confiſqués." Code penal.

CHAP.

CHAP. XXI.

Of other Crimes relative to the Perſons of Individuals.

INJURIES and abuſes, which relate to the perſons of private ſubjects, are properly liable to penal laws; for in their example and tendency they are dangerous to the public morality, and ſubverſive of the political rules of right.

§ 1. By the ancient law of England, and, I believe, by the cotemporary laws of all Europe, the offence of maiming was puniſhed by the rule of retaliation, an eye for an eye, a tooth for a tooth [a]. "*Mes, ſi la pleynte ſoit* "*faite de femme qu'avera tollet a home ſes* "*membres, en tiel caſe perdra la feme la une* "*meyn par judgement, come le membre dount* "*ele avera treſpaſſé.*" We find the ſame inſtitution

[a] Diodorus-Siculus relates a curious caſe, which happened in conſequence of a law made by Charondas to the ſame effect. L. xii, c. 17.

ſtitution in the law of the twelve tables, "*Si* "*quis membrum rupit, ni cum eo pacit, talio* "*eſto.*" The obſervations made on this ſubject by one of the diſputants in Aulus Gellius are curious and deciſive. "*Præter enim* "*ulſciſcendi acerbitatem ne procedere quoque* "*exſecutio juſta talionis poteſt, quod enim per im-* "*prudentiam factum eſt, retaliari per impru-* "*dentiam debet. Sed ſi et prudens ruperit, ne-* "*quaqam patietur altius ſe lædi, aut latius,* "*quod cujuſmodi librâ atque menſurâ caveri* "*poſſit, non reperio; quin etiam ſi quid plus* "*erit, aliterve commiſſum, res fiet ridiculæ atro-* "*citatis, ut contraria actio mutuæ talionis oria-* "*tur, et adoleſcat infinita quædam reciprocatio* "*talionum.*"

This barbarous mode of puniſhment, with the pecuniary compenſations which attended it, having gradually fallen into diſuſe, Mayhems became puniſhable by fines and impriſonment[o]; and ſo continued till the 5th of

[o] Rot. Clauſ. Anno 13 H. III. m. 9. "*Henricus Hall & A. uxor ejus capti ſunt et detenti in priſonâ de Evilcheſter. eo quod rectati fuerunt quod ipſi abſciderunt virilia Johannis* monachi, *quem idem Henricus deprehendit cum prædictâ A. uxore ejus.*"

H. IV

H. IV. c. 5. which made it felony to cut out the tongue, or put out the eyes, of any of the king's ſubjects, of malice prepenſe. "The miſchief (ſays Sir Edward Coke [p]) "before this ſtatute was; that when one had "been beaten, wounded, maimed, or rob-"bed; the miſdoers, to the end that the "party grieved might not be able to accuſe "them, did cut out their tongues, or put "out their eyes, pretending the ſame to be "no felony."

But the great ſtatute on this ſubject, at preſent in force, is the 22d and 23d of Charles II. c. 1. which enacts, "that any perſon, who, by lying in wait, *ſhall ſlit the noſe*, or cut off or diſable any limb or member of any ſubject of his majeſty, with intent in ſo doing to maim or disfigure, ſhall ſuffer death without benefit of clergy."

I have ſpecified this particular proviſion in favour of the noſe, for the ſake of an obſervation. The caſe of Sir John Coventry deſerved great indignation; but *lawgivers ought not, in conſequence of a particular enormity, to neglect the uniform diſpenſation of juſtice.* The

[p] 3 Inſt. p. 62.

ſtatute

ſtatute book is not the proper repoſitory of hiſtorical facts [q].

As to the general purport of the act; the offences deſcribed in it are certainly heinous; and the penalty, though in the extreme of ſeverity, is perhaps not diſproportionate to the audacIouſneſs of the crime.

§ 2. "The crime of wilfully and malici-"ouſly ſhooting at a perſon" is alſo made capital [r], though neither death nor maim ſhould enſue.

It is of dangerous conſequence to make the attempt to commit a crime, and the actual perpetration of it, equally penal. An aſſault in any other manner, with intent either to maim or murder, is conſidered only as a miſ-demeanor; and it deſerves obſervation, that *the wording of this proviſion, though directed againſt an enormity of a local and very different nature, comprehends the caſe of duelling with piſtols.*

[q] See the preamble to the 9th Ann. c. 16. relative to the perſons of privy counſellors.

[r] 9 Geo. I. c. 22.

Preme-

Premeditated aſſaſſination is capitally puniſhed by the law of France[s], though it ſhould reſt only in the intent, and not be followed by any actual homicide.

§ 3. The forcible abduction and marriage of women deſerves, in all ſtates, a ſevere animadverſion; and it is made a capital felony in our law, *if* done for lucre; or *if* the woman have ſubſtance in money or lands, or be heir apparent to her anceſtors. Theſe hypothetical proviſions are liable to exception; but it is unneceſſary: for the marriage act hath at leaſt had one good effect, in making this offence extremely difficult to be committed.

§ 4. The forcible taking, and the decoying by falſe pretences, any man, woman, or child, from their own country, and ſelling them into another, ſeems to be one of the greateſt crimes below the degree of murder, that can be committed againſt individuals. By the Jewiſh, and by the Roman law[t], ſuch offenders were capitally puniſhable.

[s] Ordonnance criminelle de 1670, tit xvi. art. 4.
[t] Exod. xxi. 16.—ff. xlviii. 15. 1. and—Cod. ad legem Fabiam de Plagiariis, l. ix. t. 20. l. 7. and c. 16.

It

It is remarkable, that in England, where the nature of our ſituation and commerce makes this crime eaſy to be committed; and where the freedom of our conſtitution makes it peculiarly offenſive; it is not mentioned in any ſtatute, but left as a mere miſdemeanor at the common law.

§ 5. Aſſaults, Woundings, and falſe Impriſonments, may be proſecuted in our law both as public crimes, and private wrongs. For in theſe inferior offences againſt the perſon, it hath been thought reaſonable, not only to aſſign thoſe marks of public diſapprobation, which, for the ſake of example, are due to all diſturbances, and oppreſſions of a public nature, but alſo to leave to the party aggrieved that private ſatisfaction, which is due to him for the mere civil injury.

On the conviction of ſuch offences by indictment, the proportion of the puniſhment depending on the circumſtances of the caſe is neceſſarily entruſted, under certain reſtrictions, to the diſcretion of the court. If therefore the proſecution appear reaſonable, it is not unuſual to recommend to the offender, before judgement, to make a pecuniary ſatiſfaction to the party injured; who thereupon releases his right to a civil action, and the punishment by the court is moderated accordingly.

This practice, which is founded in humanity to both parties, is exercised with the utmost caution, so as neither to lessen the efficacy of public example, nor to multiply violent prosecutions for the sake of private lucre. It is well observed however, that the exercise of such a power "ought to be "confined to judges in the superior courts "of record, and ought never to be allowed "in local and inferior jurisdictions [n]." Above all, it should never be suffered, where the testimony of the prosecutor himself is necessary to convict the defendant; for by such means the rules of evidence are entirely subverted, the prosecutor becoming in effect a plaintiff, and being suffered to bear witness for himself.

§ 6. I should observe, that, by the 9th Anne, c. 16. to *assault*, strike, wound, or attempt to kill, any privy counsellor in the execution of his office, is made felony with-

[n] Commentaries, B. iv. 357.

out

out the benefit of clergy [w]. *It would be a good general rule, to give at first a temporary limited duration to all new laws, which are capitally penal*; and particularly to those, which are made on the spur of the occasion.

§ 7. It is with much reluctance, that I undertake the mention of certain other crimes relative to the person, which, in their nature and tendency, are very prejudicial to the well-being, morality, and safety of society.

The crimes, to which I allude, are founded in the abuse of that passion, on the due regulation of which depend the existence, and much of the happiness of mankind.

The offence of rape is secret in its kind, and generally confined to the knowledge of the party injured; whose testimony is therefore competent, because frequently the only adducible proof of the fact. The charge however is in most cases supported by the collateral, and concurrent testimony of time, place, and circumstances; and the mere

[w] There is another law still existing relative to felonies against the king's council. 3 H. VII. c. 14.

affirmative oath of the woman is rarely thought ſufficient to convict.

The well-known words [x] of Sir M. Hale on this ſubject are very deſerving of attention. "It is the excellency of the trial by "jury, that they are the triers of the credit "of the witneſſes, as well as of the truth "of the fact: it is one thing, whether a "witneſs be admiſſible to be heard; another "thing, whether he is to be believed, when "heard."—"It muſt be remembered, that "this is an accuſation eaſy to be made, and "hard to be proved; *but harder to be de-"fended by the party accuſed, be he never ſo "innocent.* And we ought to be the more "cautious, becauſe the heinouſneſs of the "offence many times tranſporteth the judge "and the jury with ſo much indignation, "that they are over-haſtily carried to the "conviction of the perſon accuſed, by the "confident teſtimony of ſometimes falſe "and malicious witneſſes."

The ſame learned writer hath alſo ſaid, "that this crime ought to be ſeverely and "impartially puniſhed with death;" and

[x] Hale, vol. i. p. 634.

we may allow it to be one of thofe unhappy inftances, in which it is neceffary to facrifice the life of a fellow-creature to the fecurity of good citizens, and the peace of fociety. But it muft alfo be admitted, that it is a crime peculiarly liable to vary in the degree of its atrocioufnefs, according to the circumftances of the cafe, and therefore peculiarly open to the divine prerogative of pardon.

This crime was a felony at the common law, and had a punifhment (faith Sir E. Coke) [y] "under fuch a condition, as no other felony had the like."

The offender was adjudged "*amittere oculos,* "*quibus Virginem* [z] *concupivit*; *amittere etiam* "*tefticulos, qui calorem ftupri induxerunt.*" As good reafons might be given for cutting off the legs and arms of the offender, as for putting out his eyes. The idea of caftration is more obvious, but liable to two objections;

[y] 2 Inft. 180.—See the Myrror, c. 4. § de Homicide. And by the laws of Alfred, "Servus fi fervulam ftuprârit, Virga virilis ei præciditor."

[z] "Item fequitur gravis pœna corporalis, fed fine amiffione vitæ, vel membrorum, fi raptus fit de concubinâ legitimâ, vel aliâ quæftum faciente fine delectu perfonarum; *has quidem oves debet rex tueri pro pace fuâ*; et licet meretrix fuit anteà, tum temporis non fuit, cum nequitiæ ejus reclamando confentire noluit." Bracton, l. ii.

it is pernicious to ſociety from the example of barbarity, and inconſiſtent with that decency, which the law always ought to preſerve.

The latter conſideration ſhould never be neglected. It was an inſtance of the wiſdom of the Emperor Theodoſius, that he aboliſhed the infamous puniſhment of women taken in adultery, then uſed at Rome; by which they were proſtituted in the public ſtreets to all comers, a Bell ringing during the execution of the ſentence [a].

In the ancient law of England, excluſive of the puniſhment inflicted on the raviſher, his horſe, greyhound, and hawk, were alſo ſubjected to great corporal infamy; "*Equus* "*ejus ad dedecus ſuum dedecorabitur, caudâ,* "*quam propius natibus poſſit, abſciſſâ; eodem* "*modo canis leporarius dedecorabitur, et ac-* "*cipiter ejus perdet beccum, ungues, et* [b] *cau-* "*dam*:" but the woman, that was raviſhed, might prevent all the penalties, if, before judgement, ſhe demanded the criminal for her huſband. The Roman law was in the

[a] Pufendorff, viii. 3. 27. Socrat. Hiſt. Eccl. l.v. c. 18.
[b] Staunford, 22. B.

ſame

ſame ſpirit; "*Rapta raptoris, aut mortem, aut indotatas nuptias optet*;" upon which there aroſe what was thought a doubtful caſe, "*Unâ nocte quidam duas rapuit, altera mortem optat, altera nuptias.*" In the judgement of common ſenſe the deciſion is evident.

In the conſtruction of this crime the Roman law made no diſtinction between ſeduction and force; "*Sive volentibus ſive nolentibus tale facinus ſit perpetratum* [c]." In modern

[c] The ancient Laws of England treated every ſpecies of Incontinence with great ſeverity.—"Edmondus rex adulterium affici juſſit inſtar homicidii." Leg. Edm. c. 4. "Canutus rex hominem adulterum in exilium relegari juſſit, fœminæ naſum et aures præcidi." Leg. Cnuti, c. 6, & 50. "*Vidua ſi ſe non legitime commiſcebat* xx s. *emendabat. puella vero* x s. Domeſday, Tit. Ceſtre.—"It is (ſays Fleta, l. ii. c. 5.) the office of the Marſhal, in time of peace, to exact from every common woman found about the court four pence on her firſt apprehenſion, *and to forbid her the court.* On the ſecond, he is to oblige her by dureſs to abjure the court. "Tertio, conſiderabitur quod amputetur illi treſſoria et quod tondeatur; quarto, amputetur illi ſuperlabium."—Sir Edward Coke cites a record, in which Edward the Third commands the Mayor of London to remove all ſuch women from the neighbourhood of the Carmelite brethren in Fleet-ſtreet. And "under Hen. VIII. thoſe infamous women (he adds) were not allowed chriſtian burial when dead, nor the rites of the church whilſt they lived." A. D. 1650, it was enacted by the then prevailing powers (who were certainly ill

 qualified

dern nations, where the intercourſe of the ſexes is more promiſcuous, this ſeverity would be very extenſive in its conſequences. The Engliſh law hath made force neceſſary to the crime; and it was made felony without benefit of clergy in a female reign.

There was a degree of good ſenſe in the puniſhment inflicted by the Athenian laws on the raviſhers of unmarried women; "*Raptor virginis mille drachmis* (about 32 l. 6s.) *multator; et virginem, quam vitiavit, ducito.*" It appears

qualified for the rational and deliberate work of legiſlation) that "if any man ſhall from and after the four and "twentieth day of June following have the carnal know- "ledge of the body of any virgin, unmarried woman, "or widow, every ſuch man ſo offending and confeſſing "the ſame, or being thereof convicted, as aforeſaid, "ſhall for every ſuch offence be committed to the com- "mon jail, without bail or mainprize, there to con- "tinue for the ſpace of three months: and every ſuch "offence is hereby adjudged felony, and the perſon or "perſons ſo offending ſhall ſuffer death, as in caſe of "felony without benefit of clergy." Scobell's Acts and Ordinances, p. 122.

By the ſame act, adultery, in the *firſt* inſtance, is made felony without benefit of clergy.

The law of Howel Dda on this ſubject was written in a milder ſpirit. "*Si quis concubuerit cum ancillâ invito ejus* "*domino, dabit domino ejus* XII *denariis pro quâlibet vice,* "*et cum illâ amplius non concumbet.*" L. i. c. I.

appears however from a paſſage in Terence, that the latter part of the law was confined to Athenian citizens.

D. *Ah Stulte! tu de pſaltriâ me ſomnias*
Agere: Hic peccatum in virginem eſt civem. M. *Scio.*
D. *Eho! Scis? et patere?* M. *Quidni patiar?* D. *Dic mihi,*
Non clamas? non inſanis? M. *Non, malim quidem.*
D. *Puer natus eſt.* M. *Dî bene vortant.* D. *Virgo nihil habet.*
M. *Audivi.* D. *Et ducenda indotata eſt.* M. *Scilicet.*
D. *Quid igitur facies?* M. *Domi erit.* D. *Proh Divûm fidem!*
Meretrix et materfamilias unâ in domo [d].

§ 8. The above-mentioned caution of Sir Matthew Hale is peculiarly applicable to the proof of certain other crimes of a very deteſtable nature; the mere mention of which is diſgraceful to the human ſpecies.

The facts to which I allude are at preſent felonious, and without benefit of clergy, by 5 Eliz. c. 17 [e]; in the conſtruction of which ſtatute, *agentes et conſentientes pari pœnâ plectantur*; and this agrees with the law of Mo-

[d] Ter. Adelph. IV. vii. 8. & 28.
Siquid ego erga Te imprudens peccavi, aut natam tuam,
Ut mihi ignoſcas, eamque uxorem mihi des, ut leges jubent.
Plaut. Aulul. IV. x. 62.

[e] This act revived the 25 H. VIII. c. 6.

ſes,

ſes, "*Qui dormierit cum maſculo coitu fœmineo,* "*uterque operatus eſt nefas, et morte mori-* "*atur* [f]."

It hath been ſuggeſted by ſome ingenious writers, that ſevere penalties affixed to the conviction of crimes, the diſcovery and proof of which may be eaſily evaded, are more likely to add fuel to the guilty flame, than to extinguiſh it [g].

The idea is plauſible in theory, but doth not appear to be well ſupported by experience.

It is a maxim (ſays Buſbequius) among the Turks, ſeldom to make inquiries after ſecret criminals, being unwilling to ſeek occaſion for ſcandal; the ſeverity of their laws is directed againſt open breaches of the peace of ſociety. To this may be added, that, in the hiſtories of the Turks, we read accounts of Turkiſh ſeraglios without a woman within the walls.

[f] Levit. xx. 13.

[g] "*Veteres pœnarum ſatis adverſum impudicas in ipſâ profeſſione flagitii credebant.*" Tacit. Annal. l. iii. c. 85.

The profligacy of the Athenians on this ſubject is well known; and the partial reſtrictions eſtabliſhed by Solon certainly had no tendency to a *forcible* extirpation of it. "*Servus ingenuum puerum, ne amato, neve aſſectator; qui ſecus fâxit, publice quinquaginta plagarum ictus illi infliguntor.*" It was an obvious inference to the people, that the purſuit prohibited to ſlaves was proper only for citizens. Again, "*Siquis liberum atque ingenuum puerum produxerit, dica ei ſcribitor, convictus morte multator* [h]." The ſeduction of any other rank was not in any degree penal.

Corn. Nepos ſays of Alcibiades, "*quod ineunte adoleſcentiâ amatus eſt a multis, more Græcorum*:" and that "*Laudi in Græciâ ducitur adoleſcentulis, quamplurimos habere amatores.*"

The Edict of one of the later Emperors on this ſubject is delivered with great energy of expreſſion: "*Quid deſideratur ubi ſexus perdit locum? ubi amor quæritur nec invenitur? ubi ſcelus eſt id, quod non proficit ſcire? ju-*

[h] See Petit, Leg. Att.

"*bemus insurgere leges, armari jura gladio ul-*
"*tore, ut exquisitis pœnis subdantur infames,*
"*qui sunt, vel qui futuri sunt, rei*[i]."

§ 9. I ought to have observed, that the English law describes this offence as commissible "with Man or Beast;" under the latter part of the expression many persons have suffered death.

The unavoidable and general detestation of mankind will always be a strong barrier

[i] Cod. ix. 1. 9. 31. See also Nov. cxli. t. 24. "de his "qui *luxuriantur* contra naturam." "Apud Gothos castra-"bantur," Leg. 8. Westg. l. iii. 25. This crime is called by the Myrror "une peche mortelle encontre le roye le ciel, que cry vengeance, et que pluis est horrible, que porgiser mere," p. 252. There is a very indelicate profusion of learning on this subject in Mr. J. Fortescue Aland's report of the case of Wiseman, who was tried and convicted *de hoc crimine cum puellâ*. A very learned person is there said to have thought the peculiar circumstance of the case a great aggravation of the crime; "For it seems (said his "Lordship) a more direct affront to the Author of na-"ture, and a more insolent expression of contempt to his "wisdom, condemning the provision made by him, and "defying both it and him." Fortescue's Rep. p. 93.

"Nefando non naturalis impudicitiæ crimine qui damnatur, in rogum ardentem impositus flammis absumitor." Jura Danica, l. vi. c. 13.

"Messrs. Bruneau le noir, et Jean Diot convaincus de ce crime ont été brulés en place de Gréve le Lundi, 6 Juillet. 1750." Code penal. 238.

againſt ſo horrid a crime; but it may be a queſtion, whether the public proſecution thereof be founded in wiſdom. Some have thought it unſafe, and likely rather to ſollicit the attention, than to deter from the crime. "*Sapienter feciſſe dicitur Solon cum de eo nihil* "*ſanxerit, quod antea commiſſum non erat, ne non* "*tam prohibere, quam admonere videatur*[k]:"— "*præterea* [l] *videmus ea ſæpe committi, quæ* "*ſæpe vindicantur. Summâ prudentiâ altiſſimi* "*viri et rerum naturæ peritiſſimi maluerunt,* "*velut incredibile et ultra audaciam poſitum,* "*ſcelus præterire, quam, dum vindicant, oſten-* "*dere poſſe fieri. Facinus aliquando pœna mon-* "*ſtravit: periculoſum eſt oſtendere civitati,* "*quanto plures mali ſunt.*"

CHAP. XXII.

Of Crimes relative to Property.

§ 1. UNDER this head, the offence of wilfully burning the houſe of another is conſidered as of the blackeſt ma-

[k] Cic. Orat. pro Sext. Roſc. Amerino, c. 25.
[l] Seneca de Clement. l. i. c. 23.

lignity; being fatal to the ſecurity of the innocent occupier, dangerous to the lives and poſſeſſions of perſons even unknown, unlimited in its conſequences, and merely malicious in its motive.

By the ancient laws of England [m], it was a felony, and one of thoſe capital offences for which no ranſom was allowed; and Briton tells us, that perſons convicted thereof were burnt to death; probably under the idea of retaliation, or at leaſt to make the puniſhment ſavour in ſome degree of the crime [n]. Such whimſical connections have frequently influenced the minds of Lawgivers. It might, for inſtance, be difficult to conceive, why the 22 H. VIII. c. 9, [o] ſhould direct the crime of wilful poiſoning to be puniſhed by boiling to death, were we not informed by the preamble, that John Rooſe, a cook, had been lately convicted of throwing poiſon into a

[m] Leg. Cnuti, l. 61.

[n] "Iſſint que ils ſoient punies per meſme le choſe, dont ils pecherent." Brit. fol. 16.

[o] The ſame ſtatute forced the name of high-treaſon upon the crime of poiſoning. And in 33 H. VIII. Margaret Davy, a young woman, was attainted thereof for poiſoning her miſtreſs. And ſome others were alſo boiled to death in Smithfield, on the 17th day of March in the ſame year. 3 Inſt.

large

large pot of broth, prepared for the biſhop of Rocheſter's family, and for the poor of the pariſh; and the ſaid John Rooſe was, by a retroſpective clauſe of the ſame ſtatute, ordered to be boiled, perhaps in his own kettle[p]. But I return to the deſcription of Arſon, which is given by the Myrror, in the following extenſive terms[q]: "*Ardours ſont, que ardent citie, ville, maiſon home, maiſon beſte, ou autres chatelx, de leur felony, en temps de peace, pur haine ou vengeance.*" In ſubſequent ages it underwent various alterations, both in its definition and puniſhment; and at length by the 9 Geo. I. c. 22, made perpetual by 31 Geo. II. c. 42, it was, with many other offences, made felony without benefit of clergy, to "ſet fire to any houſe, barn, or out-houſe, or to any hovel, cock, mow, or ſtack of corn, ſtraw, hay, or wood."

I have given a literal tranſcript of this clauſe, as a ſtrong inſtance of the vague, unfeeling, undiſtinguiſhing careleſſneſs with which penal laws are compoſed, even in the moſt po-

[p] Obſervations on the Ancient Statutes, p. 406.
[q] Myrror, c. 1. § 8.

lished times. The penalty should in all cases, if possible, bear some proportion to the malice and mischief of the offence; but every idea of proportion is obliterated, when the same degree of guilt and punishment is assigned to the incendiary of a populous town, and to the destroyer of a small heap of dried grass.

The same severity is shewn, by the abovementioned act, to all persons "who shall cut down, or *otherwise* destroy, any trees planted in any avenue, or growing in a garden, orchard, or plantation, for ornament, shelter, or profit;" though, by a former act, it continues only a clergyable felony, to set on fire any wood, underwood, or coppice. And by the 10th Geo. II. c. 23, persons maliciously setting on fire any mine, pit, or delf of coal, are made guilty of felony without benefit of clergy.

§ 2. "He that by night breaketh and en-"tereth into a mansion house *with intent to* "*commit a felony*[r]," is deemed by the laws of

[r] Co. 63. And therefore an indictment for breaking into the house of A. B. with intent *ad verberandum ipsum* A. B. is no burglary, because it is no felonious intent. But

of England to commit burglary, and is, in the degree of his offence, the next object of inquiry.

Exclusive then of the permission given by our law to the alarmed inhabitant to kill his assailant [s], the sword of justice is also drawn against such assailant, and punisheth him with death, in case he should, by superior strength, or otherwise, escape alive from the execution of his purpose; and not only the Principal is made guilty of felony, without benefit of clergy, but also the Accessary before the fact.

The atrociousness of this crime consists chiefly in the terrors brought upon those who are found asleep and defenceless; and are deprived of that security in which they have a natural confidence.

For this reason the indictment must charge the house to have been a mansion-house at

But the opening of a door by a servant in the night time to come into his master's chamber, with intent to kill him, was by all the judges agreed to be burglary. Kel. p. 67.

[s] It was in like manner, one of the Laws of the twelve tables, "Si noctu furtum sit, jure cæsus est."

the time of the burglary; yet it may be doubted, whether our law hath not in ſome degree departed from this idea, in holding that, "where the owner quitteth his houſe *animo* "*revertendi*, it may ſtill be conſidered as his "manſion-houſe, though no perſon be left "in it, nor found there at the time of the "fact committed [t]."

There muſt be both an actual breaking and an entry to complete the crime. And here alſo it ſhould be obſerved, that Sir M. Hale ſeems to ſpeak with an inadvertence, and latitude, very unuſual to his temper in caſes capital, when he ſays, that if a hole be made in the houſe one night, with intent to commit a felony, and the ſame breakers enter the next night through the ſame, they are burglars: "for the breaking, and entering, were "both *noctanter*, though not the ſame night; "and *it ſhall be ſuppoſed*, that they brake and "entered on the night when they entered,

[t] Comment. B. iv. p. 225. and Foſter, 77. who ſpecifies the long vacations of lawyers, and the ſummers of citizens, as inſtances of ſuch quitting *animo revertendi*. "The breaking in ſuch caſe (ſaith Sir Matthew Hale) is burglary, and the indictment *ſhall ſuppoſe* it domus manſionalis." Hale, P. C. vol. i. p. 556.

"*for*

"*for* the breaking makes not the burglary, "until the entry."

I am perhaps miſtaken in thinking there is a degree of ſeverity in this opinion; for it certainly hath not been the inclination either of Sir M. Hale, or of thoſe who have followed him [u], to *ſuppoſe any thing* that ought not to be ſuppoſed, againſt a perſon under a capital accuſation. Yet it ſhould ſeem, that in the interval between the breaking and the entry, it is the duty of the occupier rather to repair the damage, than to leave it a temptation to further attacks: and conſiſtently with this it hath been holden, that if a perſon leaves his doors or his windows open, it is his own folly and negligence; and, if a man enters therein, it is no burglary.

Opening the caſement, unlatching the door, picking the lock, gaining admiſſion by falſe pretences, going down the chimney [w], which

[u] Commentaries, B. iv. p. 226.

[w] In the trial of a priſoner at Cambridge, Sir M. Hale "was doubtful whether this was burglary, and ſo were ſome others; but upon examination it appeared, that in his creeping down, ſome of the bricks of the chimney were looſened, and fell down into the room, *which* (ſays he) *put it out*

which is as much closed as the nature of things will permit, are all severally Acts, which, in construction of law, amount to an actual breaking.

The entry may be previous to the breaking; for, by Stat. 12 Ann. c. 7. if a person enters into, or is within the dwelling-house of another without breaking in, either by day or by night, with intent to commit felony, and shall in the night break out of the same, this is declared to be a burglary.

It is holden, that, to put a hand or a hook in at the window, to draw out goods, is a burglarious entry [x]. And this is another instance

out of question, and direction was given to find it burglary. Vol. i. p. 552.

It would not be easy for any man, whose understanding hath not the advantage of a professional education, to conceive how the nature of the crime should be varied by so trivial an accident. Such deviations of sound sense into sophistry are too often the consequences of legal reasoning.

[x] See the case of Gibbons, as reported by one of the judges who tried him. "It appeared in evidence, that the prisoner in the night-time cut a hole in the window shutters of the prosecutor's shop, which was no part of his dwelling-house, and putting his hand through the hole, took out watches, and other things, which hung in the shop within his reach; but no entry was proved, otherwise than

ſtance in which the conſtruction ſeems to have exceeded the true idea of the offence.

I have expreſſed the more anxiety on this ſubject of burglary, becauſe the ſelfiſh ſenſibilities of mankind may be too apt to excite an incautious indignation againſt the perſons accuſed thereof; and becauſe the liſts of capital executions ſhew it in fact to be peculiarly fatal to Engliſhmen.

If the exiſtence of thoſe who are convicted of this offence be really dangerous to the ſafety of ſociety, it is certainly both juſtifiable and proper to puniſh them with death; but this criterion of ſeverity ought moſt ſtrictly to be regarded.

It deſerves obſervation, that the puniſhment of breaking on the wheel, as practiſed in France, was firſt introduced and applied againſt this offence by Francis the Firſt, A. D. 1534, in the following words: "*Tous ceux* "*qui auront été duement atteints et convaincus*

than by putting his hand through the hole. This was holden to be burglary, and the priſoner was convicted." Foſter, p. 108.

"*par Justice des dits délits, crimes et maléfices,*
"*seront punis en la maniere qui s'en suit: c'est*
"*à sçavoir les bras leur seront brisés, et rom-*
"*pus en deux endroits, tant haut que bas, avec*
"*les reins, jambes et cuisses, et mis sur une roue*
"*haute, plantée et élevée, le visage contre le ciel,*
"*où ils demeureront vivans, pour y faire peni-*
"*tence tant et si longuement qu'il plaira a notre*
"*seigneur les y laisser; et morts, jusqu' à ce qu'il*
"*en soit ordonné par Justice: afin de donner*
"*crainte, terreur, et example, à tous autres de*
"*n'échoir ni tomber* en tels inconveniens."

This punishment is applied by the same edict to highway robberies; and the same form of words is constantly used at this day [y].

Though burglary may be committed without any abduction of the property of others, either intended or completed; yet in general, so audacious a breach of the peace of society is commenced *causâ lucri*, and consequently attended by theft; in which case it is a mere aggravated species of larceny.

[y] Code penal. p. 101.

§ 3. Lar-

§ 3. Larceny, when considered as a generical term, is the felonious taking and carrying away of the personal goods of another [z].

The felonious intent cannot be presumed from the wrongful possession; it must result from the evidence given, that the taking was committed *animo furandi* [a]. "I would never "(says Sir M. Hale) convict any person for "stealing the goods *cujusdam ignoti*, merely "because he would not give an account how "he came by them, unless there were due "proof made that a felony was committed "of these goods." *Tutius semper est errare ex parte Misericordiæ, quam ex parte Justitiæ.* This worthy Judge, though unfortunate in cases of witchcraft, was in every instance peculiarly anxious, that persons really innocent might not be entangled under those presumptions, which many times carry great probability of guilt.

[z] "*Contrectatio rei alienæ fraudulenta, cum animo furandi, invito ejus domino cujus res illa fuerit.*" Bracton. l. iii. 150. Fleta, l. i. 36. Hale Hist. P. C. ii. 290.

[a] For it is no felony by our law, if A find the purse of B in the highway, and take it and carry it away, and this with all the circumstances that may prove it to be done, *animo furandi*, as denying it, or secreting it, &c. But by the Swedish law it is felony.

If the felonious intent ſhould be clearly proved, ſtill it will not amount to a felonious taking; unleſs it ſhould appear, that the poſſeſſion was gained without the conſent of the owner.

It may at firſt view appear, that this diſtinction hath many exceptions in the law of England; as in the caſes of ſervants embezzling their maſters goods to the value of forty ſhillings [b]; of perſons having the cuſtody of the king's ammunition or habiliments of war, and embezzling the ſame [c]; of a gueſt robbing his inn or tavern of a piece of plate ſet before him [d]; of a lodger running away with furniture from his lodgings [e]; who are all ſeverally puniſhable, as felons guilty of larceny. But it ſhould be obſerved, that, in all ſuch inſtances, the taking is actual; the

[b] By 21 H. VIII. c. 7. See alſo 33 H. VI. c. 1. which act is ſtill in exiſtence, and inflicts an attaint of felony on the ſervant's default of appearance to anſwer to the maſter's executors in a civil ſuit.

[c] 31 Eliz. c. 4. & 22 C. II. c. 5. which takes away the benefit of clergy from this offence, ſo far as it relates to naval ſtores. See alſo 1 Geo. I. c. 25.

[d] Hale, H. P. C. vol. ii. p. 506. Hawk. P. C. vol. i. p. 90.

[e] Stat. 3 & 4 W. & M. c. 9.

offender

offender having only the liberty of uſe, and not the poſſeſſion, by delivery.

Very different[f] is the offence of A who rides away with a horſe, which is lent to him by B; or of the Carrier, who ſecretes, and converts to his own uſe, the pack, or parcel, which is delivered to him. *The property here is ſevered from the poſſeſſion*[g]; and ſuch perſons are guilty only of the violation of a civil truſt, and are puniſhable accordingly. Yet it hath been ſaid by Sir E. Coke, and adopted by other writers, that, if the carrier openeth the bale of goods, and taketh *only a part*[h] thereof, it is ſo manifeſt an evidence of the *animus furandi*, that it amounts to larceny.

[f] I venture to uſe this expreſſion, though the very learned Obſerver on the Ancient Statutes hath expreſſed a doubt, whether any reaſonable line of diſtinction can be drawn between the caſes here placed in oppoſition. Obſ. p. 371.

[g] The poſſeſſory property of the carrier, in the goods delivered to him, is ſuch, that he may maintain either an action of treſpaſs or indictment, as for his own goods, according to the circumſtances of the caſe, againſt any one that taketh them from him. See Kel. 39.

[h] 3 Inſt. 107. Comment. B. iv. 230.

— ὅσω πλέον ἥμισυ παντός.

It

It must be confessed, that, by the civil law, such breaches of trust, amounted in general to larceny. "*Si creditor pignore, sive is, apud* "*quem est deposita, eâ re utatur; sive is, qui* "*rem utendam accepit, in alium usum eam* "*transferat, quam cujus gratiâ ei data est;* "*furtum commisisse videtur.*"

There must be an abduction or carrying away; but a bare removal of things taken, though immediately interrupted by detection or apprehension, satisfieth this part of the definition.

It would lead me into an endless intricacy of discussion, were I to enter upon the detail of the several species of property, which come under the idea of the personal goods of another.

No larceny could be committed at the common law on chattels real, or things adhering to the freehold. This narrowness was founded rather on the prejudices of legal language, than on the conclusions of reason; and hath been remedied by various statutes. The stealing of writings, relating to a real estate

eſtate, ſtill continues only a treſpaſs[i]; but in general, the law on this point hath run into the oppoſite extreme of ſeverity; and many things are become objects of larceny, which ought never to have been conſidered in that predicament.

It may be a ſufficient proof of this laſt aſſertion, that the ſtealing by night of any trees, or of any roots, ſhrubs, or plants, to the value of five ſhillings, is by 6 Geo. III. c. 36. made felony in the principals, aiders, and abettors, and in the purchaſers thereof, knowing the ſame to be ſtolen. There is another milder act, c. 48, relative to the ſtealing of timber trees, ſhrubs, &c. by day or by night. It is undoubtedly true, that *mild puniſhments are the beſt ſafeguards againſt ſuch delinquencies.*

Bonds, bills, notes, &c. are, by ſtat. 2. Geo. II. c. 25. and very properly, conſidered, with reſpect to larceny, of the ſame value as the money, which they repreſent.

[i] See the caſe of the king againſt Webſter. Trin. 13 G. II. in B. R. Stra. 1133. It was found by the ſpecial verdict, that the defendant had ſtolen a commiſſion to ſettle boundaries, and alſo another parchment relative thereto, each value one penny. The queſtion was fully argued; and it was determined, not to be a felony.

I have

I have heretofore occaſionally cited many of our very harſh proviſions relative to game. Larceny may alſo be committed of all valuable and domeſtic animals, as horſes [k], oxen, ſheep [l], hens, geeſe, &c. and of all animals *feræ naturæ*, proper for food, and known ſo as to be reclaimed.

It is enacted by ſtatute 37 Ed. III. c. 19. "That if any perſon findeth any hawk, that is loſt of his Lords, he ſhall forthwith bring it to the Sheriff of the county, who ſhall make proclamation; and that if any ſteal any hawk, and the ſame carry away; it ſhall be done of him as of a thief, that ſtealeth a horſe or other thing." The concealing and carrying away is adjudged a ſtealing by this act, "In reſpect, ſaith Sir E. Coke [m], *of the* "*noble and generous nature and courage of* "*faulcons*, ſerving *ob vitæ ſolatium* of princes, "and of nobler and generous perſons, "*to make them fitter for great employments*."

In judgement of law, a man may, under certain circumſtances, be ſaid to have taken the goods of another; though he himſelf hath

[k] Stat. 1 Edw. VI. c. 12. 2 and 3 Edw. VI. c. 33. 31 Eliz. c. 1.

[l] Stat. 14 Geo. II. c. 6. 15 Geo. II. c. 34.

[m] 3 Inſt. p. 109.

the

the general property in the goods taken. A delivereth goods to B to keep for him, and then ſtealeth them, with intent to charge B. with the value of them. Or, A having delivered money to his ſervant to carry to ſome diſtant place, diſguiſeth himſelf, and robbeth the ſervant on the road, with intent to charge the Hundred. Both theſe caſes are larceny[a] in A: "For the money and goods are taken "from thoſe, who have a ſpecial temporary "property in them, with a wicked and frau-"dulent intention."

§ 4. I have now given the general deſcription of larceny, and am next to conſider its different ſpecies or degrees of enormity.

Of burglarious larceny I have already ſpoken; the next in degree is Robbery, or "the open and violent taking of money or "goods from the perſon of another, by "force, or intimidation."

If the thief, finding the thing taken of little value, ſhould return it; or if, after taking it, he ſhould drop it through fear or by accident; ſtill it is a robbery: for *the*

[a] Foſter, p. 124. Hale, vol. i. p. 513.

outrage

outrage offered to the rights of ſociety doth not vary in its nature, becauſe ineffectual in its conſequences.

A taking of the goods of another in his preſence only, as in the caſe of taking parcels out of a waggon, amounts to taking from the perſon, if done by putting him in fear; and "the law, *in odium ſpoliatoris*, will preſume fear, where there appeareth to be a ſufficient ground [o] for it;" requiring only, that the fact be attended with thoſe circumſtances of violence or terror, which in common experience are likely to induce a man to part with his property, for the ſafety of his perſon.

The benefit of clergy is taken from this ſpecies of larceny, whereſoever committed, by ſtat. 3 & 4 W. & M. c. 9; and the value of the thing taken is immaterial. An attempt to commit this offence is, by ſtat. 7 Geo. II. c. 21, made a felony, tranſportable for ſeven years.

This crime certainly is a very audacious violation of the ſocial compact, and proper to

[o] Foſter, p. 129.

be ſeverely puniſhed by the laws of ſociety; yet it may be doubted, whether it be of that heinous kind, which requires the *ultimum ſupplicium*; particularly when not aggravated by perſonal injuries to the party robbed. We have many inſtances of a peculiar generoſity in the nature of Engliſh robbers; but it deſerves conſideration, whether it be not dangerous to ſociety, to leave ſo little diſtinction between the puniſhment of ſimple robbery, and robbery perpetrated with murder [p].

§ 5. It cannot be too ſtrongly inculcated, that capital puniſhments, when unneceſſary, are inhuman, and immoral; an obſervation very applicable to the puniſhment, inflicted by our laws on the crimes, which I am next to mention.

Private larceny from the perſon, of any money or goods above the value of twelvepence is deprived of the benefit of clergy by the

[p] "A la Chine les voleurs cruels ſont coupés en morceaux, les autres non: cette difference fait que l'on y vole, mais que l'on n'y aſſaſſine pas.

En Moſcovie, ou la peine des voleurs et celle des aſſaſſins ſont les mêmes, on aſſaſſine toujours; les morts, y dit on, ne racontent rien." L'Eſpr. des Loix, xvi. c. 6.

the 8th Eliz. c. 4.[q] "that the fraternity "or brotherhood of cutpurſes and pick-"pockets (as they are deſcribed in the preamble) "may not continue to *live idle* by "the ſecret ſpoil of good and true ſubjects." A public and well-regulated work-houſe would have been a more proper remedy for this offence. "The puniſhment of robbery, "not accompanied by violence, ſhould (ſays Beccaria) "be pecuniary; he, who endea-"vours to enrich himſelf by the property "of others, ſhould be deprived of part of "his own. But this crime, alas! is com-"monly the effect of miſery and deſpair; "the crime of that unhappy part of man-"kind, to whom the right of excluſive "property hath left but a bare exiſtence." It would be abſurd then to extort pecuniary ſatisfaction from thoſe, who are already ſtruggling in the extremity of want; but there would be no abſurdity in the infliction of temporary impriſonments, with compulſion to labour; a mode of puniſhment, which, by inducing a habit of induſtry, and by

[q] The reaſon aſſigned by L. C. J. Kelyng for the framing of this ſtatute is not ſatisfactory. See Kel. p. 70.

the

the effects of that habit, would be equally beneficial to the criminal and the public.

§ 6. Larceny from the houſe, whether privily committed without violence, or openly in the day time, and therefore in neither caſe amounting to burglary, is nevertheleſs by the laws of England made capitally penal in almoſt every inſtance; and this by a multiplicity of ſtatutes, ſo complicated in their limitations, and ſo intricate in their diſtinctions, that it would be painful on many accounts to attempt the detail of them. It is a melancholy truth, but it may without exaggeration be aſſerted, that, excluſive of thoſe who are obliged by their profeſſion to be converſant in the niceties of the law, there are not ten ſubjects in England, who have any clear perception of the ſeveral ſanguinary reſtrictions, to which on this point they are made liable.

A modern writer, whoſe Book is peculiarly calculated for the general benefit of mankind, hath, by a diligent collation of the ſtatutes to which I allude, reduced this chaos to ſome degree of order. I ſhall tranſcribe from his account, that the benefit of clergy is now denied upon the following ſuppoſed aggravations of larceny[r]; viz. "in all larcenies "above the value of twelve-pence from a "church, or from a dwelling-house, or booth, "any person being therein; in all larcenies, "to the value of five shillings, committed "by breaking the dwelling-house, though "no person be therein; in all larcenies to the "value of forty shillings from a dwelling-"house, or its out-houses, without breaking "in, and whether any person be therein or "no; and in all larcenies to the value of five "shillings from any shop, warehouse, coach-"house, or stable, whether the same be "broken open or not, and whether any per-"son be therein or no. In all these cases, "whether happening by day or by night, the "benefit of clergy is taken away from the "offenders[s]."

§ 7. These severities have, with great plausibility, been ascribed[t] to the increasing opulence of the kingdom; and indeed there seems

[r] Commentaries, B. iv. 220.

[s] Stat. 23 Hen. VIII. c. 1. 25 Hen. VIII. c. 3. 1 Edw. VI. c. 12. 5 and 6 Edw. VI. c. 9. 39 Eliz. c. 15. 3 and 4 W. and M. c. 9. 10 and 11 W. III. c. 23. 12 Ann. c. 7.

[t] Observations on the Ancient Statutes, p. 375.

sufficient

ſufficient reaſon to believe, that ſanguinary laws are the probable conſequence of national proſperity. Senſibility ſleeps in the lap of luxury; and the legiſlator is contented to ſecure his own ſelfiſh enjoyments, by ſubjecting his fellow-citizens to the miſeries of a dungeon, and the horrors of an ignominious death. Still, however, he feels a tacit diſapprobation of the laws, which he hath enacted; and even, when injured, heſitates to bring the offender to juſtice. He knows, that the puniſhment is diſproportionate to the offence; or, at leaſt, if humanity be obliterated by intereſt, he foreſees, that the puniſhment cannot be inflicted without raiſing the indignation of ſociety againſt the accuſer. The delinquent therefore is diſcharged without proſecution; he repeats the crime, under the expectation of repeated mercy; he becomes gradually familiar with diſhoneſty; and at length falls a victim to that prepoſterous ſeverity of the law, which hath ſo long been the ſubject of his mockery. It is a property inſeparable from harſh laws, that they are neither regular, nor expeditious in their execution; conſequently, that they flatter the hope of impunity, and, equally injurious to the ſociety and to the criminal, tend to the fatal multiplication both of crimes and of punifhments.

Exclufive of the feveral larcenies which I have already defcribed, and their refpective penalties; it is, and hath been from the year 1109, the law of England, that in general all perfons guilty of larceny above the value of twelve-pence fhall be hanged. "*Animadverte autem in quantam afperitatem, ex rerum temporumque viciffitudine, lex antiqua abripitur. Quod enim olim* XII *vænit denariis, hodie fæpe* XX *folid. imo* XL, *vel pluris eft; nec vita hominis interea charior, fed abjectior.*" This well-grounded complaint was publifhed by Sir Henry Spelman, above a century ago; during that long interval the grievance hath been gradually increafing, and ftill remains unredreffed.

But the error lies deeper. *Money, which in its nature is of fluctuating value, is in no cafe proper to be made the ftandard-meafure of criminality.* When the punifhment of the offender depends on the value of the thing ftolen, the adjudication of the law is vague and uncertain. Mercy alfo is admitted under the fhield of interpretation; the impulfes of benevolence are oppoſed to the obligations of religion; and jurors are taught to trifle with their oaths, and to call ſuch trifling "a kind of pious perjury."

In fact, upon trials of larcenies ſo limited, it is commonly found to be the chief anxiety both of judges and of jurors, to reduce the crime below its real predicament, by reducing the conviction below the value affixed by law. Such an anxiety is the natural conſequence of laws, which, by an abſurd diſtinction, make a trivial difference between two ſums the criterion of a capital crime; and enact, that a penny more or leſs ſhall be equivalent to the life of a man.

In ancient times, larceny was puniſhed in ſome caſes with the loſs of a thumb[v]; in others with the pillory, and the loſs of an ear: in others with demembration, by cutting off the hand or foot[w], but this only after repeated acts. At length, by our Saxon laws,

[v] Corone, 434. 10 H. III. Briton, xxiv. 6.
[w] Laws of K. Ina, Lambard, l. xviii. *Si paganus ſæpius furti inſimulatus ſit, ei manus et pes præciditor.* This mode of puniſhment was alſo much uſed in the reign of Hen. II. Bened. Abb. p. 132. Hoveden, p. 549.

it was nominally, when of the value of twelve pence, punished with death; but the penalty was redeemable by pecuniary composition, which was called *capitis æstimatio*. By the laws of Ethelbert this composition was a threefold restoration, besides a fine to the king; and, if the thing were stolen from the king, the restoration was nine-fold; but by the 9th of Hen I. it was enacted [x], "*ut si quis in furto* "*vel latrocinio deprehensus fuisset, suspendere-* "*tur; Sublatâ Weregildorum, id est pecuniariæ* "*redemptionis, lege.*"

§ 8. Forgery, which is defined to be the fradulent making, or alteration, of a writing, with intent to prejudice the right of another, is also a crime against property.

It appears to have been a species of the *crimen falsi* among the Romans; but it is rarely mentioned by them, or in the laws of other ancient nations; and the reason is obvious.

The increase of modern riches, the invention of paper, the many complex securities, and representations of property, the institu-

[x] Leg. Anglo-sax. p. 304.

tion of national funds, and rules of written evidence, have all contributed to render forgery a consideration of great extent and importance. The offender, by 5 Eliz. c. 14, is punished with forfeiture to the party aggrieved of double costs and damages; with standing in the pillory, and having both his ears cut off, and his nostrils slit, and seared; with forfeiture to the crown of the profits of his lands, and with perpetual imprisonment. *I have cited this statute*, which extends only to certain forgeries therein described, *merely as proper to be repealed.* At present, " the imitation of stamps, in order to defraud the Stamp-Office; the antedating of a deed of conveyance in order to over-reach a former deed; an alteration in the name and description of the premises conveyed, or in the sum of money secured by bond or other deed, or in the limitations of an estate intended to pass; all these acts, and others of the like nature, tending to establish a false and fradulent title to property, whether in the name of a real or fictitious person, are forgeries[y]; and there is hardly a case of this kind,

[y] It is also a felony, without benefit of clergy, to make a false entry in a marriage register; to alter it when made; to forge or counterfeit such entry, or a marriage licence, or to aid and abet such forgery; to utter the same as true,

kind, possible to be conceived and described, which hath not, in the course of the present century, been made a capital crime. The statutes for that purpose are innumerable; for, exclusive of many general provisions, it is become usual, upon the issuing of new bills of credit, lottery-orders, army-debentures, &c, to add a special clause of forgery relative to the subject then in question. Here, therefore, if any where, may be applied the observation, *Pluit super populum laqueos legum accumulatio*[z].

§ 9. There is also a great variety of injuries against private property, which are in no degree fraudulent, but merely malicious; under this head the crime of Arson, which is capitally punished, is of the blackest dye; because destructive both of life and property. It hath, however, been thought expedient by the English legislature, to extend the same degree of severity to many mischiefs of very inferior criminality. Such are the offences, of

knowing it to be counterfeit; or to destroy, or procure the destruction of, any register-book of marriages, or any part of such register-book, with intent to avoid any marriage. 26 Geo. II. c. 33. § 16.

[z] De Augm. Scient.

of persons destroying turnpike gates upon roads, or posts, rails, or other fence, or fences, belonging to such turnpike gates, or the sluices, flood-gates, or other works of navigable rivers; of persons cutting any hop-binds growing in a plantation of hops; breaking down the head or mound of any fish-pond, whereby the fish are lost and destroyed[a]; *killing, maiming, or wounding any cattle*; such also is the offence of wilfully and maliciously tearing, spoiling, cutting, burning, or defacing the garments or cloaths of any person or persons, which is in like manner made a felony, though within the benefit of clergy[b]. If the legislature had not given repeated and deliberate proofs of a different sentiment, the punishment of death would seem by no means applicable to delinquencies which are merely in the nature of civil trespasses.

The second Stat. made in the 12th year of Q. Ann. c. 18. is less liable to exception.

[a] Stat. 9 Geo. I. c. 22.

[b] 6 Geo. I. c. 23. which is intituled, "An act for the further preventing robbery, burglary, and other felonies, and for the more effectual transportation of felons." The clause relative to cloaths *is to be found* in the last section.

All

All persons making any hole in any vessel in distress, or stealing any pump of such vessel, or who shall wilfully do any thing tending to the immediate loss or destruction of such vessel, are thereby declared to be guilty of felony without benefit of clergy.

CHAP. XXIII.

Of Crimes of positive Institution.

§ 1. EVERY wanton, causeless, or unnecessary act of authority exerted by the legislature over the people, is tyrannical, and unjustifiable; for every member of the state is of right entitled to the highest possible degree of liberty, which is consistent with the safety and well-being of that state[c].

With this observation I proceed to instances from which this part of my subject will receive its easiest and best illustration

[c] *Mens et animus, et consilium, et sententia civitatis posita est in legibus. Hoc fundamentum est libertatis quâ fruimur, hic fons æquitatis. Legum denique idcirco omnes servi sumus, ut liberi esse possimus.* Cic. Orat. pro Cluent.

In

In the year of Rome 671, L. Flaccus, being chosen Interrex, declared Sylla perpetual Dictator, ratified whatever he had done or should do by a special law, and empowered him to put any citizen to death, without accusation, hearing, or trial. On this law Cicero made the following comment, "*Omnium legum iniquissimam, dissimillimamque legis, eam esse arbitror: veruntamen habet excusationem, non enim videtur hominis lex esse, sed temporis*[d]."

When Lepidus celebrated his triumph over Spain, he commanded the whole Roman people *to rejoice upon pain of Death*; "*Sacris et epulis dent omnes hanc diem; qui secus fâxit inter proscriptos esto.*" This proclamation must be considered in the nature of a temporary Law, and, as such, was both absurd and tyrannical.

The Decemvirs authorized creditors to cut in pieces the bodies of their insolvent debtors. One would wish to persuade one's self, for the credit of humanity, that this was

[d] De Leg. Agrar. iii. c. 2.

only

only a figurative permission to divide the effects[e].

The Emperors, Arcadius and Honorius, forbad upon pain of death all applications in favour of the guilty. They little considered, how unworthily the hand of Power is employed, in closing the eyes of Justice against Mercy.

A Man was capitally punished at Athens, for having killed a sparrow, which, to escape the pursuit of a Hawk, had taken shelter in his bosom: And the Areopagites put a Boy to death, for having picked out the Eyes of a little bird. The former case was thought a proof of a mind incorrigibly depraved; in the latter, "*non videntur aliud judicâsse, quam id signum esse periculosissimæ mentis, et multis malo futuræ, si adolevisset*[f];" or, in the words of a more elegant writer[g], "*il ne s'agit point là d'une condamnation pour crime, mais d'un juge-*

[e] Tab. III. l. vi. "If the debtor be insolvent to several creditors, let his body be cut in pieces on the third market-day. It may be cut into more or fewer pieces with impunity: Or, if his creditors consent to it, let him be sold to foreigners beyond the Tiber."

[f] Quinctil. Inst. l. v. c. 9.

[g] L'Esprit des Loix, l. v. c. 19.

ment

ment de mœurs dans une republique fondée sur les mœurs." Such might be the motive; but such motives are not of that urgent necessity, which can authorize a legislature to place the life of a man in competition with that of an insignificant bird. It must be confessed indeed, that, by the laws of England, the malicious killing or wounding of any cattle is at this day capitally punished[h]; but severities so preposterous confound every idea of proportion between the enormity of crimes, and the extent of their punishments.

It is a Law at Venice, that those, who carry fire-arms about their persons, shall suffer death[i]. This law is founded in apparent utility; nevertheless it is contrary to the nature of things, to make the bare possession of the means of mischief equally penal with the most criminal use of those means. I have before observed, that it is high-treason by the law of England to have in possession

h 9 Geo. I. c. 22.

i *Charondas lege cavit, ut si quis conciones cum ferro intrâsset, continuo interficeretur. Interjecto deinde tempore, gladio accinctus, ex rure domum repetens, subito indictâ concione, sicut erat in eam processit: ab eoque qui proxime constiterat, solutæ a se legis suæ monitus. "Idem ego illam inquit sanciam," ac stricto confestim gladio seipsum transfigit.* Valer. Max. vi. 5. Diod. Sic. xii. 19.

an

an inſtrument, or other tool, not of common uſe in any trade, but proper only for coining.

Fleta mentions an ancient Engliſh law, which commanded every perſon contracting marriage with a Jew to be burnt alive. The blood of a Chriſtian family was ſuppoſed to be contaminated perhaps by ſuch a contract; but it would be difficult to prove, that any human Tribunal had a right to inſiſt on ſuch an expiation[k].

A law of the Viſigoths[l] compelled the Jews to eat every thing dreſſed with pork, but would not permit them to taſte the pork itſelf. In this we trace all the wanton cruelty of deſpotic enthuſiaſm.

[k] In the Chapter "of Crimes relative to Religion," I ought not to have omitted Sir Edw. Coke's argument for the uſe of fire in caſes of hereſy. 3 Inſt. 43. "*As he*, that is a Leper of his body, is to be removed from the ſociety of men, leſt he ſhould infect them, by the King's writ *de leproſo amovendo: ſo he*, that hath *lepram animæ*, that is to be convicted of Hereſie, ſhall be cut off, leſt he ſhould poiſon others, by the King's writ *de hæretico comburendo*."

[l] L. xii. tit. ii. § 16.

§ 2. The

§ 2. The pursuit of this subject might be amusing; but I return to the laws of England now in force, some of which I shall mention without any observations.

Every person shall forfeit his goods and chattels, lands and tenements, to the King, and shall be imprisoned during life, who shall be convicted of having acted as a broker, or agent, in any usurious contract, where more than ten *per cent.* was taken [m]; or, who shall obtain a patent for the monopoly of gun-powder [n]; or who, being a counsellor, or other officer in the courts, shall practise without having taken the new oaths of allegiance and supremacy, and without subscribing the declaration against popery [o].

All persons shall be guilty of felony, who shall *assemble* armed to the number of three, for the purposes of smuggling [p]; or, who shall serve a foreign state without taking the oath of allegiance [q]; or, who shall bring into the realm Gally-halfpence [r]; or who shall

[m] 13 Eliz. c. 10.
[n] 16 Car. I. c. 21. and 1 Jac. II. c. 8.
[o] 7 and 8 W. III. c. 24.
[p] 9 Geo. II. c. 35. § 13.
[q] Jac. I. c. 4. § 18.
[r] 3 H. V. c. 1.

transport

transſport wool out of England; or who, being watermen, ſhall take[s] a greater number of paſſengers than are allowed, *if*[t] *any be drowned.*

It is felony without benefit of clergy, to remain one month in the realm, being an Egyptian; or to be found in the fellowſhip of Egyptians; and Sir M. Hale takes notice, that thirteen perſons were executed for this offence in one aſſize at Bury. It is equally capital, if any perſon ſhall wilfully break any tools uſed in the woollen manufacture, not having the conſent of the owner[u]; or ſhall maliciouſly cut in pieces or deſtroy any manufacture of linen cloth or yarn, either when expoſed to bleach, or dry[w]; or ſhall wander, being a mariner, without the teſtimonial of juſtices[x], or ſhall knowingly receive, relieve, or maintain, Prieſts or Jeſuits[y]; or ſhall, during the term of tranſportation to the

[s] 10 Geo. II. c. 31. § 9.

[t] In this caſe the criminality is founded on the hypotheſis of a caſual event; in like manner it hath been adjudged treaſon to break a priſon, *if any perſon be in durance under an accuſation of treaſon*, though the priſon-breaker did not know that ſuch perſon was impriſoned for any ſuch offence. Hale's Hiſt. P. C. vol. i. 141.

[u] 12 Geo. I. c. 34.

[w] 4 Geo. III. c. 37. § 16.

[x] 39 Eliz. c. 13. § 4.

[y] 27 Eliz. c. 2. § 4.

British

British colonies, voluntarily go into any part of the French or Spanish dominions[z]; or shall be found in disguise in the act of passing with prohibited or uncustomed goods; or shall forcibly hinder, obstruct, assault, oppose, or resist, any of the officers of the customs, or excise, in the seizure of any such goods[a].

It would be easy to collect considerable additions to this dismal catalogue; but the instances already given form a sufficient foundation for the following remark.

§ 3. Positive laws are those, which do not flow from the general obligations of morality, and the general condition of human nature; but have their reason and utility, in reference to the *temporary* advantage of that particular community for which they are enacted. Every law therefore, which comes under this description, ought to have a limited duration; and should not be suffered to remain a burthen upon the people, when the grievance, for which it was framed, hath ceased, and is forgotten.

[z] 20 Geo. II. c. 46. § 1. [a] 19 Geo. II. c. 34.

The accumulation of sanguinary laws is the worst distemper of a State. Let it not be supposed, that the extirpation of mankind is the chief object of legislation. *Nous lisons de quelques empereurs de Maroc, qui uniquement, pour faire parade de leur adresse, enlevent d'un seul coup de sabre, en se remettant en selle, la tête de leur ecuyer.*

CHAP. XXIV.

Of the Composition and Promulgation of Laws.

§ 1. IN the course of this inquiry, I have attempted to state the original contract of society, the institution of penal restrictions, and the different effects of different penalties upon the sentiments of mankind: the nature also of criminality, the several species of crimes, and the particular degree of correction, to which, morally and politically, each crime ought to be subjected, have in their turn been considered.

But

But these are the ground-works only of the system of government; the promulgation and execution of penal laws are the superstructure.

Here then we discover new matter for examination; too multifarious indeed, and too important, to be brought within the compass of the present design. I shall confine my attention therefore to the outlines only of this part of my subject; still anxious to establish the rights of humanity upon the principles of reason and benevolence; principles, applicable only to the legislation of those happy communities, where the good of all is the great object of all; and which bear no reference, either to that unnatural mode of government, which is known by the name of Despotism; or to those abused Aristocracies, which seek the gratification of a few in the desolation of many. Passive obedience hath no principles. Man is not created to submit to the arbitrary caprice of creatures like himself: "It is necessary to make a bad subject, in order to form a good slave [b]."

[b] L'Esprit des Loix.

§ 2. On the promulgation of every new law, it ſhould not eſcape the attention of the lawgiver, that *public virtue is the love of the laws* [c]. For the love of the laws is followed by the love of our country, and is conſequently productive both of rectitude of conduct, and purity of morals. Public virtue, thus defined, is the true end of government; but harſh and ſanguinary laws have a tendency to check the attainment of this end; for they cannot be executed without raiſing the indignation of the ſufferer, and the abhorrence of his fellow-citizens. Vague and uſeleſs laws have the ſame evil tendency; for it may with truth be affirmed, that public virtue bears a proportion to political freedom [d]; and that political freedom decreaſes in proportion to the uncertainty and multiplicity [e] of penal laws.

[c] "*Nec verò ſolum, ut obtemperent homines obediantque magiſtratibus, ſed etiam ut eos colant diligántque, præſcribimus, ut Charondas in ſuis facit legibus.*" Cic. de Legibus, l. iii. c. 2.

[d] The ignorance of the people alſo diminiſhes in proportion to the increaſed freedom of the government.

[e] And therefore it rarely happens, that very flouriſhing States retain a great degree of liberty; for the laws neceſſarily bear a relation, not only to the principle and nature of the conſtitution, but to the opulence, extent, and populouſneſs of the country.

§ 3. It

§ 3. It is essential to political freedom, and consequently to public virtue, that no man be compellable to do any thing, to which the laws of society do not compel him; or to abstain from any thing which the laws have not prohibited. Hence results a general right to do with impunity any action, not prohibited by antecedent law; for every penalty must in its nature commence *in futuro: Moneat Lex oportet, priusquam feriat.*

When the Duchess of Norfolk was attainted by the parliament[f], for having known and concealed the vicious life of Catharine Howard before her marriage; she was attainted for a concealment, which, without the spirit of vaticination, she could not know to be criminal. Her conduct had been in itself innocent; her guilt was then first created by the legislature; and she was in fact punished for having eyes, ears, and a grand-daughter. Retrospective laws are generally unjust.

§ 4. It is also essential to political freedom, that the mandates and prohibitions of law be

[f] Stat. 33 H. VIII. c. 21.

not extended to any action, not immoral in its nature, nor prejudicial to the well-being of society in its consequences.

When the Russians resented the attempt of the Czar Peter to cut off their beards, their resentment did not arise from a belief, that Liberty consists in the privilege of being exempted from the rasor; but they misconceived the attempt to be founded in the mere wantonness of power; and their reason, uncultivated as it was, informed them, that, in matters of indifference, unrestrained freedom is one of the indelible privileges of mankind.

When by Stat. Jac. I. it was made felony for any person infected with the plague, to go abroad or converse with company; it was impossible to object to a severity, which, though fatal to individuals, was essential to the general safety of the people. But when in the eighteenth century it is made a capital crime to cut down a cherry-tree in an orchard; the thinking part of mankind must listen to such a law with irreverence and horror: for they know that the evil to be prevented is

by

by no means adequate to the violence of the Preventive.

Under this head it may be obſerved, that laws very ſevere in their nature, but originally not inconſiſtent with ſound policy, are ſometimes ſuffered to retain their force, long after their ſubject-matter hath ceaſed to be of any conſequence to the intereſts of ſociety. Such, for inſtance, is that ſtatute [g], under which it is at this day a capital offence, to give corn, cattle, or other conſideration, to the Scots for protection. It would be eaſy to produce many other inſtances equally exceptionable. And this is the neceſſary conſequence of having given an unlimited exiſtence to laws made for the correction of preſent evils. In the promulgation of ſuch laws it ſhould be obſerved, that they are founded in the momentary exigencies of ſociety, and reſemble that neceſſity, which, in caſes of extreme famine, obliges men to eat each other. They ceaſe to eat men, in ſuch caſes, as ſoon as bread can be obtained [h].

[g] Stat. 43 Eliz. c. 13.
[h] See the French Commentary on the M. Beccaria.

§ 5. It is farther essential to political freedom, that the laws be clearly obvious to common understandings, and fully notified to the people.

Anciently the laws were composed in verse, which were frequently sung in public[i], that men might remember them. The laws of the twelve tables were so well known, that, in the time of Cicero, children learnt them by heart in the first rudiments of their education[k]. At Athens the laws were written upon tables in large characters, and hung up in public places on the walls. The invention of printing, and the easy circulation of printed papers, have made these precautions unnecessary in our times; but, in England, the effectual promulgation of the laws is much retarded by the manner in which they are formed. It was well observed by Lord

i Aristot. Probl. § 19. & Horat. Ars Poët. 395.

"Fuit hæc sapientia quondam
Publica privatis secernere, sacra profanis;
Concubitu prohibere vago; dare jura maritis;
Oppida moliri; *leges incidere ligno.*
Sic honor et nomen divinis vatibus, atque
Carminibus venit."

k "Discebamus enim pueri duodecim tabulas, *ut carmen necessarium*; quas jam nemo discit." De Leg. ii. 23.

Bacon,

Bacon, that the mandatory clauſe ought always to be placed at the beginning of the ſtatute; yet thoſe tedious preambles, which ſeem to have been derived from the ancient method of paſſing laws by petition, are ſtill retained, though frequently ill-connected with the ſubſequent parts of the law, to which they are prefixed. When the laws are imperfectly known, they are feared, not loved. For, when the people firſt learn the law by fatal experience, they feel as if the Judge was in effect the Legiſlator; and as if life and liberty were ſubjected to arbitrary controul: the idea of inſecurity is ſpread through the whole ſociety; and the ſenſe of ſafety, in which political freedom is founded, ceaſes to exiſt. Upon the ſame principle, the ſame will be the conſequences, where the law is imperfectly and indefinitely expreſſed. The ſtile therefore ſhould be clear, and as conciſe as is conſiſtent with clearneſs; general terms alſo ſhould be particularly avoided, as liable to become the inſtruments of oppreſſion. Under the act 14 Geo. II. c. 6. ſtealing ſheep, "*or other cattle*," was made felony without benefit of clergy; but theſe general words,

"or

"or other cattle," being considered as too vague to create a capital offence, the act was properly holden to extend only to sheep.

§ 6. It hath been said, that the dread of evil operates more forcibly on the mind, than the expectation of good [l]; and *therefore*, that the sanction of laws must consist rather in penalties, than rewards [m]. But it may be offered, perhaps, as a more obvious reason for the establishment of penalties, that obedience to the law is a matter of duty, demandable from the subject, and unnecessary to be purchased by the allurements of gifts and privileges. Be this as it may, every law must have both a directory and compulsory part [n], and without the latter will be imperfect [o]. The wayward minds of the people must be deterred from disobedience by the frightful images of pain and infamy.

[l] Locke on Human Understanding, B. ii. c. 21.

[m] Pufendorff, B. i. c. 6. § 4.

[n] Which other writers express by the word "*vindicatory*."

[o] "*Inter leges quoque illa imperfecta esse dicitur, in quâ nulla deviantibus pœna sancitur.*" Macrob. l. ii. c. 17.

It is unſafe to leave the meaſure of corporal puniſhment indefinite; but when ſhame only is the penalty, a greater latitude of expreſſion is admiſſible. If the penal ſyſtem were good, ſhame would be the certain conſequence of diſobedience to law. The Valerian law was revived in the year of Rome 453, and was expreſſed in ſtronger terms than before: "*Siquis autem adverſus ea feciſſet, nihil ultra, quam improbe factum, adjecit: id (qui tum pudor hominum erat) viſum, credo, vinculum ſatis validum legis* [p]." Diodorus Siculus [q] pretends to have preſerved certain laws of Zaleucus, in which the puniſhment of infamy is implied in a manner ſtill more indeciſive.

"Let not a free woman, *unleſs ſhe be drunk*, "be attended by more than one ſervant. "Let her not go forth from the city in the "night, *unleſs when ſhe goes to proſtitute herſelf* to her Gallant. Let her not wear rich "ornaments, or garments interwoven with "gold, *unleſs ſhe be a courteſan.*"

[p] Liv. Hiſt. l. x. c. 9.
[q] Diod. Sic. l. xii. c. 20.

The

The hiſtorian cites other laws of the ſame kind; and obſerves, that they were attended by very beneficial effects [r].

It would be eaſy to purſue this ſubject to a very conſiderable length. I ſhall conclude however in the words of Lord Bacon [s]:

"*Lex bona cenſeri poſſit, quæ ſit intimatione*
"*certa, præcepto juſta, executione commoda,*
"*cum formâ politiæ congrua, et generans vir-*
"*tutem in ſubditis.*"

[r] Οὐδεὶς γὰρ ἐβούλετο, τὴν αἰσχρὰν κόλασιν ὁμολογήσας, καταγέλαστος ἐν τοῖς πολίταις εἶναι. Ib.

[s] De Augm. Scient. l. viii. c. 3.

CHAP.

CHAP. XXV.

Of the Execution of Penal Laws.

§ 1. SOLON is recorded to have ſaid, that he had accompliſhed his ſyſtem of laws, by coupling juſtice together with ſtrength[t]; by which he meant to imply, that the legiſlative power would be of little avail without the aſſociated and effectual exertion of the executive. This idea may be extended; and one may aſſert, without the imputation either of cruelty or preſumption, *that the ſtrict execution of every unrepealed law is the part both of wiſdom and of mercy.*

It had better be ſaid, "*perquam durum eſt,* "*ſed lex ita ſcripta eſt*;" than "*lex ita ſcrip-*" "*ta eſt, ſed non valebit.*" Cruel laws are ſuffered to exiſt, becauſe they are rarely enforced: for the ſame reaſon they are diſregarded by the people; and laws more cruel

[t] Ὁμȣ Βίην τε, καὶ Δίκην συναρμόσας. Plutarch. Vit. Solonis.

are

are made, becauſe thoſe already exiſting are found ineffectual [u]. Thus it is, that errors of the moſt fatal tendency are accumulated through many centuries; a truth, of which the conduct of criminal proſecutions in this country is a ſtriking example. The Engliſh courts of judicature have long been eminent for the extraordinary wiſdom and probity of the Judges. Benevolence hath a natural prevalence in ſuch characters; but benevolence ceaſes to be a virtue, when it induces them to forget that they are not authorized to interpret the penal laws; and that they are entruſted with the execution of them by a Legiſlature actually exiſting, and alone competent to ſuch interpretation [w].

If Larceny, when amounting in common apprehenſion to the value of twelve-pence,

[u] A ſtate ſo circumſtanced may be deſcribed in the words of Tacitus, "*Antehac flagitiis laboraſſe, nunc legibus.*" Tacit. Annal. l. iii. c. 25.

[w] This idea is very ſtrongly inculcated in Diod. Sic. l. xii. c. 16. "Charondas illos, qui in criminalibus judiciis legis conſilium non verba ſpectant, compeſcuit; ne cavillationibus auctoritatem legum labefactarent. Nam legum latori cedere honeſtum, argutias vero alicujus civis prævalere omnino abſurdum, exiſtimabat. *A legis igitur præſcripto, licet male admodum ſcripta eſſet, ut nullo modo diſcederetur, vetuit. corrigendi autem poteſtatem fecit, ſi quâ correctione indigeret.*"

had regularly received the judgement of death according to law, a law ſo abſurd would not now exiſt; and Pilfering, deſtined to a more adequate, but certain correction, would no longer be encouraged by the confidence of impunity. Many inſtances of a ſimilar kind have occurred in the courſe of this work.

" In England, ſays Monteſquieu [x], the ju-" rors determine, whether the perſon accu-" ſed be guilty of the crime ſubmitted to " their inquiry; if he be declared guilty, " the Judge pronounces the puniſhment in-" flicted by the law on that particular of-" fence; and for this purpoſe, it is only ne-" ceſſary for him to open his eyes." The learned writer was only acquainted with the theory of Engliſh law.

§ 2. But let not theſe obſervations on the danger of impunity be miſapplied; they relate merely to the ſtrict conduct of tribunals in the courſe of proſecution and conviction; to that fixed, invariable adminiſtration of juſtice, which is beſt calculated to make the penal ſyſtem reſpectable. God forbid that I

[x] L'Eſprit des Loix, l. vi. c. 3.

ſhould

ſhould confound the duty of the judge, which is to be directed by the letter of the law, with that prerogative of pardon, which reſides in the breaſt of the ſupreme magiſtrate; and which, when properly exerted, participates the beſt attribute of heaven! Yet it ſeems neceſſary to remark, that every diſproportionate ſeverity of the penal laws hath a tendency to familiarize the minds of princes to the exertion of this prerogative; and conſequently to lead them in many caſes to the abuſe of it. When ſuch inſtances happen, the rightful ſecurity of the people becomes a ſacrifice to the ſovereign. It hath been well ſaid, that "Clemency is a virtue which ought "rather to reſide in the code of laws, than "in the private judgement of any indivi-"dual:" Yet we muſt allow, that, even in the mildeſt ſyſtems of which human ſocieties are capable, there will ſtill exiſt a neceſſity of this diſcretionary power, founded in the poſſible circumſtances of every conviction.

§. 3. *Intereſt reipublicæ, ne delicta ſint impunita.* But let not this conſideration be ſuffered to induce an intemperate zeal, either

in

in judges or prosecutors, to punish the person accused, because a crime hath been committed. If the proof be doubtful, let the wretch be left, if guilty, to be his own punisher; let him be left to the censure of that internal tribunal, whose judgement is incapable of corruption, and whose terrors cannot be evaded by cunning, or collusion.

It is a political truth, that, *when the laws are good, those, who deserve punishment, rarely escape the arm of Justice.*

"Cur tamen hos Tu
Evasisse putes, quos diri conscia facti [y]
Mens habet attonitos, et surdo verbere cædit,
Occultum quatiente animo tortore flagellum?
Pœna autem vehemens, ac multo sævior illis,
Quas aut Cæditius gravis invenit, aut Rhadamanthus,
Nocte dieque suum gestare in pectore testem [z]."

---

[y] The same idea is finely expressed by our own poet, who seems to have possessed the singular power of turning his genius to every train of ideas, of which the mind of man can be capable:

"Tremble, thou wretch
That hast within thee undivulged crimes,
Unwhipt of justice: hide thee, thou bloody hand;
Thou perjur'd, and thou simular man of virtue,
That art incestuous: Caitiff, to pieces shake,
That under covert and convenient seeming
Hast practis'd on man's life."

[z] Juv. Sat. xiii. ver. 193.

§ 4. The firſt ſtep towards the puniſhment of offenders is their formal accuſation. In all governments, which have any mixture of political freedom, this accuſation ſhould, as in England [a], be public. Private informers are the proper inſtruments only of deſpotic governments. Every idea of liberty and ſecurity is loſt, when the ends of juſtice are ſuffered to be ſought by ſuch means. It is the part of wiſe and moderate Legiſlators, anxiouſly to preclude [b] every poſſible avenue to falſe accuſation and calumny.

§ 5. In

[a] The firſt depoſitions before the Magiſtrate are generally taken in the face of the country; and the finding of the indictment by the Jury is ſtrictly in the nature of a public accuſation; for the names of the Witneſſes are indorſed on the Record, and ſo delivered into the Court, that they may be publicly examined, and confronted with the priſoner in the courſe of the trial.

And here I ſhall digreſs in ſome meaſure from my ſubject, to obſerve, that, though the accuſation tranſmitted to the Court is afterwards to be ſolemnly tried and determined; yet grand jurors ſhould remember always, that it is their duty to conſider fully the weight and credibility of the evidence laid before them; and that they are not authorized to expoſe a fellow-citizen to the ſhame, expence, and danger of a public trial, upon the vague ſuggeſtion of a mere probability.

[b] Yet it may be doubted, whether a wiſe and good writer did not uſe a very exceptionable, and dangerous latitude of expreſſion, when he ſaid that the falſe accuſer ought to ſuffer the ſame puniſhment to which the perſon

§ 5. In the proceſs ſubſequent to the firſt accuſation, ſome delays are beneficial; (when Beccaria ſaid otherwiſe, he conſulted his own heart, and forgot the imperfections of mankind;) they are beneficial, becauſe a certain interval is neceſſary between the crime alledged and the trial, that popular prejudices may ſubſide into ſound reaſon; that judges may not be heated by the recent recollection of the fact; and that proſecutors may rather ſeek the ends of juſtice, than the gratification of revenge. The enormity of the crime in queſtion ſhould be the meaſure of this interval. When the fact charged is very atrocious in its nature, a proportionable delay is requiſite; not only, that the firſt paſſion of the people againſt the offence may evaporate; but that a ſufficient time may be given for the preparation of proof on the part of the Public, and juſtification on the part of the Accuſed. Reaſon and the rights of humanity demand, that the ſtrength and ſtrictneſs of proof be increaſed in proportion to the enormity of

perſon accuſed would have been expoſed in caſe of conviction. "Ogni governo, e republicano, e monarchico, deve al calumniatore dare la pena, che toccherebbe all accuſato." Dei Delitti, e delle Pene, § 16.

An aſſertion, which, if reduced to practice, would prove a fatal check to all criminal proſecutions!

 the

the crime in queſtion. The more trivial delinquencies are leſs incredible in their nature, and leſs important in their conſequences both to the Public and the Party; they are therefore proper for a more immediate diſcuſſion. But in neither caſe ſhould the interval be ſo great as to deſtroy that promptitude of puniſhment, which is requiſite to make the ſuffering of the offender the apparent conſequence of his offence.

§ 6. I will not affirm that the ſame diſtinction ſhould be our guide as to the infliction of puniſhment after trial and judgement. If the crime be of an inferior nature, it ſeems certain, that the puniſhment proportioned to it ſhould be immediately inflicted. We ought in ſuch caſes to ſpare the corroding torment of expectation, which can neither tend to the private amendment of the criminal, nor be exemplary to his fellow-citizens; and to promote as much as poſſible that uſeful aſſocation of ideas, which may check the frailty of the people, by holding out the image of unavoidable and immediate puniſhment. *The impreſſion of terror diminiſhes in proportion to the diſtance of the object.*

But

But how far it may be proper to allow a longer interval, when a capital judgement is the consequence of conviction, is a question, on which it is difficult to reconcile the language of political utility with that of religion. The immediate execution of the criminal may possibly give a more salutary shock to the sentiments of his fellow-citizens, than the same horrid spectacle can produce, when the circumstances of the crime are in some degree faded on the memory, and when compassion hath taken the place of indignation. Yet what are the feelings of a serious mind at the sight of a fellow-creature thus cut off,

"With all his crimes broad blown, as flush as May;
"And, how his audit stands, who knows, save heaven;
"But in our circumstance, and course of thought,
"'Tis heavy with him [c]."

§ 7. There are certain possible contingencies relative to the criminal, which should in all governments be admitted as good reasons in stay of execution. Of this kind is the plea of insanity; in regard to which,

[c] Shakespeare, Hamlet.

the benevolence of the Engliſh law hath been already mentioned. The plea of pregnancy is entitled to a ſimilar indulgence, though not admitted to operate ſo abſolutely in our law, as in the law of Egypt [d], and of ancient Rome [e]. "If a woman (ſay the writers on the Engliſh law [f]) hath once had the benefit of this reprieve, and been delivered and afterward become pregnant again, ſhe ſhall not be entitled to the benefit of a further reſpite for this cauſe." Such is the doctrine of our law, and uſe hath taught us to read it with tranquillity and indifference; though in truth no reaſon can be given as to the firſt reprieve, which will not apply equally to the ſecond.

[d] The reaſons for this indulgence are clearly and fully ſtated in Diod. Sicul. l. i. c. 77.

[e] ff. xlviii. 19. 8.

[f] "And when a woman commits high-treaſon, and is quick with child, ſhe cannot upon her arraignment plead it, but ſhe muſt either plead "Not Guilty," or confeſs the charge. She cannot alledge it in arreſt of judgement, but judgement ſhall be given againſt her; and if it be found by an inqueſt of matrons, that ſhe is quick with child, (for *privement enceint* will not ſerve) it ſhall arreſt and reſpite execution till ſhe be delivered; *but ſhe ſhall have the benefit of that but once, though ſhe be again quick with child.*" Co. 3 Inſt. p. 17.

§ 8. By

§ 8. By the laws of the Romans [g] the Executioner was forbidden, not only to appear in the Forum, but even to have any habitation in the City; and this was enacted, that the minds of the people might not be familiarized to the Idea of capital executions. Upon the same principle, it was not unusual to put the Malefactor to death in a secret dungeon, which was called Tullianum. It seems more advisable however, on many accounts, that the punishment of death should in every instance be publicly inflicted; and it is a certain proof of some defect in the mode of infliction, when it ceases to be considered as the most solemn and affecting scene that can be exhibited.

[g] "Carnificem non modo foro, sed etiam coelo hoc ac spiritu, censoriæ leges, atque urbis domicilio carere voluerunt." Cic. Orat. pro Rab. c. 5.

CHAP.

CHAP. XXVI.

Of the Importance of this Subject.

IT cannot have escaped the notice of my readers, that the ideas, which in the course of this inquiry I have endeavoured to establish as principles of penal law, have not been stated as abstract propositions; but rather as argumentative inferences, interwoven with, and to be collected from, observations on the penal systems of different governments. My attention hath at the same time been most particularly turned to the English code of laws; and many melancholy instances have concurred to shew that the reformation of that code is become an important and almost necessary work. I know, that many will conceive such a reformation to be impracticable; I know, that the minds of some will startle at the idea of innovations; I know, that others will shrink from the supposed difficulty:—Yet I am convinced, that the undertaking is neither impracticable, unſafe, nor difficult [h].

Under this conviction it hath been my object, by frequent appeals to reaſon and benevolence, to engage thoſe ſenſible and good minds, which are ever ready to ſympathize with him who pleads the cauſe of humanity. To excite the attention of that more nume-

[h] The Britiſh Conſtitution is the pride of every Briton: to ſecure, to fortify, to perpetuate that excellent ſyſtem of government, is the buſineſs of every Briton. It may be pardonable therefore in me to point out, what I conceive to be the beſt method of accompliſhing the reformation in queſtion; leaving the execution of that method, or the adoption of a better plan, to thoſe who lie under the more immediate engagements both of intereſt and duty.

The learned Obſerver on the Ancient Statutes was certainly well founded in ſuggeſting that a reformation of the Engliſh Law can never be effectually carried on, without the aſſiſtance of able Lawyers, not members of the Legiſlature. With ſuch aſſiſtance, it might perhaps be eaſy to frame ſeparate declaratory ſtatutes relative to each claſs of crimes, comprehending all the deſcriptions and degrees of each crime, with their proportionate puniſhments. Every ſuch declaratory ſtatute ſhould be attended by a ſupplemental Bill, repealing all prior proviſions relative to the claſs of crimes in that ſtatute contained. It ſeems ſuperfluous to point out the many collateral good effects, which might ariſe from this method of ſeeking the end propoſed.

The repeal of particular ſtatutes, without ſuch preparatory caution, will be found a mere palliative remedy; which may tend indeed to abate the ſymptoms of the diſeaſe, but from which a radical cure cannot be expected.

rous clafs of men, who are diftracted by the cares, heated by the action, or diffipated by the pleafures of the world, may be wifhed, but is not to be expected: though nothing is more certain than that the fubject of thefe enquiries deferves the attention of every man amongft us. "For no rank, no elevation "in life, no conduct how circumfpect foever, "ought to induce any reafonable man to "conclude, that the penal fyftem doth not, "nor poffibly can concern him [i]." A very flight reflection, on the numberlefs unforefeen events which a day may bring forth, will be fufficient to fhew that we are all liable to the imputation of guilt; and confequently all interefted, not only in the protection of innocence, but in the affignment to every particular offence, of the fmalleft punifhment compatible with the fafety of fociety.

It muft ever happen, that many private members of the ftate will regard the imperfections of the laws with indifference till they experience their effects. What in fuch men muft be attributed to inability or neglect

[i] Fofter's Crown Law, Pref. p. 3.

only, may in others, perhaps deſerve the appellation of a breach of truſt. Be this as it may; it highly concerns the ſafety of every individual, as well as the general morality and happineſs of the people, that the innocent be protected againſt unmerited ſeverities, and that the guilty be conducted with certainty to puniſhments proportionate to their crimes.

Theſe Ends can be attained only when the penal ſyſtem is good. Under ſuch a ſyſtem, they who offend againſt the Laws, and they only, have reaſon to fear: whilſt thoſe happier members of ſociety, who deſerve ſecurity, enjoy it in the full perfection to which the rectitude of their conduct hath entitled them.

THE END.